Praise for *Life Well Spoken:*

"Kris Prochaska writes from her heart as she teaches readers how to tell the difference between the voice of God inviting them to their true purpose and the small critical voices of fear and self-doubt that seem so much louder. She shares in real life terms—no sugar coating—that the discernment can be challenging, and she provides information tools that will bring about amazing transformation."

— Karen Lynn Maher, Book Writing Coach and Creator of the *Expert*Book™ Made Simple Series

"Keep this book close by because you will refer to *Life Well Spoken* over and over. It is like having twenty-four-hour access to Kris' insight and wisdom on the knowledge we all seek: moving past our own fears and living in alignment by embracing our God given purpose. Kris speaks to you at the soul level; her words and story resonate deeply and motivate you to get started in a long awaited transformation."

— Stacie Beam-Bruce, LICSW, CHT, Centerpoint Hypnotherapy & Counseling

"Grab a cup of tea or something stronger and settle in for a read that will change the course of your life forever. In *Life Well Spoken*, Kris shares real life examples of how she and others have made the decision to listen to their own inner authority and portrays how taking small steps or slightly reframing even one belief can change everything for the better. You'll find yourself reading along, nodding your head, and saying, "Hell, yeah," as if Kris were in the room with you. This book is a brilliant blend of practical guidance and spiritual soul searching."

— **Debbie Whitlock, Cash Flow Business Coach at Fast Track CFO, and Seattle Radio Host**

"Kris Prochaska's book, *Life Well Spoken,* is one of those books that I highlighted more often than not—I might as well have highlighted the entire thing! As I read this powerfully honest book about how we all really need to be living our fullest lives, I laughed out loud, nodded along, and was deeply impacted. Kris's sassy style is engaging and purely authentic. It is going on my list as one of my most quotable books!"

— **Jessica Butts MA, Psychotherapist, Owner of Accomplish Magnificent Things**

"I know Kris personally and professionally and she's the real deal. You'll feel supported and in good company as you read Kris' personal stories and interviews with others who have learned to listen and follow their own inner authority. Her book helps people understand intuition and how to listen to it. She shares the tools and techniques for hearing and understanding your inner truth and shows that listening to one's Inner Voice is essential for good health, wealth, and a joyful life!"

— **Krista Hopper, Senior Business Systems Analyst and Project Manager**

"Keep this charming book handy for moments when those voices of shame, guilt, or doubt start drowning out your wise Inner Voice. In *Life Well Spoken*, Kris Prochaska sets out on a deep, honest, and revealing exploration of what it means to be stuck in the 'middle,' the uncomfortably familiar place that lies between passive, blind acceptance of what happens to us and being conscious thought leaders fully in tune with our intuition. With her sparkling style and her fun and curious intelligence, Kris shares inspiring and instructive stories of her personal transformation, professional experience, and the journey she's taken to discover and trust her own Inner Voice, and she makes sure you learn how you can, too."

— **Madeleine Eno, Writer & Marketing Strategist at In The Write Place**

ALIGN WITH POSSIBILITY

LIFE WELL SPOKEN

Free Your Inner Voice
and Prosper

Chelsey —
Trust your
Inner Voice,
Always.
xoxo,
Kris

Kris Prochaska, MA

AVIVA
PUBLISHING
NEW YORK

Life Well Spoken: Free Your Inner Voice and Prosper

Published by:
Aviva Publishing
Lake Placid, NY
518-523-1320
www.avivapubs.com

Edited by Tyler Tichelaar, PhD.
Cover and Interior Design by Fusion Creative Works:
www.fusioncw.com

Address all inquiries and book requests to:

Kris Prochaska, M.A.
support@krisprochaska.com
www.krisprochaska.com
www.LifeWellSpoken.com

ISBN 978-1-935586-94-4 (soft cover)
ISBN 978-1-935586-95-1 (eBook)

Library of Congress Control Number 2013954323

Disclaimer

In order to protect the confidentiality of my clients, their names and other identifying information have been changed. Sometimes the details have been altered as well, but the essence of the story or example remains the same.

The interviews herein are from colleagues and friends, who share their experiences of what happened when they listened to their Inner Voice versus what happened when they ignored it. In all other stories, the names have been changed to protect the identities of my clients.

I dedicate this book to Mike, Eli, and Anja.

Words cannot express how much gratitude
and love I have for each of you.

You inspire me to choose consciously every day.

I love you with all my heart and soul.

Acknowledgments

This afternoon I went for a walk. The sun was out at 4:30 p.m. four days before Thanksgiving. The mountains have snow while here in town it's cold and dry. I'm living in my dream town with people I love dearly. I am doing what I came here to do in this lifetime and I love it. I am healthy and fit. I have people in my life who are smart, talented, successful and deeply spiritual. I am blessed.

I inhaled the smell of juniper, sage, pine needles and crisp fallen leaves. The beauty of this place and the path that brought me here still takes my breath away daily. Every tear shed, every challenge, every choice that didn't sit well with others, every experience that clarified who I am and every interaction with others who are living in harmony with their Inner Voice, (or not) influenced me in some way. Within the enormity of this appreciation and bird's eye view I had this afternoon, of the past, and of the scenery before me. It was so easy, and felt so natural to think: "Oh, thank you God for all of this. I'm so grateful."

God got me, right away. No words were necessary. Words can be clumsy and awkward, way too limited for the feeling I was experiencing. My heart was bursting to full and I could feel so much excitement, antici-pation, and love—both for the possibility of this project and my ideas for sharing it with you all, and for the sunset experience I was having in the moment. I felt, and feel, infinite gratitude and appreciation for my family, for my friends, for the people who contributed to this project, for the people whom I have yet to meet and serve, and those for whom I am already blessed to serve.

Then, later sitting here attempting to capture on paper those bodily feelings of warmth, grace, potential and possibility, Love, gratitude, deep knowing of Truth, and absolute faith that all is well, no matter what, I wondered, "How do I convey that to my family, my friends, contributors, editors, coaches, and colleagues?" Listing names with a thank you in front seemed paltry compared to recognizing who you *truly* are. It's easy for me to say thank you to God when I'm alone in nature. But when God comes through other people, through my lover, my children, my friends, my family, through you listener, and you, reader (I can feel you all); sometimes I am so blown away by the intimacy of it, the presence of the Divine in you, that I lose my ability to speak—I feel so humble and overwhelmed at once. My heart swells and hurts at the same time…the infinite and swiftly fleeting converge in a moment and I'm not sure which to hold onto—so I let them both go, and trust we will meet again someday. When we do, words will not be needed because we'll look at each other and simply know: "I got you."

So, until that time comes, I will do my best to say thank you in writing.

I wish to extend a heartfelt thank you to all of the contributors of Inner Voice stories (you can find their website information in the Resources section): Roma Anjoy, PhD, Lynn Baldwin-Rhoades, Beth Buelow, Jessica Butts, MA, Elizabeth Case, Dr. Perry Chinn, DC, Maria Dykstra, Jaquline Fairbrass, Megan J. Huber, Tabitha Jayne, Dianne Juhl, Karen-Lynn Maher, Jennifer Pearson, Mike Prochaska, Julie Ramage, Nadhira Razack, Megha Rodriguez, Kristin Thompson, Marty Ward, Rachel Whalley, MA, and Debbie Whitlock.

Your stories are our stories too. It was truly a pleasure to interview each of the folks who shared their stories of when they listened to their Inner Voice, and when they didn't and what were the results. The themes throughout those stories and experiences were simple, yet profound. I wish I could have included all the interviews in this book in their entirety. I had to make the difficult choice not to include all of the interviews, not because they weren't compelling, but rather to keep the book a manageable length! You can find the interviews and new ones as well at www. LifeWellSpoken.com.

I'd like to say a special thank you to my Board of Direction: Jessica Butts, M.A., Karen-Lynn Maher, and Debbie Whitlock. Jessica who keeps me real with lots of love and a healthy dose of humor; Karen-Lynn who keeps me accountable to my purpose and who reminds me that my family is my priority—not work; Debbie who coaches me and has taught me that nothing is more powerful than a woman with a dream and the money to make it come true. Thanks to my other coaches: Darla LeDoux for teaching me to be real and above all—believe in myself; Anne Presuel who helped me trust my intuition; and Kristin Thompson who helps me be a better speaker and share this message with the world. Thank you to Patrick Snow who helped me get started with this project, and a special thank you to Karen-Lynn Maher of Legacy One Authors for making sure it got finished! It is because of Karen's love and belief in my message that you are holding this book now.

And, of course, thank you to my family and friends. A big shout out to Angela and Sundy who helped me by watching my kids when I needed to work or write. Your support and love for my children eased my stress so I could create. Thank you for that. To Paul & Renata: Thank you for understanding and for ensuring that pancake Sunday happened even when I wasn't at the cabin because I was home writing. It felt good to know Mike and our kids were safe, well-fed, and happily enjoying the "golden cabin" while I wrote. Thank you to my parents, sisters, and in-laws who, while they haven't always agreed with what my Inner Voice has guided me to do, continue to love and support me anyway. It is within these closest relationships that I have the hardest time being vulnerable and expressing how much appreciation I have for each of you.

Mike, you and our children are my toughest teachers. You expand my capacity for love and break down barriers around my heart everyday. You call me out when I speak from my little voices, and reflect back to me infinite love when I'm aligned with my Inner Voice. This is a priceless gift. I don't know too many men who would do what you do for me, and for us. Thank you. Eli and Anja—I love you *infinity-Google-plex!* Thank you for teaching me that fun and play are how to best access the Inner Voice and are at the heart of a prosperous life. I want to be like you when I grow up.

I have so much gratitude and a special place in my heart for my clients who are committed to their own healing and transformation. You are changing the world every step you take to knowing yourself and living your truth and it is my deepest pleasure to serve you all. Last, but far from least, thank you God for designing me perfectly to do the work I am meant to do in this world and for providing everything I've ever needed to serve you through helping others share their own unique expression of Your voice.

From My Heart To Yours,

Contents

INTRODUCTION

Enough Is Enough

"You are not a piece of crap."

"Stop arguing for your limitation."

I tried to convey these ideas to a woman in her forties who, obviously wounded and more than a little drunk, was caught up in the familiar litany of reasons why her life wasn't working, why she was hurt, broken, and unloved.

Yes, not the best time to try and break through the fog of a self-imposed prison, I know, but sometimes enough is enough.

Sometimes there comes a time when someone, even ineffectively, has to remind you...

YOU ARE ENOUGH.

Are you done? Done with the old story of why this or that didn't work, this person or that person didn't love you, or loved you inappropriately? Are you done with beating yourself up and trying to fix what's "wrong" with you? Have you had enough yet?

Recognize that as a human being, you have forgotten. You have forgotten who you *truly* are.

Your parents and caregivers forgot too.

It's okay. I think it's by Divine design for us to have forgotten.

Now it's time to remember.

Is there darkness in the world? Yes. Evil? Most definitely.

Do people do stupid, unfathomably ridiculous, horrible things to each other? Yes. Do most people do these things without realizing what they are doing?

I believe so.

In the Buddhist tradition, ignorance is one of the main "sins" that creates *maya*, or the world of illusion. It's what has us forget who we truly are, and what we are capable of as forces of Love in the world.

When I have my down times, the times where I get foggy, fearful, and my mind gets eff'ed up because those little voices in my head are so loud, that's when I forget who I am, I forget who my kids are, and I forget who other people are. It happens.

In those moments I forget that we are all Divine beings, connected, all One, and I say things and do things that display my ignorance.

I feel shame. Guilt. I cringe inwardly and draw myself smaller so as not to be seen.

Living that way pretty much sucks. So I have made a choice. It's a choice I remind myself of daily. This book is about that choice and how to practice it yourself. I made a choice to be free from those little voices, and from that one choice I have been shown not only what has kept me a prisoner, but others as well, especially my clients. I've seen things I didn't want to see. I tried to turn away, to act like that wasn't a part of me, but one can't go on pretending forever because eventually, when you find yourself out of alignment with your heart and soul, the first thing you must do is practice freedom through choice.

The choice is to wake up and remember.

I wish I could say that waking up happens in an instant and you never go back to sleep. I think it *can* and *does* happen that way for some folks. And with the right tools and information, a person can wake up quite suddenly! But for most of us, it's more of a process and a practice.

This book is both—a process and a practice. It's about "freeing" that which truly can never be encumbered, except through our forgetfulness and ignorance. You are already free. This book will show you how to experience that freedom.

If you so choose...

> *"Somewhere in there, among the worries, questions,*
> *advice and advertising jingles, lives your intuition,*
> *your true 'inner voice.' You can hear it to*
> *the extent that you give it your attention."*

> **— Martha Beck**

SECTION 1

Getting Oriented

CHAPTER ONE

Meeting in the Middle

*"When I was 17, I read a quote that went something like,
'If you live each day as if it were your last, someday you'll most certainly
be right'...since then...I have looked in the mirror every morning and
asked myself, 'If today were the last day of my life,
would I want to do what I am about to do today?'
And whenever the answer has been 'no' for too many days in a row,
I know I need to change something... Your time is limited....
Don't let the noise of others' opinions drown out your own
inner voice. And most important, have the courage to follow your heart
and intuition.... Everything else is secondary."*

**— Steve Jobs, June 12, 2005,
Stanford Commencement Address**

I started writing this book at a time when my whole business was falling
apart and my relationships were strained. I was far too serious, uptight,
and focused on doing the "right" thing vs. doing what my heart was
calling for. It was showing up in my bottom line, my stress level, and
my relationships. "More play, less work!" was what my Inner Voice was
screaming to me (as were my kids and husband!).

I had run myself ragged trying to keep up with emails, tele-classes, coaching programs, speaking, launches, networking, caring for my kids, trying to be there for my husband, seeing clients, trying to get enough sleep, and dealing with perimenopause, thyroid issues, and adrenal fatigue symptoms. In short, I was burnt out and felt put out at every turn. My nerves were raw and there were days when I could actually feel my soul being sucked or drained out of my body. My clients were getting the best parts of me, while my family and my own body, mind, and spirit suffered.

This hectic life was not what I had signed on for when I decided I wanted to be in business for myself! I just wanted to help people. When did it get so damn complicated to do that? As I grew and expanded, it seemed there was always another hurdle to overcome. I never got to rest. It felt a lot like being in labor with my kids. Little to no rest, lots of work, and never being sure when the reward would come and the pain would end.

I knew I couldn't keep up this pace much longer; my heart was skipping beats and I was increasingly anxious. Whereas in the past I would have used any one of my grounding, soothing, or energy techniques and kept moving along, I was finding that I couldn't stay focused long enough to use my own medicine. My thyroid medication wouldn't stabilize, I was either over- or under-medicated, and I had a hard time sitting still long enough to meditate and do the breathing that I knew would help my stress level. I felt like a big huge fraud. Here I was helping people with their stress and beliefs, and doing good work with them—they were feeling better and making progress—while I was getting more stressed and my financial situation was getting worse and I couldn't seem to pull out.

I kept focusing on what was wrong and trying to find some way to "fix" it—and me. I hired therapists, coaches, and went to several different doctors over a ten-year period. I spent thousands of dollars trying to figure out how to stop feeling so darn empty and frustrated. I was sick and tired of feeling sick and tired, and nothing I did seemed to work; in fact, the more I tried, the more elusive my desires and goals became. I had so much shame about where I was that I tried to keep my stress and health issues hidden. I definitely hid my financial situation as well. Until I couldn't anymore....

My primary thought and feeling was: "There must be something wrong with me." (Because other people seemed to figure out how to balance everything—people who had much harder lives than I did.) Why was I so miserable and crabby all the time? Being a tenacious gal, and having made some big commitments with my coach, I kept going—determined to push through, to find a way out of the quiet hell I was living inside.

I kept getting intuitive hits that I needed to change it up, and I would— for a while—but something would pull me right back into the vacillation dance again, and I couldn't seem to break free. I was stuck. I could see where I wanted to go, what I needed to do (or at least thought I needed to do—because it's what all the "experts" were saying), but I either couldn't make it happen or always felt like I was just a little "off the mark," even when I nailed it.

Three big aha's happened then, within the span of about five months. The first was that I saw a woman speak at a women's networking event. The message she taught was similar to mine—we both teach about mindset, how important it is, and how our emotions and thinking can either liberate us or hold us back. This woman is brilliant. Her story amazing: She grew up in an abusive home, left that home as a teenager to live on the streets, was pimped out at a young age, and knew things most young women should never know. Long story short: A teacher believed in her, gave her books to read, food to eat, and something each of us needs if we are truly to break out of whatever hell we may find ourselves in—belief in her worth, until she could believe in it for herself.

As I sat and listened to this woman, who now has her Ph.D. (plus several other advanced degrees), who teaches at Stanford, and who was making nearly half a million a year as a coach at the time when I saw her speak, I thought how amazing her life and story are. How inspiring she is, how incredible, literally, to go "from the streets to Stanford" and be where and who she is today. I have so much respect for her.

But...I couldn't relate to her story. As I drove home from the event where I heard her speak, I was thinking about my own life story. About what I'd overcome in my life, about how hard I'd worked, and how sometimes it seemed like I really hadn't come that far because my life hadn't been as dramatic as hers—I hadn't made a huge leap in environment like she did, or come from literally surviving and wondering whether I'd make it through another night alive, or starving because I had no food for a couple of days. My story wasn't physically about life or death, it wasn't so...well, simple.

Around the time I heard her story, I also heard a couple of other people share their stories of living on the streets and then turning it around. Having hit bottom, they created their lives out of nothing. I was thinking about their stories, and I felt something profound, liberating, and a little scary: *When the only thing you have left to lose is your life, things get pretty simple.* There's no more bottom than that, and the only way out is up. Period. A person knows right where he or she is because there is nowhere else to go.

I thought about my own life. I thought about the times when it felt like life or death—those were the times when I was terrified at an ego level of being ridiculed, rejected, uncomfortable, or ashamed. And I was usually able to avoid really experiencing those things by playing it safe, flying under the radar, and doing whatever I needed to do to fit in or deflect attention off of myself. I saw how being stuck in this "middle" place between being led by my emotions (an *emotional follower mindset*) and being totally clear, spiritually dialed in, and trusting my value, my intuition and the process (a *thought leader mindset*) was exactly where I'd been. The middle is a disorienting place. It's foggy and confusing because there is no bottom, and there is no "top." It all blends together in this no-woman's land of conjecture, constructs, and conflicting thoughts, beliefs, and emotions.

The second insight I got was that I was focusing on the wrong thing, literally. I kept focusing on what's wrong, trying to "fix" it, but the problem never went away. I began to think that with all this focus on what's wrong, maybe I was creating the vicious cycle. I saw that we cannot make someone or something all right by focusing on what's wrong. It just doesn't work that way.

The painful part of this realization was that I had spent my whole life solving problems. I was very good at it. I had been studying psychology since I was in middle school. I was trained to diagnose and figure out what's wrong with people (not in my grad school program, which was more philosophically based, but in my job as a research assistant at the University of Washington and later as a therapist in private practice). In my family while I was growing up, the focus was on "fixing" and finding solutions. I was steeped in it!

The other challenge with this insight was that most marketing is focused on the pain people are in and trying to solve some problem that people are having. I knew if I were to hold true to my belief that we can't make something or someone all right by focusing on what's wrong, then I'd have to do it in my marketing as well, as much as I could. There aren't many models for this out there!

Finally, the thing about this insight that really freaked me out was: If I'm not fixing what's wrong, or solving some problem, then why the hell would anyone want to pay me? What value do I have? What exactly do I do? I really had no idea. All I knew was what I knew, and I certainly didn't know who I'd be if I were doing something that didn't involve solving a problem or making someone feel better by addressing what's wrong in his or her life or business. I know deep in my heart that I am a healer. I always have been, but I also knew I was being called, and am still being called, to heal in a different way—to acknowledge and understand and help people to see that nothing is inherently wrong or broken about them.

I knew I had to focus on something different, but what?

During this time, I was developing my ideas about the little voices and the Inner Voice, and the continuum of consciousness between emotional follower and thought leader. In short, someone in an emotional follower state of mind is listening to the little voices of fear, doubt, shame, guilt, criticism, judgment, etc. and is overwhelmed by—led by—these emotional states OR the person is so closed off to her emotions and not allowing herself to feel or experience any kind of emotion that she is ruled by the subconscious mind. On the other end of the spectrum is a thought leader who is deeply connected to her intuition, and to Source, and is someone who is the "primary creative force" in her life (as Robert Fritz describes it in his book *The Path of Least Resistance*).

Thought leaders listen to and live from their Inner Voice. Someone in the middle, who is *managing the middle* as I call it, vacillates between the emotional follower and thought leader consciousness so much that she is stuck, frustrated, and maybe even numb. She listens to the little voices and the Inner Voice and often can't discern between the two, or she is terrified of following what her Inner Voice is guiding her to do because the little voices still hold reign over her inner boardroom. These are the "worried well" people—the folks who do not meet criteria for some mental health disorder, or who are having a difficult time functioning. They are people who are simply stuck—stuck in the middle, listening to the little voices, and wondering, "How did I ever get here?"

I knew intuitively that learning to listen to and speak from the Inner Voice was the answer to years of therapy and time on the couch processing and focusing on the little voice stories, but I still didn't know how to "do" that.

Turns out it has nothing to do with *doing*, and everything to do with *being*.

Our human being, that is. I was introduced to *Human Design*, a synthesis of four esoteric systems of understanding the human experience (Astrology, Chakras, the I Ching, and the Kabbalah), blended with the science of quantum physics and genetics. I began studying the life charts in Human Design and realized that it's all right there: the blueprint for how we are meant to express Spirit, how we are meant to lead ourselves, and be in relation to one another—based on our unique design at birth. Our purpose, strengths, and access to inner wisdom are all there in our unique chart. I saw how we kept trying to "fix" something that was never broken in the first place. Everything changed personally and professionally from that point on.

The third "aha" that happened is that I was listening to a teacher describe our "relationship" to money and how we cannot serve two masters. In other words, we cannot serve money and God. We can only serve one, and most of us serve money but think we are serving God. Holy heck! A divine two-by-four right in the third eye! I saw what had happened. My coach had asked me what I was a "stand" for in the world. I declared that I was a stand for God being expressed through each individual unencumbered (even though I didn't really know what that meant or looked like). Although I didn't grow up in any formal religious tradition, I knew this was what I was called to do—to live from and speak from my Inner Voice and be a stand[1] for others doing the same. In essence, I said, "I'm serving God, the Divine in each person, come hell or high water," but subconsciously, I was serving money.

Here's how this realization showed up. This service to money was all totally subconscious for me. I had no idea it was happening until I saw it. (This is still hard for me to admit, especially publicly, but I'm guessing there are some other folks for whom this story will resonate, so I share it in hopes that it will open up some space in your heart as well.)

I'm not sure when it happened, but I think the seeds were planted when I first had a home-based business and began my journey into the world of entrepreneurship. This money servitude grew as I began to make more money and become more discerning about whom I worked with and how I spent my time. While discernment is absolutely essential to success, when you choose and act from the perspective of your ego, it's no longer discern-

---

1 By be a "stand" for something, I mean that no matter what, a person stands in her own conviction and inner knowing that this is what needs to happen right here, right now, and she won't back down in the face of any fear or opposition or wave that threatens to push her over.

ment or valuing yourself and others clearly, but rather seeing and choosing from a limited point of view. It is a fine line.

Somehow, I started to see the world and people only in terms of how could they help me, or how I could make money by being in association with this person or organization. I was trying to "get" without (or before) "giving." I know I'm not the first person to think this way—I've run into people who were blatantly obnoxious in this mindset. I like to think it wasn't totally what was going on for me, but as I got busier, truth be told, I started to see everything I did in terms of how the situation would benefit me. Even when I told myself it was about service first, it all became about money.

Including parenting.

Here is where it really gets painful. I found myself wanting to work and put off being with my kids because I had this almost frantic feeling inside that was something like "If I don't focus on these clients or people outside my home, they won't pay me, so I better serve them first. Oh, and I have lots of meetings and things to do, so I gotta do that too, and then there's writing, blogging, calling, etc." It started innocently enough, my kids asking me to play, to read to them, just to *be* with them. My husband was asking for the same thing. I would engage, but not really. I'd often be thinking of all the things I had to *do*. I wasn't fully present all the time.

Then I noticed at some point that my little family stopped asking me to join them, but not really. They had asked, they wanted me to be there, and then at some point, they had sort of given up on me. That's when I realized I had monetized my relationship with my family—on some level, it was running in the red, but I had to make some money so I could keep the mad machine going, and since my husband and children weren't paying me, they would just have to wait.

Thank God, I figured this out before it was too late. Seriously. That's all I kept thinking.

Thank God it's not too late.

Right about the time this last aha hit, it seemed like my business was truly falling apart. I had agreed to do a joint venture with a gal, but a week and a half before the event, she sabotaged it (and she acknowledged it), and we ended up canceling it. She sabotaged it, but deep down, I had known it wasn't a good fit months before, yet ignored all the red flags and my Inner Voice.

That week, I also had one of my favorite clients end our time together. I felt a lot of loss, and although I knew I had done some of my best work with her, I knew she needed to work with someone else on the issues she was dealing with because they were not my specialty. I could have easily thought, "Oh, no! This is a sign that something's wrong! I should just quit now!" Instead, I asked myself, "What's right about this?" And I realized that God was realigning my schedule and life to fit what I wanted and to help me fulfill my part of the deal to be a stand for Source to come through each person. I knew I was close to a breakthrough, and I also knew I had to start with me, and my family.

This playbook, as I call it, is how I did it. This book is about how I aligned myself with my Inner Voice and let go of any fears or objections to *consciously being* a living temple of God. This process is a practice, and it's not about perfection or even "arriving" anywhere or suddenly being ready to "launch" or move forward or have all your ducks in a row. Those damn ducks never really line up anyway, but they do get pretty closely bunched up—enough to keep herding them along as you take one step at a time in the dark.

On second thought, one way to line up your ducks quickly is simply to get a reading of your Human Design chart. You'll at least be able to see the patterns much more quickly and then take action to get rid of the ducks that don't fit and bring in some more that do! There are resources at the back of this book that describe how to get that chart created for free and have a reading done if you so choose.

This book can be used for your own personal exploration and escape from the middle, or it can be used in the context of a group setting (i.e., Inner Voice Circles). Throughout, I share some short stories and ideas as a jumping off place for you to explore what these stories bring up for you, and I offer questions to reflect upon, either on your own or with others. It will only work if you wholeheartedly engage in creating a new conversation within yourself and with others. Sometimes, it's awkward learning a new language and practicing it out loud, so I encourage you to have fun with it!

Here's what's cool: Although this is life and death work (death to the ego!), it doesn't have to be so serious. In fact, play is one of the best ways to engage the Inner Voice. For those of you who, like me, cringe at the thought of play much like we cringe at the sight of a blank piece of paper awaiting our ideas and expression, I welcome you.

I guarantee that this process of exploring and coming into alignment, into harmony, with your Inner Voice will bring you riches beyond measure, the least of which is money.

"As long as I remain on good terms with my 'other self'
I shall be able to acquire every material thing that I need.
Moreover, I shall be able to find happiness and peace of mind.
What more could anyone else accomplish?"

— Napoleon Hill

CHAPTER TWO

Obstacles and Opportunity

*"Every great leader of the past, whose record I have examined,
was beset by difficulties and met with temporary
defeat before arriving."*

— **Napoleon Hill**

Obstacles and opportunity are part of the game. We all know that, and yet, why do we spend so much time resisting them? Each time I have met with an obstacle and really engaged with it (meaning I didn't put my head in the sand or avoid it), I have learned from it. Each time I have said, "Yes" to an opportunity, especially those that take me out of my comfort zone and where I have no idea whether they will actually pay off, I grow and my business grows. Sometimes not right away. Sometimes immediately.

One of my friends, Debbie Whitlock, financial expert for women and business coach, has had a similar experience. Here's her story:

Kris: Can you think of a specific time when you felt like you really ignored that Inner Voice, and what happened?

Debbie: Yeah. I knew that...when I had my life insurance agency, my sweet [Inner] Voice was saying, "Look, honey; we've got to make a change, and we've got to make it quick. If you don't..." Essentially the summary of the message was financial peril will befall you.

My ego, the other team that runs the joint, was just like so in denial that we fought that message for a long time. Fortunately, in a moment, as it usually is, of absolute weakness, bathroom floor praying to God kind of moment, the voice came back in again and said, "Okay, okay, I have the answer. I've had the answer. I'm here, just trust me." When I started listening to that I was able to extract myself from a really toxic professional contract.

It didn't make sense at the time, Kris. It was the most frightening thing I had ever done. What do you mean? I'm turning in a contract that generates nearly a million dollars of revenue into my business and this is supposed to make me happier? Giving up a nearly seven figure revenue opportunity is supposed to eliminate my financial peril? Please help me understand.

Kris: Yeah, exactly. It really flies in the face of complete rationality, doesn't it?

Debbie: Yeah. What I realize now, five-and-a-half plus years later, is that nowhere did the voice say, "Oh, and when you make this decision by the way, multiple seven figures are going to come back to you. So don't worry about it, sweetie; you'll be fine."

But what it did say was, "You make this decision and release yourself from that arrangement, which is not in alignment with who you are and the purpose that you're meant to serve on this planet. We promise, promise, promise, promise, we will show you the way to get where you're going to be with much better grace and ease than you ever thought was possible." Sometimes I still question that because, trust me, nearly seven figures was a whole lot better than low six figures. But I have faith. I still have faith.

Kris: What about the grace and ease? Or life satisfaction?

Debbie: Kris, that's a huge piece. The first thing that happened once I listened to that little voice and I trusted, was I began a journey that let me stop trying to fit my square self into the round hole of the life that I had "bought."

Kris: Wow, that you had *bought.*

Debbie: Mm-hmm. When I was able to kind of let go of that. It's not easy and I still am working on that piece of it, but when I think back on that, I know that that was as much the money piece. One of my big takeaways was that you don't have to try so goddamn hard. Things actually do come much easier now than they ever did before.

Kris: So that was a huge result for you then.

Debbie: Huge.

Kris: What I really love about this is that while things are coming easier and there are days where you have better grace and ease...What would you say would be the biggest benefits that you've gotten from that, that weren't like a direct relationship to, "Okay, I gave up seven figures and now I'm making seven figures doing what I love." It's more like, "I gave that up and I got blessed with ____."

Debbie: Confidence.

Kris: Priceless.

Debbie: Mm-hmm, yeah. The confidence that I have today—I wouldn't trade that confidence for the kind of revenue that I had between 2003 and 2007, 2008. I wouldn't trade that for those five years at all. I will take my leaner financial lifestyle professionally. Actually, my margin's much bigger than it was before. Oh, by the way, the confidence that I have in who I am now is completely based upon who I am. Not what the rest of the world wants me to be. That [Inner] Voice helped me find that.

Kris: Wow. Isn't that really what we all want, and we'd pay anything for it.

Debbie: Mm-hmm. Yeah, absolutely. And oh by the way, as it relates to business, I believe that I can, and I will, be back at that knocking on our seven-figure revenue friend. But because I'll be in such a completely different place and because I already am in a completely different place, the ease at which that will happen—no more square pegs round holes.

Kris: Exactly.

Debbie: It won't feel like you're pushing that big boulder. That's probably the biggest thing for me, Kris—as it relates to a kind of entrepreneurship in our lives—is that life doesn't feel like I'm pushing the big fucking boulder up the hill every day anymore. You've got to lean into stuff, and you still have to work at it. Trust me, it's not coasting down the hill of easy street. You definitely get to lean into things, but it's that efficiency theory that when you're doing the thing that you're meant to do, it just isn't so hard anymore.

...I'm sure it's a cartoon somewhere that I've seen. But it's that you climb the corporate ladder only to realize that your ladder was leaning on the wrong building kind of thing. It was sort of that deal. It was like I had climbed the ladder, and I got to the top of the ladder only to realize that I was on the wrong building.

Kris: Yeah. You're like, "Oh shit."

Debbie: "Oh shit, I'm supposed to be over there." Thankfully, I was just at a place where I was ready to surrender. I think that's the other thing—I think we all come to this place where we surrender and we say, "Okay, okay. I don't know. Me and my ego, we can make a mess of things super fast. So what if we bring in some skilled professionals here?"

Kris: Exactly. It's like trying to do surgery with a chain-saw.

          I wrote that down actually, when you said you came to a moment
          of absolute weakness. That knees on the floor come to Jesus
          moment where we surrender. …The end result, is that the Inner
          Voice comes back in again. We do have to totally surrender.

Debbie: Right. Here's the beautiful thing, no matter how much I ignored
          her, she never left me alone.

Kris: It makes me want to cry.

Debbie: How beautiful is it that we have that inside ourselves that no
          matter how mean and messy we can be to ourselves, that she never
          leaves us alone. So whether we're knees down on the bathroom
          floor, or in my case I was sitting in my real uber-cool loft office in
          downtown Seattle looking out at the city skyline and having my
          complete breakdown on my desk.

          She never left me alone. She was always there, quietly, gently
          whispering, "I have the answer. I have the answer when you're
          ready." There's no judgment in it. I think that's the biggest thing
          that I've taken through all this over the last five years is that the
          grace and compassion that that voice shows me is the grace and
          compassion I want to show myself, the human.

Kris: Absolutely. I love that you brought that up because I think of that
          Inner Voice as the voice of God. It knows exactly who we are,
          what we're meant to do, the next best step, what our purpose is.
          It knows exactly who we truly, truly are and when we're living
          congruently with that and when we're not. I just love that you
          really pointed out how unconditional that love is.

          I wonder, why do you think that there are people who can't listen
          to it? Is it that they can't accept that amount of love in their lives?

Debbie: I think that is a piece of it. I think that they've never truly experienced perhaps complete passion and absolutely selfless love. I think that they also live in their head. I think of my head as where my ego and I hang out, and my heart is where that voice and my spirit hang out.

So when I was living all in my head, I couldn't get it. I just couldn't get it. Until I started to consider that perhaps there was another way; life just didn't have to be so damn hard; there had to be another way. It was almost like there had been something sort of faintly tapping at me, but I didn't know where it was and I didn't know what it was. The sound was almost annoying at times.

Then the moment that I had my breakdown in my office looking out at the city skyline, it was almost like in that moment there was a crack in the door, and it was like what is the essence of that was finally able to come in and I was able to hear. It wasn't a tapping. It wasn't something that was irritating. It was actually just a gentle voice inviting me to consider something else. So I think when we can get out of our heads, and I still spend a fair amount of time up there—

Kris: Oh yeah, I'm sure we all do.

Debbie: But now there's the ego and my spirit, that voice, there's a two-way communication now that I never had before.

Kris: I love that you brought that up. Even just as we're sitting here talking about it and listening to you talk about it, it sinks me into my heart just listening. It really is a soft place, and there's so many places that have sharp edges in the world these days.

Our perception is that we need to protect ourselves, and being right or looking good and all of these things are sharp edges. They're not soft places. If we're constantly in this place of always being and feeling the sharp edges, it's really scary to sink into that soft place.

Debbie: Yeah, it is. The other thing that I would say as sort of my loving words of encouragement to somebody else who is reading this and thinking, "No, not for me. I don't know anybody else like that." Here's the thing. When you open yourself up to this possibility that there's something inside you that already knows, you will be shocked and overwhelmed with how many people you start to run into who operate from exactly that same place. When you find other people who are doing that, it gives you the confidence to do and be more of that.

Opportunity often comes disguised as temporary defeat—as some obstacle that cannot be overcome, nor that we want to engage in, because the outcome is unknown. And yet, that is where the true wealth is. When we own the perspective of our Inner Voice, and we live from that place, owning *all of it*, both the obstacles and the opportunities and how we got ourselves into this mess in the first place, then we get to see a way out, and take action to be free. And prosperity really does come.

CHAPTER THREE

The Playing Field

"When you are adrift from your core, the space between your surface and your depth fills up with anxiety. Too much time away from your inner home leads to homesickness."

— Carrie McCarthy & Danielle LaPorte

When I first began studying mindset, I often felt frustrated because it seemed like something was missing. I couldn't quite put my finger on it, but it seemed like there was this crucial piece of information that other people seemed to understand that I didn't, and they weren't sharing what that crucial piece was (or they weren't aware of it themselves!).

I realized after I began studying Energy Psychology and how our thoughts (beliefs) and emotions create our reality, that there are a number of components, or elements, that affect each other and our overall mindset beyond just our thoughts and emotions. I saw that when one of these elements was out of harmony, a person's mindset was often negatively affected as well. In other words, the person struggled with emotional upset and physical, energetic, and spiritual imbalances. Thinking positively, let alone staying positive and clear, was really difficult, and taking action that was in alignment with the person's goals and vision was also really challenging.

Pasteur, on his deathbed, rescinded his life's work of proving that germs are the cause of disease by saying, "It's the environment." He recognized that he had spent all his life focusing on the wrong thing, trying to kill and cure the germ, when the environment (in the body) was the most defining influence on whether or not a person, once exposed to a germ, would become ill.

This situation is no different with our thoughts and beliefs.

We must create an environment internally that is steeped in Love, Security, and Self-Esteem (the Inner Voice) and create an environment externally (with people, places, and activities) that support listening to and speaking from our Inner Voice.

Why is this essential?

If you do the internal work, but you don't take actions in the external world that support the internal shifts, you will struggle. You'll likely fall back into patterns that I described above and find yourself still stuck in the middle (that place between emotional follower mindset, where you're led by the little voices, and thought leader mindset, where you're led by the Inner Voice).

In order to help my clients, we—the client and I—needed to create an internal and external environment that supported his or her new beliefs and emotional "balance," and for that we needed a road map. I found that when I teased apart the Five Key Elements that make up a person's world (body, mind, emotions, spirit, and energy) and looked at her "world" as really being a reflection of her mindset, it was much easier to figure out which element was out of harmony or alignment with not only the other elements, but also the main issue/vision/goal that she had. It also helped me to understand even more deeply how our mindset is a reflection of who we are *being* while we are doing what we are doing because there's action and then there is intention (the energy behind the action), and that is a subtle nuance that my clients really found helpful as well.

In the Five Elements of Chinese Medicine[2], the elements all affect one another through flow and control cycles. Each element is related to physical, emotional, and mental characteristics as well as energy and spirit. In the chart below, I have replaced the Chinese Five Elements with the Five Key Elements that make up a person's Aligndset™. The Aligndset™ Map brings awareness to all the parts of our human experience that affect our point of creation: the intersection of our body, thoughts, emotions, spirit, and energy, which help us manifest our vision (or goal). I call it an Aligndset™ vs. simply "mindset" because when these Five Key Elements are in alignment, there is a harmony, and ease in our lives. If any of them is really out of whack, it pulls the others off course too. They are so closely intertwined, in fact, that it's difficult to tease them apart. The Aligndset™ Map, and this book, is my attempt to do so in order for you to understand where you may be out of alignment yourself and how to bring yourself back into alignment easily and quickly.

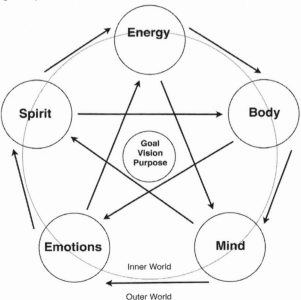

2 The Chinese Five Elements (and the respective elements of AligndsetTM) are water (emotions), wood (spirit), fire (energy), earth (body), and metal (mind).

While the relationship between the location of the traditional Chinese elements and the Aligndset™ elements is interesting, it's not important for understanding the map or using it effectively. Just know that I consciously matched up each element, and sometimes, there is a direct relationship, and other times, an indirect relationship between them.

What is important to understand is that all the elements of one's Aligndset™ affect and are affected by our inner world (or how we see ourselves, and how we see ourselves relative to our goal/vision), as well as our outer world (the people, places, and interactions we experience around us). As we take action toward fulfilling our goal or vision, we directly influence our outer world and the people, places, and experiences in it, and these in turn will influence us. **It is a huge flow and control cycle**, not only between the elements themselves (as indicated by the arrows between the elements), but also between our inner and outer worlds (as indicated by the small circles being half in the larger circle and half outside the circle). How we interpret this influence is our choice, and this ability to choose is what sets us apart from all other animals on the planet.

Energy is the cornerstone of the Aligndset™ Map—not our beliefs or thoughts as most people teach relative to mindset. We are energetic beings first and foremost, and while our thoughts and feelings are important, it's the energetic vibration of thoughts and feelings and the energetic interaction between us and other people that really make the difference. When we know our energetic make-up and how energy flows through us, when we know how we best access our inner authority, or Inner Voice, then creating an external environment that is in alignment with us, our purpose and the way we "roll" in this lifetime creates ease and joy like nothing else. Another way of saying it is this: if you're tired of trying to change the way you think in order to achieve success, you're in the right place! Changing how you relate to the world based on your energetic design is much easier and a hell of a lot more fun.

This choice and insight into our unique design is what will also, ultimately, free us from the middle mindset, a place that doesn't really exist in reality, but more a state of being and belief that is somewhere between what I call *emotional follower* and *thought leader* on a continuum of consciousness.[3]

An *emotional follower* is someone who is led by her emotions (with no awareness of what these emotions are telling her), and who follows others blindly because she gets mired in the drama and confusion created by overwhelming emotions that make no sense. She's unable to discern between what she actually thinks and believes because her thoughts and beliefs are so heavily influenced by others and the tapes running through her head that, frankly, she doesn't even know the difference between what she thinks and what she feels. It's all the same. She feels completely out of control and like a victim to the circumstances and people in her life. What distinguishes her from the "middle" is that she is unaware—nor does she care to know—that there is another way to see the world. In the "middle" there is some awareness of responsibility, but it's not consistent. An *emotional follower* takes no responsibility for her thoughts, emotional reactions, or her behaviors. One could say she is ignorant, but not at all blissful.

I want to be clear about one thing: I am not saying emotions are bad—quite the opposite. They are the juice of life and help us to create lives full of meaning, purpose, pleasure, and holiness. As human beings, we live in an emotional universe. It's like the air we breathe. Emotions are simply waves of energy and information; however, they are so potent they can rock us to our core if we don't understand them and how they flow through us. They can also derail us when we don't allow ourselves to experience them, or try to push some away and only feel certain ones, or when we are designed in such a way as to reflect back the emotions of others, but we take those emotions on and process them even when they are not our emotions in the first

---

3 You can find out where you are on this continuum of consciousness between emotional follower and thought leader by taking the Aligned Voice Assessment at www.krisprochaska.com/assessment.

place (more about that later!). *Whatever we limit, or lack awareness of, we are led by.* In other words, if we limit the range of emotions we allow ourselves to feel and experience, then the ones we disallow and shove down will be the ones that run the show. We will be led by them instead of informed by them. If we are not aware of where the emotions are coming from and what they have to teach us, we'll be led off track by them, instead of gaining wisdom and clarity while playing in the waves.

On the opposite end of the spectrum is the *thought leader*. She is a woman who is wholly conscious and aware of how her thoughts, beliefs, and emotions create her reality. She takes full responsibility for herself and for her results. She can discern between her emotions and her thoughts, and she observes when there is an imbalance in her thinking because she notices the results she's getting and makes course corrections in her thinking and her behavior in order to get new results.

She is selfish in that she takes care of herself, and she is mindful of herself and the affect she and her thinking, emotions, energy, and actions have on others. She takes care of herself because it feels good, and because she recognizes that without her valuing and nurturing herself, she doesn't have a healthy business or fulfilling relationships.

She makes the changes necessary to alter the outcome on behalf of not only herself, but on behalf of others as well. She may be a thought leader in the way most of us think of it: as someone who is on the leading edge of thought and creation, who innovates and influences large numbers of people and as *someone who drives results through sharing her ideas*. As she evolves on the continuum of consciousness, she becomes what I call a *quantum-thought leader*, because she knows that who she is *being*, and her level of clarity, composure, and emotional equanimity in the face of stress and chaos has a radical and immediate effect on the world around her. Either way, she knows and recognizes that she already influences large numbers of people, even if indirectly, by managing her own thoughts and emotions and leading herself wisely, both as a matter of course and as an example to others—especially her kids. A thought leader follows her own inner authority no matter what. She is deeply connected to and guided by her Inner Voice. Her emotions, rather than pulling her this way and that, are information for her. She allows all of her feelings to be present, judging none of them, and not trying to escape either. She is the primary creative force in her life, and she owns that.

Between these two states of consciousness is the middle. The middle is a sinister place. It is the land of vacillation between emotional follower and thought leader mindsets, and it's extremely difficult to navigate. Why? Because the signs are not well-marked. There are lots of "comfortable" places in the middle that feel so nice and snuggly, and soothing. We often just want to sit down and rest a while there. It's like the "waiting place" in Dr. Seuss' *Oh, the Places You'll Go!* There's a lot of waiting around in the middle, and plenty of people to keep one company while waiting. Numbness, depression, anxiety are all symptoms of the middle. Here, you often hear people say things like: "It's okay," "I'm fine," "No problem," or "It's not that important."

The middle is a place filled with B.S., with lies, half-truths, and opinions galore. It's filled with lots of folks who actually know better, who really are "awake" and have some consciousness awareness, yet don't do anything with that awareness because that would mean *change* and *sacrifice*, and those are two things people in the middle fear the most. Folks in the middle desire change, but they often have been so "beaten down" by well-meaning "authority" figures outside of them (parents, teachers, preachers, political figures, movie-star role-models, social media, etc.) that they stay put in order to stay safe, or because they have lost hope that they could experience anything different. These folks are typically the ones who once followed their inner authority, but it was taught out of them, or punished out of them, and they just sort of gave up.

Billions of dollars a year are spent by people in the middle, who are just trying to look good, fit in, and make sure they are keeping up with the latest creature comforts. Mmmmm. The middle is juicy, and it's got a rotten under core that makes folks uneasy...they often don't know why.

There is only one way out of the middle. It's your way. You cannot follow someone out of the middle. You must lead yourself out, and yet we need the help of others to do so as well.

It's a great twist of irony that we must lead ourselves, yet we need others to help us. We need others on this journey with us for several reasons:

1. We are all interconnected. If we make a change, it affects others. Not only that; we need to surround ourselves with those who can hold the space for our vision until we are fully living it. Some of those very people will bring you the very energy and insight you need to break free.

2. We are blind. We can only see what we can see, and most of what keeps us from moving forward is that which we cannot see, but others, in their objectivity and compassion, can see. They help us remove the blinders to our greatness.

3. We need witnesses. We need to have someone hear us, hear our soul's calling, especially when we can't hear it ourselves because of fear, habits of shame, and the din of our little voices. We need others to see us as we *truly* are: both in our Divine perfection, and in our "imperfect" human bumbling—in our struggles and in our breakthroughs. We must enroll others in our vision in order to give it life, and for that, we must have witnesses and willing participants along the way. We are here for each other, not just ourselves.

As I describe Emotional Followers, Middle Managers, and Thought Leaders, please know that I'm really referring to *states of consciousness*, and they are not to be confused with a diagnosis or a label. They are on a continuum, and the goal is to spend more and more time in the higher vibrational consciousness of the thought leader. That said, we all flip back and forth between the different states, depending on our levels of awareness, focus, ability to manage our emotional reactions, willingness to observe and choose our thoughts, and our connection to something bigger than ourselves, i.e. God or Spirit.

I see this flipping back and forth as almost like the tide coming in. The waves come in, they reach the shore, they retreat, pull back, and surge forward again, each time getting a little further up the beach. The only difference is that here (unless there is some injury or extreme emotional blockage due to trauma), the tide of our ever-expanding consciousness never goes out. It just keeps reaching further up the sands of time, until we are spending more and more time living consciously. Awake. Aware. Being Love.

It's not about perfection or reaching some glorified thought leader, "I have flippin' *arrived*" status! In fact, almost as soon as the words "Hey, look at me—I'm a thought leader!" leave your mouth, you're out of the thought leader mindset because that level of talking about it is more like a middle manager (ego) who wants recognition. My opinion is this: if someone else calls you a thought leader, by all means own it. Until then, just *be* one. There is no place to arrive, for even those who spend most of their time in "thought leader consciousness" know that it's an ever-evolving unfolding of consciousness and awareness, and that's what keeps us going for it—it's fun!

All the work I do with my clients is in service to this goal—helping as many people as possible become thought leaders in their own lives through raising consciousness and freeing their Inner Voice. I don't know your path. I only know mine since I've been following it one step at a time. But I have learned some universal tools, techniques, and signs to watch out for from my own personal work and my work with my clients. And I have compiled some of them in this book for you to use on your own journey.

I invite you to listen to and speak from the only voice that will set you free: Your Inner Voice.

"What a liberation to realize that the 'voice in my head' is not who I am. Who am I then? The one who sees that."

— Eckhart Tolle

CHAPTER FOUR

Aligning with Success

"Something in human nature causes us to start slacking off at our moment of greatest accomplishment. As you become successful, you will need a great deal of self-discipline not to lose your sense of balance, humility, and commitment."

— Ross Perot

Before we jump into the Aligndset™ Map, let's take a moment to orient ourselves to the ultimate goal here.

What are we shooting for? Most everyone wants success—whether that's having a successful business, a gratifying relationship, a positive parenting experience, publishing a book, successful weight loss or healing of some other health-related issue, a feeling of having lived one's purpose and passion in life, or just a successful short-term goal in any of these areas, people want to feel successful.

The successful people I've studied[4] who have experienced breakthroughs in any of the above areas had five things in common: *Clarity, Courage,*

---

4 The people I choose to study see success as more than just a lot of money; they see it as only part of the equation, and they see being happy, connected, and joyful while on the journey of success as equally important as the end goal itself. You can find a list of authors in the references section.

and *Conviction*, which all led to *Commitment*. Finally, they all, in some way or another, aligned themselves with their *Inner Voice*, or the voice of God (their Higher Self, Spirit, Universal Truth—whatever fits for you), and allowed that to be the guiding force in their lives vs. their egos.

These folks were, or are, all thought-leaders in their own lives. They had aligned their Being with their Inner Voice, and they had taken action from this perspective in most, if not all, areas of their lives. Some are well-known authors, some are people just like you and me who started listening to and honoring their own inner authority, and they not only lead themselves powerfully, but are also leading others as well. A few of them are included in the interviews you'll find throughout the book.

Let's look at the five common characteristics a little deeper:

Clarity: They knew their intended outcome, where they were starting from, and about how far they were from their goals; they were aware of their strengths and limitations, they knew on some level that not only were they not alone in the journey, but that they were spiritual beings having a human experience first and foremost, and they drew upon this powerful knowing of their inherent value.

Courage: These people were often scared out of their pants, felt rejection, extreme loss or hopelessness, and they kept going anyway—no matter what. They lived by their heart (the root of the word "courage" is *coeur*, or "heart" in French) not by their head.

They had total **Conviction**: unshakeable faith and unwavering focus on their desired outcome. They knew absolutely their own personal truth, followed their inner authority, and believed in themselves as they practiced living by Universal Truth as well.

Commitment: Finally, they recommitted themselves to their goal or vision over and over and over again because they knew it wasn't a one-time deal but an ongoing practice.

Inner Voice: The Inner Voice is the voice of our Higher Self, Infinite Intelligence, Divine Being, Holy Spirit, God—whichever definition fits for you. All are appropriate. The Inner Voice speaks to us in several different ways, depending on our design. I used to think it only spoke to us through our gut intuition, but not everyone has access to that information in the same way. (I explain this in more detail later.) This voice knows exactly what our purpose is, why we are here, and the next best step for us to take. It knows just how valuable we really are. This voice is expansive and all-inclusive; it is infinite in its wisdom and love. It holds no judgment of itself, us, or anyone else. It sees all possibilities and all perspectives, and it has access to all the secrets of the Universe. The aspects of the Inner Voice that I have incorporated into the Five Key Elements of the Aligndset™ Map are Vision, Ownership, Influence, Choice, and Embodiment. Together, they create an acronym for VOICE.

There are many reasons not to listen to our Inner Voice, all of them compelling, none of them valid. There are the perfectly "reasonable" ways that you will be enticed to ignore your Inner Voice as well as some perfectly "unreasonable" ways to heed your Inner Voice. I include both throughout the book so you will know what to watch for. With awareness and action, you can prosper by speaking your world into being, just as you desire it to be, to live a life well spoken.

Jessica Butts, M.A., a psychotherapist in private practice, shares how dramatic it was for her to ignore her Inner Voice and then the realization that she was doing so:

Jessica: ...I think that I follow my Inner Voice a lot. I'm doing what I do because I refuse not to listen to my Inner Voice. [Before] My external world was telling me, "Don't do it, don't do it, don't do it."

           I spent the first fifteen years of my business career doing what the external world told me to do. I was deafened by my Inner Voice just saying, "You are not supposed to be doing this. This is not your path. This is not your life. This is not what you're supposed to be doing."

That living incongruently almost felt like it killed me. I'm being a little dramatic, but it was stifling. It was overwhelming. If I hadn't listened to it—it makes me want to throw up thinking about that—I would still be there. That is profoundly disturbing to me, to think that I could still be living that life if I hadn't just said, "I'm not going to do it anymore. I'm not going to live this life that I'm not supposed to be living."

The only thing that guided me there was my Inner Voice, my inner person telling me what was the life that I was supposed to be living because no one else believed it but me. Yes, I'm the only one. No one else told me, nobody else, not my husband, not my mom, not my sister. It's not even as if they were not necessarily supportive. They just don't live in me. They didn't know this profound calling to do something different.

Kris.   Yeah. It's that profound calling; I love what you said—you were deafened by it. Tell me about that. Tell me what that meant to you. How did that show up? I know you said you were getting that you're not supposed to be doing this. Is that how it was deafening, or are there other ways that it showed up that it was deafening?

Jessica: A couple of ways. Is it helpful for you, Kris, for me to share my story in this way?

Kris: Yeah, if you would like to. If you're willing to that would be great.

Jessica: Yeah. I figure for the purposes of this it might be helpful just to get the entire context of it. This actually happened to me a couple of times in my life. The first time it happened was right after I graduated from high school. I jumped into going to community college. I was just working at this retail store right out of high school, and I met this boy. I was living a life that was not my intended life. My intended life was to go to a four-year college and to go on that path of probably psychology of some sort. That's what I knew I was supposed to be doing.

I met this boy and we moved in together, and I was living this life that just literally was not my life. It was almost a balcony view sometimes of just, "Who am I?" It was deafening then too. It's interesting; it was deafening in a way of almost—this sounds really dramatic, but of this balcony view of me almost screaming down at myself of, "What are you doing? Who are you?" It was such an out-of-body perception of myself.

I realize now saying that, that that's what's happened twice, of looking down upon myself thinking, "I don't know who that person is, but it's not me because the person that's me is sitting up here in the clouds or in the balcony with my Inner Voice still connected to my spirit, but it's not connected to my body. My body is not doing what my spirit is intending me to do."

They were totally split. They were literally split into two different people. My spirit body, which had my Inner Voice, and my worldly body was living out this life that I had no comprehension of that being my life. It wasn't me.

At that time in my life—I was very young, eighteen or nineteen years old—I remember I was standing in line at Wendy's with my boyfriend at the time; we were living together. I just turned to him. I had this secret. I knew my spiritual self was still not connected to my body, and they finally converged in that moment standing in line at Wendy's. I just turned to him as if my spirit came into my body and I went, "I am going to Central Washington University. I've already enrolled. I've been accepted, and I'm moving out, and I'm going to live in a dorm."

All this came flying out of my mouth. As soon as I did it, which I'm super big on working with my clients that once you find your voice, and this is such a trite wording but I totally believe it, the truth will set you free. In that moment, I just was like, "Oh my God, here we go. I'm done and this is what I'm supposed to be doing." That was one example of it.

Can you relate to Jessica's experience of the disconnect between what her Inner Voice wanted and what her body was doing? How is it that we can live dual lives in one body? It depends on who's running the show....

These successful people I studied also overcame the main roadblocks (i.e., perfectly logical reasons to ignore their Inner Voice) in the terrain that each of us encounter along the way in our journey of consciousness: the *little voices*, *conclusions*, *constructs*, and *comparison*. It can be helpful to know just what we will encounter along the way so that when it comes up we can say: "Oh yeah, she said that would be there. Got it. Moving right along...."

Before I describe conclusions, constructs, and comparison, I'd like to delve a little deeper into the Inner Voice and little voices. It's imperative that you are able to discern between them because those little voices are really tricky!

OUR INTERNAL LEADERSHIP TEAM: MEET YOUR BOARD OF DIRECTORS

"Be mindful of your self-talk.
It's a conversation with the universe."

— David James Lees

Imagine a boardroom. In it is a large table with chairs all around it. On either side of this table sit the *Middle Managers*. These folks LOVE a problem to solve, and they thrive on drama. They can come up with a thousand reasons why something can't be done or they'll go off on tangents that will take the whole team off track. They are always asking what's wrong:

"What's wrong with me? What's wrong with them? What's wrong, or could go wrong, with this situation?"

Each one has a distinct personality, and they often act like a bunch of kids who haven't grown up, each vying for control of the room—and scared that they'll be "found out" as not good enough, or as unnecessary. They do not want to be fired, so they will create circumstances and problems to solve so they can stay in their jobs. Some are loud, some are quieter, but all play games either in back room deals or under the table, and they pretty much run the company and all the results when the CEO (that's us) is out to lunch—consciously speaking!

These *Middle Managers* have three basic goals or needs: Love, security, self-esteem[5]. They achieve these goals by sucking up to anyone and everyone they meet, playing it safe, and looking good no matter what. They are also what I call the *little voices*. These little voices are the voices of fear, doubt, shame, guilt, resentment, criticism, and judgment. They are little not because they are quiet or small, but because they make us feel small, they constrict and contract our very being, and they were most often created and programmed when we were very small children.

These little voices only have access to memory banks and collect data from the five senses (sight, smell, sound, taste, and touch), so they have a very limited view of the world and how to solve the problems that they see everywhere. They'll often rehash things over and over, trying to solve the same problem in the same way because they simply can't see any other way to do it. These little voices are why we have patterns that show up in our lives that look like self-sabotage.

Some of these little voices are the disowned parts of ourself—all parts that are stuck in time—typically (but not always) before the age of seven or eight. When we invite them in to have their say (in a specific context and intention), we can invite them to let go of their old stories and perceptions

---

5 These needs are described in David Neagle's Art of Success course and his book *The Millions Within*.

about the world, and give them a new message: one that empowers rather than sabotages our goals and desires. They are part of our inner circle, our board, and so they are valuable. I figure they are there, so there must be a reason for them, even if we don't know exactly what it is. They are part of the human experience, and they are likely not just going to disappear because we want them to.

Some of these little voices are the ones we hear outside of our own heads. They are the voices of our parents, friends, partners, colleagues, culture, teachers, society, etc. Sometimes they are well-meaning, sometimes envious and intentionally malicious. But mostly, they are ignorant (ignorant as in they don't have all the information, not as a judgment) and fear-based.

On the other end of the table, across from where we sit, there is our *Most Trusted Advisor*, or our Inner Voice. The Inner Voice doesn't seek love, security, and self-esteem. *It IS love, security, and self-esteem.* This voice has been described as the "still small voice within." I see the Inner Voice as quite big—it's our right-hand advisor after all—but the little voices of the *middle managers* are often so darn loud we can't hear the Inner Voice, and so it goes unheeded. Even so, it quietly and patiently waits for us to listen. How we listen is unique to each of us; for some it is through a gut-knowing, an instantaneous feedback system that is deeply intuitive; for others they must feel their way through it and navigate the tumultuous waves of emotion and wait until they have emotional clarity and a felt sense that "Yes, this is right for me"; still others know exactly what they want in their heart of hearts and they go get it. I will explain this in more detail later in the book.

People in an emotional follower state of mind listen to the little voices in their heads and they speak from the perspective of these little voices. They get caught up in riots and other group-think or mob mentality and "lose themselves" and their ability to treat themselves and others with respect. The little voices are both in their heads as the tapes from their childhoods, or the opinions of others, and they are also the little voices outside of themselves, often those of family and well-meaning others who say stupid shit that doesn't serve anyone. They may mean well, or may just be mean, but either way, they speak out of fear and ignorance. When people are in this state of mind, they lack discernment and cannot seem to break free from the bondage of the little voices and their negative storm.

In contrast, those folks who are in a thought leader consciousness listen to their Inner Voice, that Most Trusted Advisor who knows the next best step to take, and who leads through intuition, felt sense, gut feelings, emotional clarity, and absolute clarity of who they are and what they want in life. The Inner Voice knows our worth, and it has never stopped trying to remind us of it as well. This Inner Voice is also the voice of Spirit or God, and it knows the unique gifts and contributions each of us makes to the whole. In fact, the Inner Voice has access to everything. Amanda Owen in her book *The Power of Receiving* describes this concept as the "Big Circle" and the "little circle." The Big Circle encompasses everything. Nothing is left out. All are welcome here. This is the realm of the Inner Voice. The little circle, as she describes it, is where the disowned parts of ourself—emotions, people, and experiences we don't like—are banished. When we invite everything from the little circle into the Big Circle, then we have access to it all. Thought leaders are able to discern between the little voices and Inner Voice and have the ability to choose which one to listen to at will because they have practiced emptying the little circle.

Finally, there is us. We are the CEO, the Chief Executive Officer. As the CEO, we act on the directives we receive from the Board of Directors. So, depending on whom we are listening to and taking direction from (and speaking from!), those are the results we can expect to achieve. When we are listening to the little voices or middle managers, we get the same old thing over and over. Lack, limitation, and a focus on fixing the problem keep us spinning our wheels, and keep the problem firmly in place. On the other hand, sometimes our little voices are screaming so loud that if we keep ignoring them, they will sabotage us. So it's about finding a balance and being present with all that is in order to discern consciously the direction to take oneself.

As we attune to our Inner Voice, our Most Trusted Advisor, then we focus on where we are going versus where we have been, and we are *creating the results we want to experience* in order to take us in the direction we want to go.

When we free up our Inner Voice, and stop holding ourselves back from fear of what others will do, say, think, or feel about our expression, then our voice, our full expression in all ways we communicate, is unleashed. It is important to note that harming another with our words and full expression is *not* the expression of our Inner Voice. Our Inner Voice doesn't roll that way—only our little voices do. So when people "find their voice" it is very often used to refer to releasing the inhibition they have imposed upon themselves to give voice to the anger, resentment, and blame that has been festering deep inside for years and unleashing it on others. While speaking our truth means we have to look at the negative emotional states and inhibitions, when we are truly speaking from our Inner Voice, we are actually pretty calm and "level-headed" even about highly emotional situations.

I believe this calmness results from our actually speaking from our "high" heart—the one that knows we are all connected—instead of our bottom heart or broken heart—the pointy part of our heart that hurts and wants to hurt others as well. My son Eli came up with this analogy during breakfast one day. He was eight years old at the time. He pointed out how when people fight at the bottom of the heart, at the pointy part, they grow apart, but they finally come back together in love at the top of the heart. He drew a picture in the air with his fingers of a heart from the bottom up as he described this. I was floored. Eli, and kids in general, truly teach us some of the most amazing lessons.

It's worthwhile to note here that in the Human Design chart, the energetic center of the throat is the center of manifestation. This means that it is the place where we literally speak and express our world into being. Some people have this center clearly defined, and others do not, which, basically means, without going in-depth here, that some are designed to manifest directly and powerfully, and others are designed to make things happen in the world more indirectly. Either way, the voices with which we listen to and express through this powerful center, are the voices that will determine our reality and influence the reality of those around us. Our job is to discern whether or not they are the voices of Love or Fear.

FEAR

"The little voices never go away. You think I'll be making six figures and they'll go away, then seven figures; they don't go away, they just change. They come up in different levels, and if you haven't done the work ahead of time they'll stop you even more. As you just keep doing the work and you keep choosing not to listen to them, it gets easier. It's not that just suddenly you quiet them and they never come back; it's that you learn how to work with them...."

— Darla LeDoux

I had a series of dreams a few years back where I was in a dark house. I couldn't find my way around and there was this male voice taunting me and following me. I couldn't get away and I couldn't find the light switch. Often, just as I was about to find out who or what the voice was, I would wake up. It was very unsatisfying as well as terrifying! Over time, though, I'd get a little braver, and more courageous, and instead of running, I'd stop and turn toward the voice.

The last dream I had I recall distinctly. I was in the same house; it was dark and I could hear the voice, laughing at me, taunting me, trying to scare me. I got pissed off. I was done with this game. While it was dark, I could still somehow "see." Instead of running, I began searching for the voice. I found it in a room, and as I entered the room, I heard the voice directly in front of me. I could sense it sitting in a throne-like chair. I stood directly in front of the chair and said, "I see you. I am not afraid of you." I "saw" the voice/entity/bogeyman with my whole being. I found the light switch, flipped it...and nothing was there.

I never had that dream again.

Facing our fears is like that. When we turn toward them, instead of running, we see they are not real, but ghosts and figments of experiences long since dead.

In his book *Outwitting the Devil,* Napoleon Hill describes the devil as saying: *"One of my cleverest devices for mind control is fear...the fear of poverty, criticism, ill health, loss of love, old age, and death. Fear of poverty and death serve me the most."*

Following are some of the forms that fears come in and how their voices sound. They may sound different in your head, but just notice what thoughts and memories come up for you as you read. It's likely those memories are where your fear stems from, at least in part. It's also likely that the voices are very subtle, and because they come from the subconscious mind, we are not fully aware of them until we begin to look at the results we are getting. Often when I'm working with someone, these voices show up when we begin asking his or her body what it believes, and when, through energy therapy methods, we begin to release the charge around the fears, the voices become clear. Sometimes we become aware through a Human Design life chart reading that these are in fact ancestral fears that are part of our unconscious design. Looking at them objectively in the chart, we can begin to recognize them, and then we've literally turned the light on, and they begin to lose their power to rule us unwittingly.

1. I'm afraid I'll be *Rejected*: "What if they say, 'No'?" We question ourselves and think we must be wrong in some way to offer whatever it is we are sharing: from our thoughts to our products, services, or even ideas. Or we fear there is something wrong with our choices, or who we are and what we hold dear to us. We feel ashamed and afraid that we'll be cast out of the "tribe" or collective once again—just like we felt when we were born into a human body and felt disconnected from Source. This fear is primal. Again, when you see that how you were designed is absolutely perfect, and it's about engaging with the people and experiences that are in alignment with you and your design, all fear of rejection dissipates, because you know, deep down, there is nothing wrong with you. (Did you hear that? I'll say it again just in case you didn't get it: There's nothing fucking wrong with you.)

2. I'm afraid I'll be *Judged*: "What will they think of me?" "They won't approve or like this." "They won't let me." "No one accepts me for who I am." This fear is interesting. It really is a big fat lie because very often the only one judging us is...*us*. Yes, people will not like your decisions or be happy with the way you express yourself. It has nothing to do with you. The saying "Beauty is in the eye of the beholder" goes both ways: "The offense lies within the beholder, not outside him."

3. I'm afraid they'll find out I'm *Inadequate*. Of course, that's not how the voice sounds. It sounds more like "I don't know enough," "I'm not good enough," or "What if they find out the truth (that I don't know what I'm doing)?" (The "truth" is really a lie, disguised as "truth.") I've found that the people who are concerned that they're not good enough or don't have enough experience are very often the ones who lie to themselves the most, and who are most often actually in integrity. Why? Because they will typically take some action to make sure they have the training they need, they will ask questions, or they are so concerned with doing it right that they certify themselves into paralysis. They get certification and training after training in order to feel good enough—so much so that they never actually share their ability or gift with the world. It's the people who never question their ability, AND who don't care whether they are adequate because they just want to make a buck, who are the ones to be concerned about.

4. It's *Not Spiritual* to make money or talk about money: "I'll be punished." "It's better to be poor because poor people are more spiritual." "It's not okay to have what I want when others are suffering." "Rich people are greedy and selfish—and I'm afraid people will think I'm greedy and selfish if I have money." Do I need to go on? This fear is closely linked to the fear of being judged, but it's more a fear of some higher power, or someone else holding a power over us who will judge us for what we *do* and *desire*, versus judging us for who we *are* (as described above). God doesn't want you to be poor. How can you care

for others and make a difference in the world if you can't even take care of yourself?

5. I'm afraid to own *Responsibility*: "It's not my fault." "If _____ didn't do this to me, then I would be _____." This one is juicy! Bottom line: *What happened to us was not our fault, but what we do with it now, how we use those experiences and live our lives, is OUR responsibility, and has zero to do with others.* Understanding this truth means completely letting go of the victim mentality that makes us feel powerless. It is not easy, and yet it is so simple. Acceptance is the first step. Acceptance of ourselves, of the situations(s), of how it all went down. Acceptance does not equal approval! It is acknowledgment of what is and was without a story or desire for it to be anything other than what it is or was. It's accepting and forgiving ourselves for wanting and needing it to be other than it is or was. It's taking the steps to give ourselves *right now* what we currently need, and needed back then, so we can move forward today, without waiting for anyone else to do anything, say anything, or give us permission. It is where we find true freedom.

6. "I'm afraid of my own *Power*." This fear's voice is something like: "Power is dangerous. People in power do awful things; they hurt others in order to get what they want or make money." or, "I don't want to be seen as power-hungry." This fear is both the flip-side of inadequacy and the sister to responsibility. Most of us have such a charge around power because we've seen, or been at the hands of, someone who has misused power and hurt others. Maybe we've even misused it ourselves. I know I have, and it didn't feel good. However, this fear goes even deeper than that. It is about fully acknowledging how powerful we really are, and if (when!) we do, then we truly become a leader in our own lives. I think most of us are afraid of what that means. I know for me it means that if I am a leader in my life, then I am doing things that most other people are not doing and I will be waking up to the power and responsibility of changing my mindset. If I do *that*, then I will have to look at all the areas of my

life that aren't working and make some decisions that could then lead to losing people or things I've become accustomed to, regardless of whether or not they are supportive and beneficial. On the other hand, I could even serve at a higher level as Marianne Williamson points out in her infamous passage from *A Return To Love*:

Our deepest fear is not that we are inadequate. Our deepest fear is that we are powerful beyond measure. It is our light, not our darkness that most frightens us. We ask ourselves, Who am I to be brilliant, gorgeous, talented, fabulous? Actually, who are you not to be? You are a child of God. Your playing small does not serve the world. There is nothing enlightened about shrinking so that other people won't feel insecure around you. We are all meant to shine, as children do. We were born to make manifest the glory of God that is within us. It's not just in some of us; it's in everyone. And as we let our own light shine, we unconsciously give other people permission to do the same. As we are liberated from our own fear, our presence automatically liberates others.

Our Power is in our light. It is who we truly are. The feeling that we are powerless at some level is universal to humans, and from what I've observed, it comes in sometime around birth and possibly before. Waking up to our power is part of our journey, and one that all true leaders have embraced. The question then becomes: How will we use it? During the course of writing this book, I had the opportunity to experience a soul-retrieval with a shaman. In that retrieval, I came to understand that part of my purpose in this lifetime is/was to heal deep and long-standing ancestral trauma around power and the misuse of it, especially in the female lineage. If you know me, you know I am not much of a girlie-girl. I like make-up and beautiful things, and to get dolled-up every once in a while, but that's not my typical way of showing up. I've really had to explore what the Divine Feminine energy and power is for me, and since it's on the tips of the tongues of just about everyone in coaching and marketing these days ("Own your Divine Feminine!") I often felt that because I'm not a girlie-girl with long flowing Goddess-like hair and a wardrobe and make-up to match, that I was failing in "getting my Divine feminine power on." Then I realized that the way it shows up for me and through me is more like a guttural uh-huh deep in my sacrum and has nothing to do with how I dress but rather with my energy. The energies that are natural for me flit between playful fairy godmother/auntie who grants wishes and intuitively and lovingly downloads solutions and answers for folks and the Goddess Kali, destroyer of bullshit and blocks, who wears cowboy boots and cusses like a truck driver. My point: Own your power, whatever that looks like.

7.   "I'm afraid to be *Successful.*" Ironic, isn't it? But not at all uncommon! This is how the voice of this fear sounds: "I'll lose _____ if I'm successful." "It will hurt _____ if I'm successful." "If I'm successful, I'll have to give up _____." "What if they find out I don't really deserve to be successful, and take it away?" and "Successful people end up unhappy, their marriages end, they use drugs or drink too much, they lose it all anyway, so why bother?" I know these are pretty extreme to us logically, but remember, the voices of fear are not rational! They are based on associations made at a deep emotional level, often when we are children and do not yet have the faculty of reason working on our behalf. The fear here is loss. What will we have to give up, or lose, in order to be successful? The guilt can be huge, and the fear of being exposed as not good enough is also overwhelming and keeps people right where they are—dreaming about success, but never able to take the actions necessary to actualize it.

8.   "I am afraid I will *Fail.*" The other side of the fear of success coin, the fear of failure, is also centered around loss. The potential grief, loss of the "dream," that beautiful vision we have in our heads that feels so good, if we try and it doesn't work—the pain might be too great. For example, thinking, "What or who will I lose if I fail?" "What will people think of me if I fail?" and losing face, and having that core belief challenged of who we *think* we are (i.e., ego) all are at the

heart of this fear. There is also often a felt sense of "There must be something wrong with me," or "I must have done something wrong." And the fear is that if we've done something wrong (failed), then we'll be punished or thrown out of the tribe and lose *everything*, instead of just learning a lesson or two along the way. I think this fear also stems from the feeling of pressure that folks are not living up to their full potential (not because they can't, but because they don't know how to live in alignment with their design and purpose) OR because other people are judging them for actually living in alignment with their purpose and are threatened by it! Folks unconsciously fail so they don't have to live out that rejection and judgment and so they can stay safe in the tribe getting all the love they feel they need from others (forgetting they are Love at their core).

9. "I'm afraid it will hurt." The fear of *Discomfort*. I think this fear comes from the experience of birth. In the womb, we felt at one with our mothers, connected and even close to Source as well. For the most part, during that time we are safe and all our needs are met. I recall reading somewhere during my prenatal yoga teacher training that the baby actually sends a signal to the mother, via hormones, to begin the labor and birth process. Birthing, even under the most sacred and gentle circumstances, can be traumatic. Baby has to travel through the birth canal, and it's not an easy journey. Imagine: A grapefruit to cantaloupe-sized head through a small tube. That's not an easy journey! The trauma of birth is something universal to us all. The association of "When I make a decision to move forward (i.e., be born), it hurts!" gets deeply ingrained in our body memory, and it can affect us on many levels.

10. "I don't know what will happen." The fear of the *Unknown*. We don't know what the outcome will be or what to expect, so we resist change as much as possible. Conversely, *we are afraid to know what we know*, because if we did, we would have to change or make a decision, and all the other fears discussed above would get triggered. So, we say, "I

don't know" when someone asks us what we want, or what we are going to do, or what we feel called to do, so we don't have to change or take ownership of what we really know to be true for us, simply because we are not sure how it will all turn out. My mom told me once that if a bunch of people were sitting around and everyone threw her problems out on the table, when it came time to leave, each person would pick up her own problems and hold them close to her chest. Why? *Because they are familiar to us.*

Now that we have a better grasp of the little voices (along with the fears they express) as well as the Inner Voice, let's look at the other roadblocks that can trip us up on the journey. I call these "contractions" because they contract our energy, make us feel small and helpless, and make us start listening to and speaking from those little voices. These contractions are: *conclusions*, *constructs*, and *comparison*.

Conclusions are "logical progressions of thought" that we use to come to a decision and viewpoint about a person, place, situation, experience, etc. "This is how it is...and therefore always will be." As "logical" as they may seem, most of the conclusions we have about the world are emotionally based. They were created directly from our experiences as a young child based on the *interpretations* we made about how we felt at the time and what it meant about us and the world. Interpretations, and the process of interpreting phenomena in our world, are what we need to examine—not the phenomenon itself.

We also come to conclusions about things before they ever come to pass, and that's where we make *assumptions* about the meaning of things, or other people's intentions, and act as if that's truth without ever exploring how true those assumptions are.

Some conclusions we carry with us were passed down through our parents, teachers, leaders, culture, society, the TV, etc. Like the constructs below, these are the limiting beliefs that get passed on that we take on as truth, when in reality they are someone else's faulty interpretation or assumption about himself and the world that he shared as if it were true for everyone.

If we are not asking questions of ourselves and others and the world (which is all the mind is really good at anyway—asking questions to gain clarity through other energy centers in our body, i.e., gut, emotions, heart, etc.), then we are operating based on conclusions, and there is no freedom or heart-to-heart connection there. A conclusion I came to growing up was that logic is more important than intuition, so therefore, even if I get a strong gut feeling about something, I need to listen to what is probable or logical, instead of my intuition—because people don't value intuition. Ironically, my gut knowing is my most powerful way to access my inner authority and I've had to unlearn the knee-jerk reaction to think things through first and let go of the belief that I can't trust myself and my gut-knowing. Any time you hear yourself say, "Because," check yourself; ask some questions to see whether your reason is really true, for when you start saying "because" you're in the realm of conclusions. (Unless you're saying "because this is in alignment with my inner authority!")

Constructs are the preconceived notions that we learn from our parents, society, and especially our culture that tell us "This is how the world is" or "This is what this *is* and what it *means*." They are an attempt to make sense of the world and create a common language by labeling phenomena that becomes "solidified" through the generations through science, religion, ritual, teaching, and stories about the world. There is nothing inherently wrong with this! It's very useful in fact. For example, "tree" is a construct. It is a word that describes an idea and a physical form that we perceive with our senses. That's great if we want to point out a tree and teach a child the name for that tall, brown and green object sticking vertically out of the ground, but it is limiting because most of us, when we think of a tree, think only in terms of its physicality—what it looks and feels like when we touch it or how to use its material for building. We think of trees in relation to us and their purpose for us. But what is a tree, really? At a quantum and spiritual level, trees are so much more than the idea we have of them—but most of us miss out on that because we only perceive them relative to ourselves, and not necessarily as they truly are in all their glory. When we engage with our world through constructs only, and ignore the perceiving and receiving of the energy and information all around us, we miss out on the subtle nuances and information available to help us make powerful choices and feel connected to others and the world around us.

Another way of looking at constructs is to see them as the beliefs upon which we construct our inner world, and which directly influence the world we experience outside of ourselves. For example, if you have a certain belief about money, perhaps that it's "hard to keep around," then that is, and will be, your experience of money until you deconstruct that belief and build a new one that is more empowering.

Most of our "constructs" or beliefs about ourselves and the world are formed at an early age and reinforced over time. Like I mentioned in conclusions above, many of these beliefs are not ours—we learned them from others. We absorbed them and took them into our own subconscious structure at a young age (see more about this in Chapter 6 on the mind) and have been living as though they are true, "solid," and unquestionable. Get curious and start questioning: "Where did I learn this?" "What do I really think and feel about this?" "How do I *want* to think and feel about this?"

Comparison is judgment and trying to locate our place in the world based on who we are relative to others, versus who we *truly* are (which is a unique and Divine expression of God). We are looking for where we are better or worse, smarter or dumber, skinnier or fatter, faster or slower...you get the picture. All of these comparisons keep us fully entrenched in the world of duality, and living from the conclusions and constructs we have made about what those ideas mean. They are ideas because they are created in the small-mind or ego of human beings—not the mind of God or Source. They tell us nothing about who the person or thing is—only what it is relative to something else.

One of my friends shared how when she goes on Facebook, she can find herself in a "compare and despair" cycle really easily. It's as if everyone is doing amazing things, growing her business, being happy, and everything is just grand, while her life is in the pits. This compare and despair cycle is a conclusion-construct-judgment trap. She cannot see all of the reality of the experiences of her "friends"—so much more is happening behind the scenes! Furthermore, she is reading the posts through the filter of her constructs or beliefs, which are also not a reliable indication of what is True. What if the despair she feels is not only her ego feeling left out or less than, but her Inner Voice knowing the Truth of who she really is, and the Truth of what's possible, and the disparity between her construct and the Truth is what feels so bad—not that she's bad....

Think about that next time you're on Facebook or other social media, or watching television, or reading a fashion magazine, or you start comparing yourself to others and feeling like you're coming up short.

Comparison or judgment is where that very powerful and provocative little voice shows up the most: the inner critic. In Chapter 9, we'll look at how to deal with this inner critic as well as the other little voices, but for now, just recognize that this voice of the critic is, for all intents and purposes, trying to keep you safe. Thank it, and move forward anyway.

All three of these contractions are often used in the decision-making process that keeps us, and the world around us, limited in the amount or degree of possibility that can show up. We hold them to be truths, but they are subjective truths, because they do not stand up to the real test of Truth, which states *in order for something to be true anywhere, it must be true everywhere, no exceptions.* Most of us do not question our conclusions (or our constructs and comparisons for that matter!). We learned not to question them early on by the way. Not only that, we learned to make decisions with our mind, which is a lousy place to decide from! The mind wasn't designed to make a decision, only to gather information or ask questions in order to gain clarity from our inner authority (which does not reside in the mind). Furthermore, the mind is a binary organ: it has two hemispheres that see things very differently. It is always looking at things relative to the past or to the future; it isn't designed to be in the present. Our awareness of what to choose comes from other centers of awareness (the most common being intuition and emotion). Bottom line, it's not our fault we've been using our minds incorrectly—but in order to wake up and truly evolve both personally and as a race, we must start questioning these contractions and how they show up in our lives. Why? Because they kill off possibility and cause us all a great deal of pain in the process by feeding the fears I described above.

In the chapters that follow are descriptions of each of the Key Elements of Aligndset™ along with tips and techniques for working with each one. Alongside each element is one of the five aspects or practices of listening to, speaking, and creating from one's Inner VOICE (Vision, Ownership, Influence, Choice, Embodiment).

I've written this book to be a map for bringing yourself into alignment with your Inner Voice, but you could also use it to bring yourself into alignment with any goal or vision you may have. In fact, at the end of the book, I describe a way to design your own personal Aligndset™ Map. No matter what your life goals are—whether they relate to business, relationships, health, money, etc.—as you bring yourself into alignment with your Inner Voice, those life goals become much easier and more fun to manifest or receive.

These key elements are so closely interconnected that to bring one of them into alignment can pull the others along as well. There is no step-by-step process to transformation. We are organic beings, and transformation is an organic process. As I describe each element, you'll see how they interconnect and affect one another. I invite you to seek out all the connections yourself in your own life. It will deepen your understanding of the Aligndset™ Map and continue to breathe life and energy into it because, like you, it is a living, breathing organism that requires breath and nourishment to thrive. I recommend that you focus on one element at a time, but you'll likely notice shifts in all of them because as you focus on bringing one of them into alignment, you will necessarily and inherently be bringing the others into alignment as well.

So many authors, books, and personal experiences went into developing the ideas in this book (you can see a partial list of them in the references section), but four in particular that stand out for me are Napoleon Hill's book *Outwitting the Devil*, Bruce Schneider's book *Energy Leadership*, David R. Hawkins' *Power vs. Force*, and Chetan Parkyn's *Human Design*.

After I had designed the Aligndset™ Map, I read their works and realized that all of them describe this same journey to thought leadership and evolution of consciousness, with different ways of expressing it. Hill's interview with the devil helped me to understand the little voices and Inner Voice (he calls it "my other self"), and the seven principles he outlines in the book are closely related to the Aligndset™ Map and aspects of the Inner VOICE. The descriptions in brackets are where I address each of these principles throughout the Aligndset™ Map.

Napoleon Hill's seven principles for outwitting the Devil:

1. Definiteness of purpose [Vision]

2. Mastery over self [Which voices are you aligned with? How do you see yourself?]

3. Learning from adversity [Moving along the continuum of consciousness, releasing victimhood and stepping out of emotional follower mindset; keep going even with failure.]

4. Controlling environmental influence [Whom are you listening to outside yourself? How is your physical environment influencing you?]

5. Time: "giving permanency to positive rather than negative thought habits and developing wisdom" [Using the will and inner authority (and tools within this book) to create your reality anew each moment with consistency!]

6.   Harmony: "acting with definiteness of purpose to become the domi-
      nating influence in your own mental, spiritual, and physical environ-
      ment" [inner authority and creating a harmonious Aligndset™]

7.   Caution: "thinking through your plan before you act" (especially with
      regards to associates), learning to say, "No," becoming discerning and
      not "allowing people to attach themselves to you on their own terms"
      [breaking vows and energetic cord cutting]

In Bruce Schneider's *Energy Leadership*, he describes the internal levels of
leadership and how who you're *being* (and the energy and vibration of your
intention) is more important than the actions you are "doing." The ability
to recognize where you are and where you want to be, and then choose to
act from this higher vibrational awareness is integral to moving along the
continuum of consciousness. I'll discuss this concept more later in Chapter
9: Harmonize Your *Energy*—Embodiment.

In Hawkins' book *Power vs. Force*, he describes the vibrational frequency
of different energy levels of consciousness. Again, the message is: Increase
the vibration of your thoughts and feelings and you affect not only your
own world, but also the world around you in a positive way. You become a
leader from the heart. His energy fields of consciousness and their respective levels of vibration coincide nicely with Schneider's Energy Leadership
Index, even though they are measured and described somewhat differently.

Finally, Chetan Parkyn's book and courses on Human Design and reading
life charts was the missing piece for me. It helped me to make sense of
so many of the ideas I had, but I wasn't sure how to pull together. More
importantly, studying Human Design opened up the doorway and provided the answer I was looking for in helping people to "express God/
Spirit unencumbered" as a human being. I've been able to help people to
see themselves clearly, understand and own their unique design, including
their gifts and places to grow. Armed with a clear vision of whom they are
designed to be, I've helped folks make the necessary changes that happen as
they bring themselves into alignment with their Inner Voice and break old
patterns of relating to themselves and others while discovering their pur-

pose. It is literally an answer to my prayers to find a way to help, without "fixing" anything or anyone.

Human Design also helped me to see that my burnout was a result of committing my considerable life-force energy to people and projects that were not in alignment with how I am designed. I learned how to access and trust my inner authority and make decisions so I can be more discerning, and commit myself to my purpose in a streamlined and joyful way, and that's what I do with my clients as well.

Why all this talk of energy? If everything is energy, which it is, then simply "treating" a problem, or the symptoms of a problem, in essence throwing a bandage on it and calling it good, does very little to change the environment or the underlying core vibration of the issue. Also, what I really find powerful in all of these writings is that it is a process, and a choice, to keep moving up this scale of consciousness. That being the case, we each are where we are, and need not compare ourselves to anyone else.

Throughout the remainder of this book, the questions I ask of you, the reader, are designed to see where you are and where what you may be currently thinking, feeling, and experiencing is out of alignment with where you want to be. Then I give you specific energy techniques for radically changing your internal and external environment—some of them will be actions to take in the world, others will be simple movements and intentions that you perform on and with yourself, to change your own vibrational patterns. All are designed to help you increase your clarity, courage, conviction, commitment, and of course, alignment with your Inner Voice.

Before we begin, here is:

WHAT IS REQUIRED OF YOU:

1. A *willingness* to be present. It's about being willing in any given moment to check in with yourself honestly, get quiet enough to notice what's happening for you, and exercise your God-given right to choose a new way of being based on your intention.

2. A willingness to screw up. Yep. This expectation is especially impor-
    tant for you perfectionists out there. And I've got your number, so
    don't even try to get all-or-nothing on me, okay? This expectation
    goes back to #1—being willing to be present, here and now, and
    access your point of power, which is right in this moment. Choose
    again and again to come back in and engage, forgive yourself, and
    start over. Pretty soon you won't have to start over as much.

3. A willingness to be curious, amazed, surprised, and playful. You may
    want to hang out with a younger crowd more often (ages 4-10 or so)
    or at least some folks who are young at heart and willing to play a
    bigger game with you. The bigger game is this: Expand and embody
    all that you are, so that you have the power to choose and BE a power-
    ful creative force in your life guided by your Inner Voice living life on
    your terms.

SECTION 2

*The Five Key Elements and Inner
VOICE Aspects*

CHAPTER FIVE

Key Element #1:
Honor Your Body—Vision

"We are the temple of the living God."

— 2 Corinthians 6:16

I saw the above quote engraved in the floor of the sanctuary at Seattle University's Chapel of St. Ignatius. I knew it was perfect for opening the discussion of creating an Aligndset™ that is in alignment with the Inner Voice and leading from the heart.

Your body is a **powerful tool and source** of infinite wisdom and information.

Truly there is no separation between the mind and the body—you can experience the mind-body connection every time you think a certain thought and feel an immediate change in your physiology.

It can be easy to ignore the body's signals and wisdom, especially if you are uncomfortable in your own skin. I call that *living on the ceiling*.

Come back into your body. It is your point of power.

The body's reaction to fear is related to a system of the brain called the limbic system. It is also known as the fight-or-flight region of the brain. When the amygdala, located in the limbic system, is firing, you are either **preparing to fight or preparing to run** (or freezing and staying put!). When this system fires is usually when folks end up on the ceiling or a few feet to the side or behind themselves. Their body is there, but they are not in it! When you go to make a change in your life or business, and it is totally counter to what you've experienced in the past, it's *normal* to feel some anxiety or worry. And it's pretty common to pop out of your body, until you create an environment in there that is safe and grounded and practice staying put in your place of power.

For some people, deciding to *get out of the middle* and really take control of their thoughts and feelings can be very scary. Some part of them feels as though they are in physical danger when they make radical changes that fly in the face of what they were taught as kids, and that's where the limbic system can start firing—even when no real danger is present. It's why many people stay stuck! They literally feel like they are going to die, and so they do anything to avoid making a decision or taking action that will actually move them forward toward their goals. The only thing that is dying is the ego and its attachments to keeping the status quo.

One way to affect the amygdala directly is through Energy Psychology methods, one of which is meridian tapping. The most well-known meridian therapy technique is EFT or Emotional Freedom Technique. This method, as well as others I utilize to increase the effectiveness of EFT, is one of the most potent ways I know of to calm the amygdala. However, even if you don't know EFT or other Energy Psychology methods, you can still calm down the fight/flight reaction in the brain to help you get through the situation. These techniques won't address the underlying cause per se, but they will provide some immediate relief and help you get through a stressful situation in the moment. Then you can make a decision to take action that is in alignment with your intentions instead of defaulting to past behavior out of fear or avoidance of discomfort. For longer lasting results, I recommend clearing the underlying cause of the stress.

The body's reaction to fear is also located in the spleen energy center (as described in the Human Design system). I don't want to go too in-depth with this material here, but in the discussion of energy and being influenced and informed by energy through our interaction with other people and environments, this very brief overview may help. It is there in the spleen center that the immune system, as well as instinct and intuition, reside, and depending on whether or not you have this center "defined" in your life chart, you will experience this fear, and what to do with it differently than someone who has an "undefined" spleen center. What is helpful for you to know right now (assuming you don't know what your life chart says) is that this center, if defined, has a split second knowing whether something is in alignment with our health and wellbeing, and it is continuously scanning the environment for negative or foreign energy that is out of alignment with our health and vitality. If your center is undefined, you may be more susceptible to being influenced by the fears of others, and you don't necessarily have this split-second awareness. (You have other ways of staying healthy and full of vitality!)

I bring this up to point out again that the mind is a lousy decision-maker, and when we are talking about the hind-brain (or limbic system) in particular, it's really unreliable because it's typically firing on memories of past experiences, or future-tripping. In contrast, the spleen center (if defined) is perfectly designed to give in-the-moment feedback about whether or not there truly is a danger, and you can trust this implicitly and use this information to make decisions. Unfortunately, most people, even if they have a defined spleen center, listen to the fearful mind chatter that makes up all kinds of stories and reasons why they should be afraid, instead of truly detecting whether there is a danger. If your inner authority is through emotional clarity, then recognizing the antics of the monkey-mind that's making up stories and interpretations of the fear and the emotional rollercoaster that can ensue is how you will gain clarity about how to move forward, or choose in favor of your health and vitality.

Techniques to calm your body's reaction to stress and anxiety and get centered here and now in your body:

- **Grounding:** Feel your feet on the ground. If you can, take off your shoes. If you can go outside barefoot—do so. I recommend grass or dirt, but a hardwood floor works great too. If none of those are options, use your imagination.

  Feel your feet on the ground/floor beneath you. Spread your toes and balance weight equally on the ball and heel of each foot. Breathe. Imagine roots from the center of your feet anchoring into the Earth deeply below the surface—go all the way to the core of the Earth if you wish. Feel your connection to the Earth, to something larger than yourself. Keep noticing your feet on the ground and allow the tension to flow out of your feet into the ground.

- **Centering:** Notice that your center is just below your navel. Imagine that if you extended your arms overhead and straightened your legs below, the tips of your fingers and the soles of your feet would be roughly equidistant from this center-point. Place one palm over your "center-point" just at or below your navel and the other palm over your heart. Breathe into both of these places. Relax your shoulders, face, etc.

- **Breathing:** Sitting erect or lying down, inhale through your nose to the count of 4-5; pause very briefly—in fact, notice the natural pause vs. trying to make anything happen; exhale through your mouth to the count of 7-8. Notice the natural pause again and inhale as above. Start with 3 breaths like this and work your way up to 30 or more. Take it slow; if you ever feel more anxious breathing this way, stop immediately and breathe naturally. If you can only inhale to the count of 3 and exhale to the count of 5—no problem! Start where you are;

this is not about forcing your body to do something it's not yet ready to do—that just causes more anxiety!

Practice grounding and centering yourself this week. Go outside, exercise, play, and be in your body. Make friends with your vehicle for Divine Expression!

Both my husband and I notice that after about thirty minutes of movement, exercise (walking, yoga, biking, hiking, etc.), our intuition and creative juices really start flowing. It's almost like those 20-30 minutes of release and creating space are necessary before deeply accessing creative, juicy places in the heart and mind.

With regular and consistent movement, or sitting still in meditation, the amount of time it takes to reach that juicy place gets shorter and shorter. It becomes easier to access the Inner Voice as we regularly practice letting go of our focus on what we don't want, move to release pent-up emotions in the body, and turn our attention to what we do want to create and what feels good to us.

As I mentioned above, letting go of what you don't want is an integral step in making space to receive and experience what you do want or desire. Some of the things you need to let go of first are the very things you can't see—or won't allow yourself to see. These are typically the things you are *tolerating*.

One of the most powerful places people tolerate feeling crummy has to do with food. Be aware that what you eat, drink, and certain medications you take can affect your anxiety levels—in fact, caffeine and sugar are two big culprits in not only making anxiety worse, but also creating anxiety-like symptoms in the first place. In honoring your body, begin to notice how what you eat and drink affect your mood and your ability to relax.

Food sensitivities and allergies can also affect your body and your mood, as well as your ability to take action consistent with your intentions. Practicing mindfulness about how your body feels after eating certain foods can help, in addition to seeing a naturopath or nutritionist who specializes in food sensitivities. I have been aware for years that certain foods cause not only a physical reaction in my body, but also an emotional and mental reaction as well. I can get irritable and foggy, and unable to think straight. I've struggled with this both within myself and with others. In myself, I tend to want to eat what sets me off and creates discomfort when I want "comfort food." Ironic, I know. With others who don't understand the food-mood connection, I've subverted my own needs and eaten what was served to me in order to keep the peace between us, at the expense of peace within myself. I get how challenging this can be. Again, it's not about perfection, but about awareness and choice, and being willing to be honest with yourself and others about what you need in order to be your best.

I invite you to pay attention and ask yourself some questions that will help you to see what may be blocking a healthy internal and external physical environment. *(No need to take action on all of them yet; just be radically honest with yourself).*

QUESTIONS TO FREE YOUR INNER VOICE

What are you tolerating in/on/around your body?

What are you tolerating in your physical environment?

What are you waiting for? Is there something you've told yourself needs to happen first before XYZ can happen? (Especially in regards to what you wrote above?) Make a list here:

"When _____, then I can/will
_____."

"When _____, then I can/will
_____."

"When _____, then I can/will
_____."

Pick one thing from the list above in your body and/or physical environment and take some action on it. It need not be a huge radical action; sometimes the smallest action on something that's been stuck for a long time can make the biggest difference.

I am no longer willing to tolerate _____ in/on/ around my body.

I am no longer willing to tolerate _____ in my environment.

I have been waiting for _____ to happen before I can take action.

The action I'm committed to taking this week that would have me step out of waiting and tolerating into experiencing peace and joy in my physical body is: _____.

The action I'm committed to taking this week that would have me step out of waiting and tolerating into experiencing peace and joy in my physical environment is: _____.

And now let's turn our focus to the first aspect of the Inner Voice: **Vision**

"If you can see your path laid out in front of you step by step, you know it's not your path. Your own path you make with every step you take. That's why it's your path."

—Joseph Campbell

THE BLANK CANVAS

What do you want to create? So many books are out there on self-help and how to break free from this or that...they make it sound so easy. Decide what you want to create, what is your vision, and begin from there. Simple, right?

But deciding what we want can be the most difficult step. It's why we skip it, or come up with something that's lukewarm or a watered down version of what we really want to see in our life. Why? We carry all this information, this baggage with us. It's in our artist's box of colors if you will, and it's so easy to reach for them, especially when we are called to perform some task, like answering the question "What do you want to create?"

Most of us, frankly, don't want to get real enough with ourselves to be clear about what we truly want because many of the things we are currently experiencing are things we don't want. We've either given up wanting more or decided it really isn't worth wanting something different anyway because "I got all *this* and I didn't ask for it, so what power do I really have?"

Many folks believe that we don't deserve to have what we want, or that we are selfish if we ask for it, or that others will lose if we gain. All demonstrate belief in lack, low self-worth, and false responsibility that are frankly lies. These are lies I believed for years. Sometimes, they still show up in subtle ways, now I recognize them—and they aren't so compelling anymore.

"What power do I really have? Who am I to ask for this? How will I ever create that?" Those are not useful questions in the creation and manifestation process, and yet I think they are the ones that stop us nonetheless. An artist typically doesn't ask herself those questions when faced with a blank canvas. Depending on how she creates (either with a clear idea in mind, or freely allowing the process to unfold), there is an urge, a desire to create, without ego or the little voices involved. There is only the desire to create and express what wants to come through.

Asking yourself new and different questions, or better yet, having someone else ask you powerful questions, is how you can begin to pick up new colors, new brushes, new tools, and create something totally different on the canvas of your life.

*"My problem is that I believe the reality
I see around me is real."*

**— A Client (when sharing about the limitations she was
facing in following her dreams)**

One place to begin is to do an inventory of what you currently see in your life. Look at the relationships, environment, things, and experiences you're currently seeing around you, and **ask yourself whether you really want them**. Do you want them just as they are, or do you want them, but in a different way? Are you merely tolerating them, or are you consciously choosing them?

For instance, it could be that you want the person you're married to—you love that person and are attracted to him or her—but you don't like how things are going in that relationship. You can easily start with what you don't like in the relationship. What would you *like* to see and experience with that person? That's a great place to begin. Do not concern yourself with whether or not he or she can really *be* that person with you, or if your spouse is capable of fulfilling his or her end of the bargain. Only concern yourself with what you want to see in relation to another person, and *focus on what you must do to see that vision come to pass.* Even though you have no idea *how* it could work out or whether or not it even *will* work out that way, don't concern yourself with those thoughts. Holding the vision is what really matters.

What if you don't know what you want? *Start by making a list of what you have.* Include those things you are tolerating or "making due with." Then ask yourself whether you really want the thing or person or experience as it is. If not, what would you like to see instead?

Decide either to change or get rid of the things you don't want, including habits or ways of being that aren't working for you and/or *choose* to own each item you want to keep in your life. This includes people, by the way. I don't mean to imply that we can just "get rid" of all the people who bug us in some way or another. Everyone is in your life for some reason or other; sometimes you'll know why that is, and other times you won't until much later. Certain people not in your immediate circle simply do not resonate with you; they are the easy ones to release. Choose not to spend time with them.

"Okay. I got it," you may be thinking. "But what about the people I live with? What about my kids and other people I am in charge of caring for?" *Choose them as they are and how you are going to BE with them.* Honestly, if someone is really bugging you, that person is very likely mirroring something back to you that you don't like or want to see about yourself. Own that and you will see your relationship change with the person. I've found in these situations that it really comes down to understanding your design as well as the design of those around you and learning to work with that information. That goes for everyone in your life! Those people who came to be a mirror for you temporarily will fall away, and the people with whom you are meant to stay connected, will stay—but in a richer, more loving way.

An example: I always knew I wanted a husband and kids. Did I want them because that's what society told me to want, or because I truly wanted them at my core, in my heart? I had to ask myself that question, and what's fascinating is that I came to the realization in the process of inquiring about my husband and kids that, even though I had them, I hadn't ever really *chosen* them, not consciously at least. I simply *knew* I was going to have them. I welcomed them into my life, I received them with open arms, I wanted, and still do want them; however, this sense of knowing without consciously choosing kept me distant from them without even knowing it because it was as if I were taking them for granted, as a *given* in my life! When I really deeply connected with each one of them and who they are in the world separate from me as a wife and mother, I made the conscious choice to *choose* them both on the level of "husband" and "kids" and as Mike and Eli and Anja as individual souls—to choose to let them into my heart, not as a matter of course, but as a conscious living choice. It may sound strange, but it really changed my relationships with each of them!

This inquiry will allow you to see how much of your life has just "happened" to you, and what you've allowed into your experience, and it gives you the opportunity consciously to choose, or un-choose, each person, experience, thing, or idea that you, heretofore, just took on as a given. That's power.

Maria Dykstra owns TreDigital, an online advertising company. Her story illustrates how we can "just fall into" the next thing and then the next thing, and pretty soon we're hating where we are:

Maria: ...I was incredibly fortunate. My first job out of college was really not working at McDonald's like a lot of people do, but I worked for a very large organization. It was a non-profit organization dealing with educational exchanges. I really had a lot of fun because it was sponsored by the U.S. Embassy. I met fascinating people. It was still in Russia. That's where I met my husband, at the time. He was American. I was Russian. We were never expected to marry a foreigner. We were very much connected to our places and our families.

Well, after about two years of a long distance relationship, I actually did move to the United States. That was one of the biggest changes for me. I guess the Inner Voice at that point was ignoring the fact that I grew up in one country and was very connected to family and just moving to a different country. That was a difficult transition.

That was about fourteen years ago. The interesting part was that I stumbled into a career at Microsoft. My first job was taking phone calls for Microsoft support and I was saying, "Thank you for calling Microsoft" a hundred times a day. Think about a person who has an accent, just moved to the country, does not fully speak the language, speaking on the phone the whole day. That was really tough.

The interesting part of it was first as a contractor, I did that job, but six months later, I got hired full-time. Then six months later, I became a manager of a team, which was very interesting because I really enjoyed managing people, but I really could not stand the call center environment because it's a different environment. It's high pace. Really, people are not happy.

I accidentally stumbled into another thing. As you can see, I had a pattern of a lot of stumbling into something else, stumbling into a career. Back in 2000, I landed a job that was dealing with advertising and dealing with digital advertising. I stayed in that career from 2000 until February of 2012. It was different jobs, but it was a fascinating job because I was working with great people. I was working with creative folks. It's advertising. It's traveling. It's having to dream big and having the funds to really ask for them.

...But throughout the whole career, I was finding myself sitting in my office and sitting there and saying, "I can't do this anymore. I just can't." That's the Inner Voice and I guess it started about seven years ago. It was a very, very small voice in my head saying, "Really, I'm not sure what to do." But I felt really, really stuck. I'd think to myself, "You have a great job. You have a job that a lot of people would really, really want to have. A lot of fascinating things. Travel. Whatnot."

Seven years ago, I was looking at people who were actually leaving Microsoft and starting their own careers on their own outside, and I was looking, and this voice says, "You've got to be crazy. Why would you be leaving a job that's so great and has a lot of money and has a lot of possibilities and career growth?" I mean Microsoft is a great company.

So many places you can go and so many different opportunities people have. There's training. There's a lot of amazing support that you get. It's a really good place to be, but I was still sitting in my office, and especially the last year, I was thinking about it. I had two kids. That completely changed who I am, which was very unexpected because I was always saying, "Oh, kids, maybe. Not sure."

As a high-paced person, I always need to be on the go, and kids completely redefined that. They redefine the pace of life. They redefine the priorities, and so my last year I'm sitting in my office and saying, "I just can't do that anymore. I absolutely cannot do it anymore." Every day started with, "I need to do this amazing presentation," so I had to give myself a pep talk every morning to really say, "I have to do it. I have to do it. It's interesting. It's fascinating. Why can't you do it?"

Finally, February this year, I had to make some choices. It happened overnight. I just sat down and said, "I don't want to do a career in the corporate world anymore. I am very fortunate to have a passion for digital advertising," and that's where I was for the last many years, and I have passion for brands. I worked with amazing brands, but I don't have to do it for the big guy anymore. I can actually do all of that on my own and I can really have fun doing that.

February, that's where the whole thing happened. I just gave up. Then, actually, another thing that really helped is I read the book *Escape from Cubicle Nation*. There was a very interesting quote that talked about the levels of energy and how you can be completely spent or how you can still be tired, but not feel that you're exhausted beyond the point of return. I think that really resonated with me because I realized that I was coming home and I was completely spent. I just could not do anything. I had no energy for my life.

Now I still work—I go to bed at 2 a.m. and I get up at 7:30, but I feel I am more energized. I still want my espresso, but I can get going. I'm allowed to make choices, so everything I do is a choice. I can do it or I cannot do it. I felt like I didn't have that choice. I had to do things in my career that were not chosen by me, that I had to do for a certain reason because that's the structure that I was in.

I feel really liberated now. I was dealing with depression issues, and it was very deep depression. Overnight, again, the moment I made the choice, the moment I decided not to continue with that career, my depression got better. I'm feeling [like] I won a million dollars.

I look at the number of people who are in the same position I used to be seven years ago. A lot of my friends are very supportive, but I do see a couple of friends who have worked for bigger corporations and they're still trying to convince me to go back. It's all the subtle ways where they're looking and you can see in their eyes they're looking and saying, "Well, you're crazy. You have two kids. What are you doing? Why are you out there on your own? You could go and get your job back or get another exciting job somewhere in the industry," because again, I'm very fortunate to be in that digital advertising media business, which is fabulous with the location and has a lot of companies that are hiring.

I have options, but I really choose not to do that because I felt miserable in that job. That's my story.

Kris: Yeah, I love it. You have all these options to go back to the cubicle, if you will, and you have all these external voices saying it to you. "You're crazy. You've got two kids." What I got from your story is that you had—the picture I get in my mind is—you're standing in a candy store and you're sick to your stomach.

Maria: Yes.

Kris: All your friends are like, "I would love to be in your candy store. Look at all these great things you get to do." You're like, "Yeah, I should be loving this. I should be loving being in this candy store." The little voices, which are really childlike, are like, "Stay here. Stay here. Look at all this great candy. We'll feel better tomorrow. We'll be able to eat it tomorrow."

But every night you're going home and your Inner Voice is saying, "I cannot go back into that candy shop one last time."

Maria: ...Absolutely. With the background that I have, I grew up, or at
least the way I was raised and culturally, we don't believe in Inner
Voices. It's all about being strong. You're fortunate to have a great
job, so what's the point? Why are you complaining? Why are you
miserable? Go do that. You get good money. You get good benefits. You have a great job. What's your problem? That's how I
grew up, and for me, that was the big voice—always was there.
What's your problem? Why are you so unhappy? That was the
biggest voice that I had fighting in my head trying to understand,
"I have all of that, so what's my problem?"

QUESTIONS TO FREE YOUR INNER VOICE

What's your candy store?

Inventory your life: (Under each category, list the components, things, or
people in each one and ask yourself, "Do I really want this _____?" And/
or "Am I tolerating this?" This exercise is really about seeing yourself and
the reality you have co-created clearly, and choosing which things to keep
in the picture, and which things to transform or let go of.

- **Business** (List all aspects of your business separately; certain parts
  may be working while others are not. Also note that it may be that
  you are doing things in your business that you are simply not suited
  for, and that is why they are not working. I had to trust others to
  do the things that I'm capable of doing, but that are not in my zone
  of genius, and hire these folks to help me out even before I had the
  client load to warrant the help. I had to let go of models and pricing
  and structure that simply wasn't working for me after years of trying
  to make it work based on someone else's ideas about what's successful
  and what isn't. Be willing to blow some shit up in order to rebuild!

- **Relationships** (friends, family, colleagues, coworkers, clients, customers, neighbors) If you sense even an ounce of tolerance or obligation in
  any of these relationships, be willing to explore other possibilities for

letting them go, or letting go of some expectation you have of them or yourself. You may want to explore the cultural expectations you grew up with because they can be so ingrained and powerful that you didn't even know they were there.

- **Health** (emotional, mental, physical) What aches, pains, and hurts are you sweeping under the rug, ignoring, or putting off addressing until you have more time, money, or "space" to address them? You are worth taking care of. You are responsible for taking care of yourself—no one else is. (Unless you are a child. And you're not a child, right?)

- **Finances** (personal, business) I'll be honest with you: I avoided this for YEARS! I did not want to look at my money patterns, and where I was leaking money all over the place. Money is energy, and as soon as I began addressing it directly and stopped tolerating the barely squeaking-by model that I had been following mindlessly for years, things turned around almost immediately.

- **Leisure Activities** (alone, with others) Do you even allow yourself leisure time? Are you hanging out with people you enjoy who energize you, or do they (or the activities you're doing) drain you?

- **Spiritual Practice** (Are you feeling connected? What do you need?) Are you tolerating five minutes of meditation every other day when your ideal is twenty-minutes? Do you let the demands of your physical life pull you away from your spiritual sanctuary?

"Definiteness of Purpose" is the most important factor in turning down the volume of the little voices, or the "Devil" as Napoleon Hill describes it. When we have this definiteness, this clarity of what our purpose is, and what we are aiming for, it is much easier to take the action we need to take, and to avoid "drifting": the state of mind that allows the little voices to take hold as described by both Hill and Raymond Holliwell in his book *Working With The Law*.

Emotional Followers, and those folks who find themselves in the middle, are "drifting" without clear focus or vision.

Our active vision, our "definiteness of purpose" is akin to keeping our eyes fixed on a spot on the wall when we are doing a balancing pose in yoga class, or walking across a balance beam. To keep from falling over, we must soften our gaze and still keep our attention focused directly on that spot off in the distance so nothing can distract from our intention to stay balanced and move toward our intended aim.

WHAT'S IN THE PICTURE?

Our BIG vision may include aspects of the following: to see our kids as whole and complete, to spend heart-to-heart time with our spouse each week, or to be present with our family and friends and really listen. I think of these as ways of *being* instead of doing. Our BIG vision includes where we want to live, what we want to eat, and all manner of self-care so we can be sharp and on our game. It includes the time we spend with friends, and the quality and caliber of those friendships. At work, our BIG vision may be what and how we work and with whom, along with our purpose for doing so. It includes the amount of time we work and for what pay, the people we want to work with, the amount of money we wish to acquire through sharing our genius with others. It may include travel, clothing, vacations, experiences, and anything else you feel called to be, do, or have.

Maybe you have some really BIG vision to change the way therapy is done (or is it only me who dreams about that?), or to end hunger, or to help people make money doing what they love, or to develop a product that makes Divinely-abled people comfortable in their bodies so they can do things heretofore out of their reach. Good for you if you are that clear! You are among the very few folks with that level of clarity in this world.

What if you don't have a BIG vision? You may just have a desire not to be where you are, or to stop living life from paycheck to paycheck, or to get out of the job you are in. Or perhaps you simply have some inkling that you're not living up to your potential, while having no clue what that potential is. Maybe you have an idea that you want to help people, to serve in some way, and you know what you like to do and what you are good at, but you can see no way to make money doing it, so you just stay stuck and visionless, wondering whether you'll ever find "it."

I have had many sleepless nights wondering, searching, trying to "figure out" my BIG vision, or feeling there must be something wrong with me because I couldn't see it or find it—especially when it seemed like everyone around me was so damned clear!

It's one of those tricky things—this blindness. It's actually when we are closest to seeing our truth because there is a vacuum, and it wants to be filled. The problem is that we spend lots of money, time, and energy trying to find ways to fill it, instead of allowing what wants to be revealed to reveal itself—to allow it to bubble up from within instead of trying to find it outside of ourselves and mold ourselves to it. It's scary allowing this revelation to happen. Our little voices go nuts because they can't stand the quiet and they want to create all kinds of drama and distraction while the Inner Voice is saying very quietly, here...step here...now here...and so on.

This aspect of vision, or rather lack of vision, takes us off the topic of "What is your vision for your life?" and into a discussion of "How do you see yourself and the world around you?" It's also about how you see yourself relative to the "BIG vision" you have for your life. Do you believe you are able to fulfill it? Do you believe you are worthy of having all that you envision and desire? This facet of vision, I believe, will have far more impact on your ability to stay committed to and live your BIG vision/dream/goal than your ability to picture it in the first place.

UNIQUELY FLAWED

"When I don't show up fully, the only one rejecting me is me."

— Kris Prochaska

Like many people, I had a deep core belief that something was inherently wrong with me. Gay Hendricks, Ph.D., shares in his book, *The Big Leap,* that one of the biggest limiting beliefs is the core belief that something is wrong with us. He calls it an *upper limit problem*. I call it the "uniquely flawed or eff'ed up syndrome." It is perhaps the biggest illusion of them all—that we alone are uniquely eff'ed up and no one else is. I've seen it in enough clients, friends, colleagues, etc. to know that no one is immune from this dis-ease, and therefore, no one is unique in this way. That's great news! It helps me to remember when I've felt particularly down because I've just spent time comparing myself to someone else, that pretty much everyone I've compared myself to has or does feel the same way. This comparison is an effective use of the logical and rational mind, by the way!

Not everyone believes he or she is uniquely flawed, certainly not consciously, but I have found it in enough people to say safely that most people have some belief running the show that relates to this "wrongness" at the core. Recall that the little voices/middle managers love a good problem to solve, and so they are expert at seeking out evidence for how wrong we are, and they are, and this or that is. They want to solve it—remember?

It was because I was trying to do what I had learned from others at the expense of my own inner truth and intuitive hits that I kept trying to solve the problems I was experiencing in my business based on what the "experts" were telling me to do. The messages out there are so fearful—and compelling! "If you don't do this, you're leaving money on the table! If you do this, you're going to succeed." Of course, the implied opposite is "If you don't, you're screwed." Sure, these experts gave a good framework, but I needed something different. Something that would work for me, for my values, for my vision of the kind of life, business, and family I want, and for how I want to feel every day—for the possibility and vision I saw for myself and humanity. When I stopped trying to compare myself to others and stopped focusing on what's wrong, that's when what I truly want started to reveal itself to me.

When I started to see myself as my Inner Voice does, when I started to see my business and my relationships through the eyes of my Inner Voice, when I began listening to others through the ears of my Inner Voice, that's when my personal truth, and *the Truth,* began to reveal itself to me. Clairvoyance, clairaudience, clairsentience (clear seeing, hearing, and knowing) all became stronger and my courage to follow the guidance I receive has grown.

The spark of vision I had for my business came from my Inner Voice, but I got lost along the way and had long stretches where I built it from the little voices. That's when I got pulled off track and spun my wheels. That's when I spent a lot of time looking super-busy but getting nowhere fast, or at least it sure felt like it!

What's really fascinating to me is that my vision, while it has grown over the years, is still basically the same core vision I had first caught glimpses of when I began this process over thirteen years ago—some of those core visions are over twenty years old! I just pushed it all down thinking, "That'll never come to pass; I better come up with something that could actually happen within the parameters of my life as it is right now, or that others will be okay with, or that fits with what I think is possible." The fact that this core vision hasn't really changed much in terms of what I want—it's just grown as I've learned what else is possible—tells me that there is something to both the Inner Voice knowing what we came here to do, and that as we experience life and are open to new possibilities, the vision expands.

It also tells me that we alone decide how much light we will allow into our lives so we can see clearly the path before us—at least the next step.

QUESTIONS TO FREE YOUR INNER VOICE

What have you chosen to forget or resist because you thought it was just a passing fancy and not worth pursuing?

Whom have you been comparing yourself to so you feel as if you come up short? What if this person is reflecting back to you an aspect of yourself that is your strength, and you haven't been willing to see it in yourself or allow it into your life?

HELEN KELLER AND SEEING OURSELVES CLEARLY

Hold out your hand with your index finger out. Watching your finger, bring it closer to your face until you touch the tip of your nose with your finger. Keep both eyes open. Can you see your finger? Probably not. This is where your vision begins—but you can't see it, right? Often, it's too close to us—as close as the nose on our face—or the whisper of our own heart. Most of us are both blind and deaf and don't even know it!

We are blind and deaf to our own greatness. What we think we see and think we hear as our own is actually seeing and hearing through the filter of others around us, especially our caregivers' perspective from when we were young. We often focus on others around us and try to fit ourselves into that mold or box because we don't know how to see or listen for ourselves—*to ourselves.*

I once saw a picture of Helen Keller. She was radiant in the photo. What struck me most was the light in her eyes, the joy in her energy. Here is a woman who was blind and deaf, but I wondered whether that gave her an advantage over those of us who can see and hear the disdain and judgment from others, the criticism that we internalize at a young age from our outside world. Certainly, she had her own "little voices" to deal with—we all do—and yet I wonder: If we didn't have the visual and auditory feedback from others, would we connect to our Inner Voice more easily, more deeply, and with less editing?

Vision is not just about the grand scheme of our heart, our goals, and/or our purpose. It's also about how we see ourselves relative to others, to our big vision, and to the world. It has nothing to do with our purpose per se; it's more about what we think is possible, and whether or not we believe we are capable of making things happen. It has to do with how we innately see the world. One way we can be influenced by how we see the world is through our personality "type," such as the types observed and described by Myers-Briggs[6]. Introvert or extrovert, intuitive or sensing, thinking or feeling, judging or perceiving...these dyads and the way they approach the world are quite different and inform how we see ourselves and others. There are many other systems and "type" descriptors out there; Myers-Briggs is just one of them.

I personally like exploring the Human Design Life Chart with folks as it is completely objective, based on your date, time, and location of birth. The subjectivity comes in the process of looking at the chart and exploring just how you've seen the chart play out in your life, and how you'll choose to apply the insights and self-knowledge available to you as a result of the reading. Getting to know yourself is part of the process of developing your "right eyes" and being able to see yourself and the world as it *can be*, and as you'd *like it to be*, along with balancing that with *how it is currently* so you can make the changes necessary to get where you want to go. To live your vision, so to speak.

Following are a couple of short takes about the Inner Voice relative to introverts and intuitives based on the Myers-Briggs types. Beth Buelow, The Introvert Entrepreneur, shared with me how she sees introverts, who tend to be more internally focused, interact with the little voices and the Inner Voice:

Kris: ...You brought up something that I think is really true, and in your experience, I'd like you maybe to tell a little bit more about that: As introverts, our fabric, you said, is to listen within, both to the positive or that Inner Voice of knowing and the little voices of fear. Can you speak about this a little bit more? Do you find that introverts tend to get stopped even more by the little voices because they're so internal?

Beth: I think that we can and not only because they're so internal, but because we are hesitant to externalize them. Often when we do

6 For more information on the Myers-Briggs personality type system, check out www.my-ersbriggs.org.

vocalize them, when we do share them and put them out there, we disempower them. We make them a little smaller than they are and we can get that reality check against other things.

It would be too general to say, "Introverts are more affected by the fear voices than extroverts," but I do think we probably kind of can sit with those fear voices and let them have a little bit more power than we need to because we might feel very vulnerable in sharing those with other people.

I think once we realize that the sharing of them—I mean if we're comfortable. We have to honor that part of us that says, "Oh, it's too vulnerable. It's important for me to really process this inside before I share it," so honor that, but notice when you're getting stuck and when it crosses from introspection to self-sabotage.

Introspection is fine. Noticing: what I try to do and what I've learned to do instead of embracing the little voice is to just notice it. Instead of believing it just at face value, I question it. Then having some compassion for it and saying, "Okay, what is this trying to tell me? What is it trying to do for me because it's serving some sort of purpose?" Usually, the purpose it's serving is to protect us from hurt, from vulnerability, that sort of thing.

Once I can kind of get my head around that, I can say, "Well, what is it protecting me from? Is that a real threat? Or is that, again, something that's in my head? Is that a little voice?" I think the great thing about introverts is that we're not exactly known for our huge social circles, but we are known for our intimate social circles and having deeper relationships with people that we trust.

One big lesson I learned, and my husband actually helped me to learn this, was that's what your friends are for. Your friends are there to help you share things that are vulnerable that you are doubting or you have questions about. It's like it's an honor for most people who are true friends for one person to be vulnerable to the other.

Kris: Oh, my gosh! Yes! I get goose bumps when you say that. Absolutely.

Beth: It's an honor and so let's lean into that. Let's trust that and allow ourselves to trust that other person, trust ourselves, share what that little voice is saying so it can be transformed into more of a truth, because that's when we can say, "Okay, so what's really true?" Often, we'll say something and then we'll say, "Wow, that sounds really ridiculous, doesn't it?" Whereas in our head, it sounded huge and true and barbaric.

          When we say it out loud, it's like, "Wow, that seems a little silly, doesn't it?"

Kris: Mm-hmm. Yeah.

Beth: That's my thinking on that. I think introverts and extroverts probably equally have the little voices of fear. I think introverts can hold onto them longer and it can cross from introspection into self-sabotage. So lean into that intimate circle in order to get some of that out and turn it into something healthier.

Bottom line: We need other people to help us discern between the Inner Voice and little voices, so even if you're an introvert, "leaning into" your friends and trusted confidants and sharing, perhaps even more deeply than you would typically, will help immensely with that clarity and self-check.

Jessica Butts, M.A., therapist, and Myers-Briggs expert, shared with me her view on Myers-Briggs Type and the difference between the intuitive and sensing types as they experience the Inner Voice:

Jessica: Just to go off on another little bit of a tangent here for a couple minutes...I do believe, because you know how much I believe in type and who we are innately, I do believe that part of this is more intense for intuitive types. I do believe that.

There is a population out there that doesn't get this as much as other people, and I believe the difference is the sensors versus the intuitive. Sensing types have a gift. They are able to be in the moment and be more fully present and sometimes more accepting of the present situation than some intuitive types. That makes a difference on the scale of the type or your preference as well.

For very, very strong intuitive types, this stuff drives us. We are absolutely in tune with this intuitive part of ourselves, often more so than others. So I just think that's worth noting. When you're thinking about readers and the reader is thinking, "I don't know if I get this," that's okay because some won't. Some strong preference for sensing may think this is unusual or may not get it, they may not connect with it.

Kris: Does that mean that a sensing type might have an easier time— what do I want to say—they might have an easier time living their Inner Voice?

Jessica: No. I think it's a little different. Again, this is about strength of preference too because some sensing types get a little pissy about this because they do have an intuitive side for sure. They have intuition. They have a sixth sense. But this is again strength of preference. So I think it's less about them just living it, and more about them just accepting where they are at. So sensing types have a much better ability to accept what is.

Kris: Ah, okay.

Jessica: ...Like a job that they don't necessarily love but they are more accepting of what is than strong intuitive types. It is gut-wrenching; it is this pain that we're talking about where some sensing types, some extreme sensing types—you know what, maybe it isn't so much that they don't have it, but they do have a different personality type that allows them to be more connected with what is. Versus intuitive types who are more connected with our Inner Voice, with this gut, this instinct that we have.

Although I believe equally that it's a gift and a curse, because there are times when, man, I wish I could just sit with what is and I just truly can't. It's painful. A lot of people in my life, my mom, my sister, my husband, they're all S types and they think I'm a little cuckoo. They're just like, "Why can't you just be? Why can't you let it be?" It's because my Inner Voice is screaming its bloody head off and I can't ignore that. I think there's something certainly strong with personality type around that as well.

Kris: Okay. We might have to have a whole other discussion about that. I would like to.

Jessica: It's fascinating. You know sensing types in your life. You could just compare the way that you are to them. Where I have to take action…my sister, my mom, and my husband all just manage their jobs.

As Beth and Jessica describe, not only do introverts and extroverts receive guidance from their Inner Voice differently, but they also express differently, as do intuitive and sensor-types. Having other people around us who can mirror back to us our process and honor our differences is (I think) a great way to expand your consciousness about what's possible, and isn't that the definition of a thought leader anyway?

This voice of our Higher Self, our intuition, our heart and soul…it is visual, auditory, kinesthetic, feeling, intuitive, and just "knows" what is the next best step for us. It speaks to each of us, and while there are similarities in the method in which it speaks to us across all humanity and across our designs, we each express it differently based on our experiences, perceptions, and point of view. I call it the voice of God. We each have an Inner Voice, one that knows what we came here to Be, to Do, to experience, to share with the world. It speaks from the perspective of our purpose and our covenant with God—what God wants to express through us, through our body, in *this* world, in this dimension, third planet from the sun in this particular solar system, at this particular time. Actually...it is beyond time, and recognizes there is no time, only energy and movement. It's where we go when we dig deep and find inner strength and fortitude. It's where we speak from when our heart is open and we are loving.

Creating a vision for our life from this Inner Voice is the highest achievement we can possibly reach in this lifetime—and we don't even need our eyes or ears to do it.

QUESTIONS TO FREE YOUR INNER VOICE

How might you be seeing the world differently from others?

If you weren't blind to your greatness, or afraid to see it, what do you think might be your greatest strength and gift for the world?

Are you sharing that gift currently? If not, why not? If yes, how can you make an even bigger impact?

How do you see yourself relative to your vision or goals? Do you believe you can make them come to life?

What voices come up as you ponder these questions?

A NOTE ON VULNERABILITY

In my experience, our vision is closely tied to vulnerability in two different ways. Vulnerability as a *noun* and as a *state of being*. Our vulnerabilities (nouns) are the experiences we have had that have negatively informed us, or created a limited view of ourselves. These vulnerabilities are most often spoken from the little voices. This form of vulnerability affects our vision when we are unable to see ourselves as capable of fulfilling our big vision for our life and business. When I'm working with someone who wants to make a change in his or her life or business, one of the most common limiting beliefs I come across, especially if the change or goal is a big one, is: "I don't know who I'd be if I were successful and living my big vision." We get stuck seeing ourselves as we have *been*. (This is the vision of the little voices by the way—they can only see us *as we have been*, not as we are, or as we *could be*.) Our Inner Voice, on the other hand, is the one that gave us, and reminds us of, our big vision, our dream, our goals, our *calling*. The Inner Voice knows what we are capable of and *sees us as we can be* in order to fulfill that vision, but often we get stopped by the little voices and their limited sight. This is why it is so essential to surround ourselves with people who will listen from their Inner Voice for our Inner Voice and be a stand for it, especially when the little voices threaten to come in and send us spiraling.

QUESTIONS TO FREE YOUR INNER VOICE

What I'm most afraid people will find out about me is:

I notice that I get triggered easily by:

It really pushes my buttons when:

I feel most vulnerable when:

The second vulnerability is a state of being. In order to get clear on our vision, we need to be vulnerable and open to receive what we had experienced before we began resisting. When we stop resisting our inner truth, or even allow ourselves to stop hiding those parts of ourselves we shut down as a child, we begin to see the value in our experiences, even the painful, vulnerable ones. I call the beliefs we created as a result of those painful experiences *myths*. The willingness to examine those myths courageously and to rewrite them is one of the first steps to turning down the volume on those little voices.

Myths are the stories, the lies, the half-truths that we take as truth and live by without questioning them. They are as familiar as a favorite bedtime story, and as scary as the most terrifying horror flick you've ever seen. These myths and stories are those things that we think are us, versus something that we simply experienced. Often we hold onto a memory so tightly that it causes constriction and illness in our bodies, resentment and anger in our hearts, and miscommunication in our relationships. We all have plenty of stories, and they are stored both consciously and subconsciously. It's the ones that are stored subconsciously that really trip us up. But it's also the unwillingness to let down our guard and allow what's occurring in our world to occur without resisting it or trying to make sense of it based on something we experienced in the past. This decision to live in the present, and not through the filter of our stories, takes a lot of mindfulness and willingness.

Want different results than you've been getting? Let go of your stories—and your need to be right about them. When we need to be right about them, we are saying that we *are* the story, instead of someone who experienced the events and emotions that constitute the story. See the difference?

THE UNDERLYING STORY

When I'm working with clients, I'm often listening for the underlying story, and in between the lines of the story. As a therapist I was taught to focus on the little voices, the content of the story, as well as the emotional undercurrent. Who are the actors/players in the drama. What year is it (i.e., how old is the "star" or my client?)? What is happening, how does the person feel, and what is the outcome (or outcome from his/her perspective)? How has he/she been replaying the story over and over again, embellishing a little more each time, so each time it is told, it becomes stronger and more real than what really did happen?

As a coach, and an intuitive, I've been honing my listing to hear beyond the lines of these stories. I've been attuning my ears to hear the Inner Voice of my clients and help them make that voice louder, and the others quieter. Sometimes it takes addressing the little voices directly, and shifting beliefs—literally healing the mind and emotions. Sometimes, it means expanding the Inner Voice so it gets so loud and has such clear expression that the result is the little voices naturally begin to heal in the Divine light of the Inner Voice.

Please understand: The parts of you telling those stories and trying to enroll others into sympathizing with your role in those stories are the little voices. The stories are not you. The stories are affecting how you see yourself and the world and what is possible.

We humans are *validation-seeking missiles*. No matter what we *consciously think* we believe, we will actually *seek out and find* validation for what we subconsciously believe. This behavior can either work for us or against us!

It's like we have x-ray vision and can "read" people who are energetically a match for whatever belief we may hold. Then we wonder how we end up in the same old relationships and patterns year after year! If we don't clear the coordinates on our missile, which basically means changing our beliefs and expectations, and learning how to access our inner authority clearly, reliably, and confidently, so we can course correct on the fly, we will continue to find evidence for what we subconsciously believe everywhere, and we'll lack the discernment that helps us choose consciously whom to let into our lives. We do this with situations and experiences as well. In this way, we literally create and co-create our reality.

The good news about this situation is that when you believe and expect positive things to happen, you'll see evidence of it everywhere! The other positive thing about this cool trick we do as humans is that it becomes really easy to see what you believe: **notice what you notice**. Watch for the patterns and the people and the results that you get in your life. Pay attention. You'll begin to see exactly what you've believed, and then you can do something with that information. Until you can see the Truth, you can't do a darn thing with it.

Play a game with looking for evidence. Pick a topic or thing you'd like to see more of in your world. Maybe it's a certain animal or flower, or maybe it's a certain person or song. Just pick something that's not a huge stretch for you to imagine; this is a practice run to play with it. Pick something you love and that would bring you joy if you could see or experience more of it. Now watch for evidence of this thing everywhere. Look for it. Expect to see it; get excited about seeing it. Do this for the next week, at least, and watch how many times this thing shows up.

Did you make that thing show up, or was it already there and you just now noticed it?

Interesting question isn't it?

Stories and seeking validation now bring us to the next Key Element, *Mind*, and it's corresponding VOICE aspect: *Ownership*.

CHAPTER SIX

Key Element #2:
Release Limiting Beliefs in the
Mind—Ownership

"Strictly speaking, you don't think: Thinking happens to you."

— Eckhart Tolle

Did you know that it's the beliefs your subconscious mind holds that really run the show? You may think you deserve to have an ideal job or mate or realize your life's dream, but some part of you doesn't believe that at all—and that may be why you aren't experiencing the results you desire. You may logically know you are not going to die or be burned at the stake for sharing your intuition and gifts with others or for speaking your truth and potentially rocking the boat as a result, but your subconscious mind may be reeling at the thought! We've all heard "There's nothing to fear but fear itself," but when your subconscious mind is working overtime in fear mode—that kind of logic is totally lost.

We are so much more than what we are aware of. How they measure the following is beyond me, but it's pretty staggering: *Our conscious mind processes only about seven (plus or minus two) bits of information a second.*

Our subconscious on the other hand, processes around 40 million bits of information a second.[7]

Think of your mind like an iceberg. The part of the iceberg we see floating on top of the water is your conscious mind; you use this for logic, will, and observing data from the five senses. About 10 percent of your thought process takes place here. The other 90 percent of the ice hovers under the water's surface—that's your subconscious mind and it governs your beliefs, emotions, memories, fears, habits, body systems (like breathing, heartbeat), imagination, creativity, and your sense of "who you are." The majority of your processing occurs here.

You may think you are running the show, but it is your subconscious mind that is truly running your life. The inability to manifest what you want to achieve in your daily life due to the negative emotions, programs, and limiting beliefs held in your subconscious mind are what are contributing to your fears and stress, if not causing you stress in the first place.

Those little voices in your head that say, "Who do you think you are?" or "I can't do that!" or even "What will people think of me?" are actually your beliefs speaking. Another way to figure out what you believe is to *listen to the voices around you.* They could be those of friends, family, your partner, song lyrics, newscasters, movie stars, colleagues, etc. Do you agree with them? Do you feel uncomfortable with their words, but you continue to hang around them or listen anyway? *The people you listen to the most will often be speaking the beliefs you hold true for yourself.* The key is to ask yourself whether those beliefs serve you or keep you stuck....

To be clear, while the thoughts and beliefs themselves can and do cause stress, it's the *emotional charge behind them* that is the real culprit. We'll look at that in the next chapter when we discuss the key element *emotion.*

---

7 Taken from: *Matrix Energetics: Matrix Energetics: The Science and Art of Transformation* by Richard Bartlett, D.C. N.D.

BLIND SPOTS

"We see the world the way we feel and believe."

— Kris Prochaska

I had a client who was really worried about whether he would get a job he had interviewed for, and he was fretting about passing through all the hoops, one of which was passing a drug test (even though he didn't use drugs and rarely drank!). He was so distressed about the interview that when he received a letter that said he had passed all the requirements for the position and would not be contacted further about the matter, all he saw was that he wouldn't be contacted further. He never saw the critical piece of information that said he was hired and would begin in two weeks. He only saw that the letter was in reference to the testing and that he wouldn't be contacted. He spent the whole weekend fretting about the job, until he had calmed down somewhat and was sharing the email with a friend and reading it aloud to her. As he did this, he was able to see literally what he couldn't see only minutes before when he was so stressed out. Physically, some people experience a blind spot, a scotoma, something on the retina that creates a darkness or shadow in their vision. In psychology, the term scotoma is used metaphorically; it is literally a blind spot that only allows us to see the world, not based on what is *really* there, but what we *believe* to be there, or what we are willing to allow ourselves to see. The letter never changed, but his vision, his ability to see what was really there, did. His emotional reaction to the letter blinded him to the real message contained within.

Have you ever looked at a picture for the tenth time when you see something you have never seen before? Or maybe you've read a book or listened to a recording repeatedly and you get something new each time. It's not that the picture, book, or recording is different—you are. For this reason, it's so helpful to have a coach or someone you're working with who can see what you can't see. We all have blind spots in our own lives—even those of us who are great at seeing and hearing what others can't see or hear for themselves!

I'm as blind as the next person to my own crap and stories. I depend on trusted friends, coaches, and confidants to help me see this stuff for myself too!

QUESTIONS TO FREE YOUR INNER VOICE

How do you know if you have limiting beliefs? *Your life, or some area of your life, is not going how you want it to go.*

That's the short answer, and **here are some questions you can ask yourself:**

- How do you feel about that area of your life? Are you able to be effective?

- Do you find yourself doing the same thing over and over again— sometimes with the same people, other times with different people but with similar feelings and scenarios?

- Do you avoid taking action (procrastinate) when you know you either need to, WANT to, or are "supposed" to?

- Do you sabotage yourself every time you take action in the direction of your goals? Perhaps you feel that others sabotage you?

- Do things just "come up" and you have no control over them, and that's why you do the things you do (or don't do).

- Do you feel depressed, anxious, or like you are about to self-combust?

- Do you feel envious or jealous of others who are doing what you want to do? Maybe you think you can't do it as well as them, so you just give up without even trying....

- Do you overeat, drink too much, and/or use other substances to self-medicate?

- Are you trying to "deal" with the stress in your life in whatever way you can?

Perhaps some of your actions are helping you, and some of them aren't. Just notice whether you feel more stressed (guilty, ashamed, overwhelmed, hung-over, etc.) when you use any of the self-help efforts above. If so, then you are creating more problems than solutions for yourself.

As with most things in life, awareness is the first step in addressing and shifting limiting beliefs. I haven't met anyone yet who didn't, or doesn't, have a few beliefs running the show that she didn't even know she had. In fact, I find some of my own all the time! I used to get down on myself about it and feel ashamed of having these limiting beliefs. I thought it meant something was wrong with me (which is a limiting belief!). The truth is, I'm human—just like you. So, now I look at these negative beliefs, celebrate the fact that I see them for what they are and ask: **"Is it serving me or others for me to keep thinking this way?"** and **"What would or could be a more empowering belief to hold instead?"**

It's all in your perspective; it's in the way you perceive and what you sub-consciously *already do* believe about the world (and aren't aware of), and what you consciously *choose* to believe about the world that will determine your experience of life.

Look at the results you've been getting in your world and the feelings you feel on a regular basis or in certain situations. Both will give you an indica-tion of what you believe!

Notice where you may be listening to the little voices (the limiting beliefs and fears) instead of listening to your Inner Voice (the voice that knows your true value, purpose, and next best step to take). Then try to reframe those beliefs or fears from the perspective of your Inner Voice and see what happens to your energy, mood, and ability to take action. Is the voice speak-ing a *conclusion* (assumption or interpretation); a *construct* some "truth" you bought into that says it is this and can be nothing other than this; a *comparison* (are you judging yourself or someone else?); or some *belief* that you picked up as a kid that has no real evidence for being true? After you get clear on what the pattern or block is, take some action that flies in the face of that old limiting belief—taking action will help to reprogram your beliefs quickly!

Another technique for reprogramming beliefs and calming emotions that is rapidly gaining popularity over the last few years is EFT, or Emotional Freedom Technique. EFT and other energy psychology techniques are great ways to reprogram beliefs because they go right to the energetic root of the belief. In other words, they shift the energy and emotional charge around thoughts and beliefs that hold them in place or keep a person from seeing any other point of view.[8] One of the reasons I love these techniques is that they can be self-administered, and I do like to train my clients to do this work for themselves. That said, if you are seeking help from a therapist, coach, or practitioner who practices EFT or other energy therapy techniques, especially around beliefs and the mind, I highly recommend seeing someone who is certified or who has training in counseling. These techniques are powerful and can bring up some really deep beliefs and even trauma, and frankly, because you can learn these techniques online and there is no regulation on them at this time, some people are doing deep work with people with no training in how to recognize or work with PTSD, depression, anxiety, or other psychological issues. They think of these techniques as a magic bullet and do not necessarily know their own limitations as a practitioner and how to honor the process of their clients. I say this from experience and from having clients who have had negative experiences with other healers where we had to undo damage that was created in sessions with unqualified practitioners. These deeper psychological issues may be present or can be triggered with this powerful work if a practitioner doesn't know how to move the client to the other side and into a state of healing.

I'll step off my soapbox now.

---

8 See the resources section for websites and information about EFT and some of my favorite energy healing modalities.

OWNERSHIP IS THE SECOND ASPECT OF THE INNER VOICE

Years ago, I remember reading this quote from Woody Allen: "I'd never join a club that would allow a person like me to become a member."

It took me a while to understand what he meant by that, and perhaps because my own self-esteem was so low, I really couldn't see it—it was far too close to home. When we devalue ourselves and what we have to offer the world, we can become suspicious of anyone or any club or group that would validate us, celebrate us, or want us as a member—let alone as a leader. (This club might be your family, by the way!)

Ownership is about getting over the belief that we are uniquely defective and can't make a difference in the world. It is amazing to me how many of my clients (all of them at some point)—and my colleagues (when they are being real and authentic), and my friends, and my family, and the people I meet at parties where the conversation is more than just superficial, and even myself...are you getting that it's *everyone* yet?—feel this way deep down inside, or have at some point in their lives.

The difference is that *people who are successful own their Divine birthright, their vision, and take responsibility for believing in themselves. If others believe in them, it simply feels good, but is not necessary. The ones who struggle are still looking for someone else to tell them they are okay—all the while holding those same people at arms' length and devaluing their acceptance and love.*

Pause.

Read that last paragraph again, would you? Which one are you? The one who owns his Divine birthright or the one looking for acceptance and love?

For my birthday last year, I gave myself something that only I could give. Not even God[9], could give it to me...well, I should say God already has given it to me, but like the Woody Allen quote above, I didn't believe it.

---

9 Just so you know, you could substitute Source, The Divine, The Holy Spirit, Universal Consciousness, etc. and all would fit. Substitute what fits for you—okay? The point is that there is something, an organizing force and energy that is Holy, Divine, and while it is

I didn't want to be a part of God's "organization" because I didn't think I deserved it.

I gave myself BELIEF. I chose right then and there that I was going to believe in myself no matter what, and I would let go of the fear and the feeling that I'm not worthy or good enough, and trust that God wouldn't have put this dream in my heart or put me in this time and place with these gifts and people with whom I could share it without giving me a vision that's bigger than I could ever dream of, so if I were really to go for it, I'd have to choose to own it. Over and over and over again.

Many folks, myself included, often ask when they see a person really going for it—really going for what it is that she wants: "Who does she think she *is* to do that?" When the real question they're asking is: "Who do I think I'm *not*?"

I had such low self-esteem growing up. It determined and influenced what I ate, when, where and how; who I dated, the jobs I took, the friends I had, what I allowed into my life—and what I kept at arms' length, thinking I didn't deserve it. Low self-esteem dragged me through an eating disorder in my teens and early twenties. And in my late thirties and early forties, it dragged my family through some lousy communication. It affected my businesses, and my ability to receive money, let alone spend it wisely.

Most people probably wouldn't have looked at me and thought "She has low self-esteem," and truth be told, I didn't think so either! I was really good at spotting it in others, but not so good at spotting it in myself; isn't that always the case? I covered up my toxic shame with a false bravado that over the years both served me very well and exhausted me. It served me well because I got further and farther than many people I know—I took risks and put myself out there; I pushed my limits because I really wanted to grow. But it was exhausting because I was always fearing that I'd be "found out." I couldn't run from myself—nor could I push myself past those low

---

Universal, it is also deeply personal. If you haven't already, explore that force and energy for yourself.

feelings about who I was, what I was capable of, and what I could really offer the world.

When I learned that part of my design is to experience myself and the world through this filter of "never quite enough," I found I stopped getting caught up in that cycle. It became an "Oh, there's that pattern again, huh," instead of "I don't feel good about myself; must be I'm a bad person since I feel bad." I began to realize that all my life I had been interpreting this as a flaw in myself, instead of as a "design challenge," and something that was neither good nor bad, but just is.

I remember reading once in a book a letter from Norman Vincent Peale's wife where she spoke of the extreme lows of self-confidence and self-esteem that her husband grappled with even as he was writing and sharing about the power of the mind and Spirit. Here was a man who was a thought leader in his time. His books are still read and quoted to this day. His insights are quoted on greeting cards and inspiring messages all over the place, yet he grappled with self-doubt just like others do. Reading that letter gave me great hope and a sense of peace.

It really helped me to realize that the little voices do not go away altogether; instead, we must learn to manage them, ignore them, and reconnect to our Source, to our Inner Voice so we can keep going and not fall into the abyss of low self-esteem. Everyone feels low self-esteem at some point; if people aren't allowing themselves to feel it, then it's showing up in other destructive ways, likely toward others. When we are experiencing low self esteem, we feel as if we were the only one ever to have felt that way! Not true. Not true at all.

All that said, we are able to raise our self-esteem and value ourselves. **It's part of my life's work and your life's work, and it's a decision to believe in your own worth—simply for no other reason than you are alive and here, and it feels so much better than holding onto a story that feels crappy.** The liberating thing to realize is that you don't have to be perfect at valuing yourself to be moving in the right direction! One really good way to raise your self-esteem is through ownership. The ownership of which

I speak means truly owning your Divinity, your worth, your value. Your Divinity is inherent. It is given. No matter who you are.

"The sad truth is that 90 percent of all people—not just women—die with their music still unplayed. They never dare try. Why? Because they lack confidence in themselves. It's sad. Women have so much potential many of them never tap."

— Mary Kay Ash

When I was in direct sales, I recall a particular group training that was very uplifting and inspiring. After the training, the leader of our organization said to my upline director, "Your group doesn't think very highly of themselves, do they?" That comment really stuck with me. I thought, "That's not true; look at all the things I do to better myself! I take risks; I go get what I want!" But you know what? He was right. Because the perception I had of myself didn't fit the results I was getting. I thought I was much further along than I was.

Then I looked at how I dressed and the thoughts I was thinking and the people I was hanging out with and I realized, "He's right." Oy. That was not easy to acknowledge, but it was really freeing; because I owned it, I could do something about it!

When we own and speak from our Inner Voice, we are saying to the world, "Here I am! This is what I do. Here's what I think. This is what is important to me. This is what I need and what I want. This is my dream, my vision, my reason for being—and here's how you can help me make it happen—and get something for yourself in the process." We lay our hearts on the line and trust it will work out somehow. We also approach the world from a perspective of "It's not about me." We recognize the greatness in others because we recognize the greatness in ourselves. We see that greatness and vision in them, and we naturally want to help them realize it because there is no competition. We realize at a deep level that there is more than enough to go around, and when others reach their goals and have everything they want, it in no way undermines us or keeps us from getting what we want or desire. We find ways to lift each other up and serve each other's purpose as well.

How can we do that if we don't own our part in the scheme of things?

This process can be scary. We are looking at believing in ourselves, perhaps when we never have done it before or have no idea what it means. It's getting past the fear of rejection and feeling unworthy. If you've ever had someone make fun of something you owned or did, then you know just how frightening it can be to step up and say, "Yes, I did that," or "Yep, that's mine."

OWNING OUR CRAPPY FIRST DRAFTS AND MASTERPIECES

When I was an undergraduate art history major, I took a drawing class. Drawing was never my forte; I thought I was really more of a doodler. I didn't like to sit still long enough to draw! I will never forget the first project we had to do; it was a shadow box. Our assignment was to take a shoebox, remove one of the long sides, rest it on its other long side horizontally, glue some interesting objects in there, and paint everything white. Then, take a direct light and shine it on the box from above and draw the objects and box with light and shadow using charcoal and pencil.

I blew off the assignment. I didn't really know how to do it, and this being my first drawing class, I figured no one else was really going to take it seriously. The reality is that when I got scared, I tended to blow things off until the last minute, and then if I did a crappy job, I somehow had this excuse that I didn't have enough time to do it, so it was inevitable that it would be crappy. I'd tell myself and others, "Well, if I had time to prepare, I could have done a really good job, but since I didn't have time, it isn't a good job." (That's a good excuse, right?) I have since learned it's not a valid excuse, but it is a common one for us card-carrying perfectionists.

We had to hang our pictures up in front of the room and then everyone stood back and critiqued them. I wanted to crawl under a rock and die. My picture literally looked like a first grader had done it, and I am not exaggerating. My professor looked at my picture, turned to the class, and said in a disgusted tone, "I'm not even going to comment on this one, it's so...." I raised my hand, interrupted him before he could go on, and said, "That is mine. I apologize. I blew off the assignment and did it last minute. I would really like the opportunity to go home and do it over."

My voice was shaking, my face crimson with shame, and I was near to tears. My professor looked at me, looked at the picture on the wall, and said I had two days until the next class to redo it. In fact, we went through the critique process for the rest of the class and he gave everyone two days to revise their pictures based on the comments. Taking my picture down and having my classmates look at me like they did was humiliating, but it was worth it in the long run.

I went home and worked on that drawing with total focus and determination. I took my time, and I really *saw* the objects in the box and how the light shone on them and created the shadows. I painstakingly rendered the light and shadow until the objects popped off the page. The first time I had done it, I had just *looked* at the box and drawn an outline of what I thought was there with thick charcoal. There was no shading, no play of light. It was two-dimensional and very crude. During my revision time, I actually *saw* what was happening—I took ownership of my perception and my skills.

When we went back to class, I hung my drawing up before the professor saw me do it. I stood back and looked at the drawing compared to those of my classmates and I saw that mine truly was one of the best on the wall—in composition and rendering. My instructor was shocked when he found out it was mine, but I was beaming with pride. Not because mine was better than others' drawings, but because I knew, without a doubt—*I can draw what I see*!

It's been over twenty years since that class, and I still have those drawings to remind me of what's possible when I give it my best and take ownership—of my crappy drafts and my masterpieces.

Owning it is scary because it means we have to take responsibility—for all of it—even the results of stuff that wasn't our fault. Stuff happened (happens) to us and around us. What we do with it, the results we get with that "stuff," is all ours. *But*...If it's all mine, then I have no one to blame!

"No one to blame!...That was why most people led lives they hated, with people they hated....How wonderful to have someone to blame! How wonderful to live with one's nemesis! You may be miserable, but you feel forever in the right. You may be fragmented, but you feel absolved of all the blame for it. Take your life in your own hands, and what happens? A terrible thing: no one to blame."

— Erica Jong

Ownership can also be challenging because at some point, we folks who have been externally motivated by fear, shame, and not wanting to look bad or get into trouble, have to flip a switch and decide we are doing it for ourselves—not for some outside person or force, or reward (or to avoid punishment). When we truly own our vision, our purpose, our story, and our Truth, we wake up to the reality that we are both the see-er and the seen, the owner and the owned. We become powerful then, with the kind of power that wakes us up and lights a fire under our butts like no external authority or circumstance ever could. That is true freedom.

QUESTIONS TO FREE YOUR INNER VOICE

Where am I blaming others or circumstances for my failure or my actions?

Do I say things like, "If _____ would only be _____, then I could _____."

or "I'll do _____ when _____ happens."

or "What am I telling myself will happen if I go out there and rock it totally by being myself and telling my truth?"

It's subtle, but those are all forms of blaming. Release the blame. Own that "It's not your fault, but it is your responsibility" as my coach once told me, and then you will have the power and energy you need to create your life consciously.

OWNERSHIP = LEADERSHIP

Owning our unique vision and our point of view, owning that we know what we know, and what we know and who we are is valuable—all of that calls us to be our own authority. It calls us to be a leader in not only our business, but first in our body, in our relationships, in our dealings with the little voices and Inner Voice.

I didn't trust, or particularly respect, authority growing up. Oh, like many, I feared it, but I spent considerable time playing passive-aggressive games with those in authority, often at my own expense. I didn't trust or honor authority; therefore, I had a very hard time *being* an authority in my life. This lack of authority showed up in my parenting, in my self-care, in my relationship with my husband, in my business, and in my bottom line.

Owning our self, our vision, our purpose, and our beliefs all call us to become leaders in our own lives. Being an "expert," an "authority" in some area, puts us under the microscope of scrutiny by the masses, who very often abdicate their own authority and leadership, and instead spend time questioning and doubting others' authority when they could be stepping into their own and heeding and speaking from their own Inner Voice, their ultimate authority. I get it. I do it too. And I'm not referring to calling out the lies and inconsistencies in the leaders and gurus, politicians, and figureheads. Of course, we must question the truthfulness and consistency of their messages. Rather, I'm talking about those folks who spend all their time listening to the little voices of fear in their heads and who see the world only through this misperception, then blame leaders for their own messy lives and don't do anything to change themselves or take responsibility. But that's not you, or else you would have never picked up this book, right?

Kristin Thompson, a successful speaking and business coach, shared with me about her experience of becoming her own authority:

Kristin: There are social rules, and I grew up in a household where my dad was really big on rules and following rules, which is ironic because he had a little bit of a rebellious side himself, but at least the way he raised us, it was like there was literally this life or death feeling like if you didn't follow a rule, the whole world might implode or explode.

I can remember still to this day one time as a kid going to school and coming home, and he was livid, and I was like, "What is wrong?" He's like, "You left your driver's license on your night-stand!" I was like, "Right, okay. I'll put it back in my purse." He's like, "You could have been arrested!" That was how he felt about everything. Of course, looking back, I get it. He was just terrified that I was going to get arrested or hurt or whatever. It came from him being a protector. But what it instilled in me was this very strong feeling of, "Oh, my gosh! Any erring of any rules at any time has catastrophic effects."

So I was very conservative, as much as I was always a little bit of a rebel and I loved the rock bands and I loved music, and there was always this rebellious streak. When it really came down to it, I was a pretty darn good rule follower because of the way that I was raised, and I saw in my early career how it held me back because I didn't really take chances. I didn't follow my gut if it didn't follow the rules perfectly. I didn't use that intuition. It was like, "Well, the rule says do this." So I'd just do that, which is ridiculous.

I mean there's a time and a place (for rules), but our intuition is there for a reason. Our voice is there for a reason, and it wasn't until, really, that experience that I shared with you with having

Gavin and then launching my own company and then it became so much more intensified, that when I listened and I took this chance, boom! Something great would happen. Then that would encourage me to do it again. Then something bigger would happen, and now I'm very conscious. In the past year, I've made some decisions with how I was going to get coaching and where I was going to invest my money for event sponsorships or different things that were bold decisions, and they were big, and there was a lot of money riding on them.

I really was kind of going against the grain with what other people in my industry and my colleagues were doing. It was uncomfortable, but I felt it so strongly inside, and I'm so much more confident now that it was easy. It was really easy to say, "I don't care that all of you are going to go do this thing. This is how I'm doing it. I'm not doing it to be rebellious. I'm just doing it because this is how I just feel it. I feel it in every fiber of my body and that's how it's going to work for me. You guys can do whatever you want to do, but here's how I'm going to walk to this music."

Kris: Wow! I could see where that experience of going against the "experts and authority" with Gavin's—with your pregnancy and then Gavin's birth that that would literally break—it literally does break something. It breaks the link in our brain where those little voices are there. "I can't do that. That's against the rules. Who am I to question these authority figures?" All of that.

Kristin: Yeah, I think in a way it was truly becoming an adult, which sounds ridiculous because I was thirty-seven years old. I wouldn't want to argue. I probably should have been an adult already, but I really think it's that shift between putting responsibility on other people, which I have, I will say, and I've always been pretty good about just taking—I just take my lumps and I take responsibility for my actions. I always have, but there's that layer of rule following and stuff that I think does make it really easy to shift responsibility and say, "But I followed the rules and I listened to you, and it didn't work out." When you truly become an adult is when you stand on your own and you say, "Well, I make my own decisions." Sometimes they're going to fit in the mold and sometimes they may not, but they're my decisions and then I'm going to stand by them better or worse.

Kris: I love that "becoming an adult" because I just saw that becoming an adult does not mean at eighteen—we're eighteen or we're thirty-seven or whatever. We can still be a child if we're listening to the little voices in our heads that are often the tapes from our parents. We're still a child. As soon as we start to listen to our Inner Voice and we step into that and the responsibility for that, I think that is when we become an adult and it can happen at any time.

I mean there are probably some kids who are twelve and thirteen who are adults. I know them.

Kristin: That's right. I think it's like an onion. There are layers to the onion, and so we become adults I think in some ways, and then there are still remnants that we find here or there. I think for me that was just another layer. I think that really I tease all the time with my clients that speaking for a living, and even just being an entrepreneur, is one of the fastest paths to personal development that you could possibly take.

Where in your life have you abdicated your authority? Here are some ways it shows up for folks, in no particular order:

*   Eating when emotional or not hungry, or eating something you know will make you feel tired, lethargic, or numbed out.

*   Drinking or using controlled substances to numb your thoughts and emotions.

*   Saying one thing when you really want to say something else.

- Keeping yourself small and hiding out for fear of rejection, persecution, or criticism.

- Always putting others first at the expense of your time, money, energy, and self-esteem (devaluing yourself).

- Allowing the circumstances of your daily life to be the driving force in your schedule instead of deciding what's most important (and in business, profitable) and doing that first.

- Following the "rules" just because an "expert" or someone in authority said you should, especially when your Inner Voice says otherwise.

INTEGRITY AND OWNERSHIP

"To thine own self be true, and it must follow, as the night the day, thou canst not then be false to any man."

— William Shakespeare, *Hamlet*

Recently, a woman I have a lot of respect for did something that made my respect for her shoot up even more. I used to work for this woman at the University of Washington. She is a brilliant researcher and clinician and developed a therapy for people who meet criteria for Borderline Personality Disorder (BPD). There was always talk and speculation that she herself had been (or was) "borderline" as people put it. It didn't really matter much to me; as long as her stuff worked, I figured she must know something about what she was doing and teaching.

After years of hearing this talk about her around the UW and in clinics outside the university, I heard that she recently "outed" herself and confessed that she had in fact been hospitalized as a young woman and that all the things people had suspected over the years about her mental health history were in fact true.

Why? Why after all these years did she do a public interview and "come out" to the world? Because a client, someone who met the criteria for BPD, stood up and asked her point blank: "Are you one of us?" And, because she "didn't want to die a coward," she said, "Yes, I am."

"I was in hell," she said. "And I made a vow: when I get out, I'm going to come back and get others out of here."[10] She created her vision from her greatest vulnerability and then owned it enough to make it her life's work and go on to create a highly effective therapy for a deeply wounded population. And when she stopped being invisible, through telling her story and her truth, in one fell swoop she brought herself into integrity—in her own personal world, and the world at large. Brava!

Integrity is about alignment and having the inner and the outer persona match. It's about having the backbone and structure within to withstand the potential backlash of making a stand, being a stand, and standing up for what you believe in and are passionate about. It's about an end to false advertising and self-sabotage. It's self-acceptance, forgiveness, and ownership. It's being real, authentic, and yes, vulnerable.

QUESTIONS TO FREE YOUR INNER VOICE

If I'm here and my vision is out there, who would I need to be or become to live that vision?

What actions do I need to take?

What's stopping me?

What do I need to let go of and stop resisting?

What do I need to own that I've been denying to myself and everyone else?

And...who can I share that with right now, so I can be free of the shame?

"Be master of your petty annoyances, conserve your energy for the big worthwhile things. It isn't the mountain ahead that wears you out, it's the grain of sand in your shoe."

— Robert Service

10 http://www.huffingtonpost.com/dr-harold-koplewicz/mental-illness-stigma_b_891359.html

BUILDING THE POSITIVE

Now that you have observed where your thinking has, perhaps, been off track—what can you do to build the positive?

- Tell a new story about it. If it's a particularly challenging situation or person, I say things like "I choose to_____" or "I'm now allowing myself _____."

- Express gratitude. Using the present tense, express your gratitude for the goodness that is here, that is coming, and that you are sharing with others. Write or speak it aloud.

- Listen to uplifting music, motivational trainings or recordings, watch shows, and read books that inspire you and that focus on the positive and what's "right"[11] about the world.

- Spend time with positive people who can hold your vision or dream— who even push you a little bit to stay on track with it.

- Practice meditation. Whether you have a regular practice or are just starting out, a few minutes a day of observing your thoughts coupled with breathing can really work!

AN EXERCISE AND QUESTIONS
TO FREE YOUR INNER VOICE

First, pick **one internal** thought, belief, or idea, and **one external source** of thoughts, ideas, or beliefs and turn a deaf ear to them this week.

Some ways you can turn a deaf ear:

- stop watching/listening to news

- unfriend or "hide" a negative/annoying person on Facebook

- unsubscribe to a newsletter that annoys you or is out of alignment with your beliefs

---

11 I use the word "right" a lot, but please don't get it confused with the need to be right, or that judgmental moralistic "right vs. wrong." It's more of a "what's flowing, what's in alignment, what fits, what feels good when you hear it and speak it" kind of right.

- spend more time with positive people who are uplifting and not complaining

- schedule a 1:1 session with Kris (or other coach/practitioner if you have one) to change a belief or turn down the volume on those little voices

I am no longer willing to listen to the voice of _____ in my life anymore. This week I will _____ in order to ignore it, change it, let it/him/her go.

It is said we are the sum of the five people we hang out with the most. Who are those people in your life?

What are the things these people talk about?

What are their attitudes about life? Money? Relationships? The economy? Success?

What thoughts do you tolerate in your head? Simply notice what thoughts, beliefs, criticisms, and judgments (of yourself or others) that you have frequently.

What thoughts, ideas, beliefs, do you allow and even tolerate from the people around you? (i.e., the news, TV shows, Facebook, friends, partners, colleagues, kids, strangers, etc.)

You'll know you're "tolerating" them because they feel crummy/depressing/frustrating when you hear them; or you find yourself saying things like, "Oh, that's just how they are" while inside you're feeling annoyed or put out; or you know these people aren't positive or in alignment with where you want to go in your life or business, but you listen to them anyway and shove aside your own truth without doing or saying anything to change the situation or how you see it.

CHAPTER SEVEN

Key Element #3: Balance Your Emotions— Influence

"Tempest-tossed souls, wherever ye may be, under whatsoever conditions ye may live, know this—in the ocean of life the isles of Blessedness are smiling, and the sunny shore of your ideal awaits your coming. Keep your hand firmly upon the helm of thought. In the bark of your soul reclines the commanding Master; He does but sleep; wake Him.

Self-control is strength; Right Thought is mastery; Calmness is power.

Say unto your heart, 'Peace, be still!'"

—James Allen

Whenever someone wants to break free from the middle and become a *thought leader*, we address the ways in which she's been an *emotional follower* (someone who is led by her emotions). Remember, it's all about increasing awareness and consciousness and finding that clarity no matter what is happening within and around us. We are not going to get rid of emotions—that would be like getting rid of the air. We live, as human beings, in an emotional context. We are all communicating through the *energy* of emotions, experiencing ourselves and others through the continuously flowing waves of emotions. In the middle, we begin to see how our emotions derail us, but often we still don't have the tools to move through the emotional turmoil and stay with the process long enough to lead ourselves out of it.

For example, do you feel a "charge" every time you think of someone or a certain situation and it really stresses you out? Did you know that it's possible to reduce or eliminate that "emotional charge" so you can think more clearly, problem-solve more effectively, and *feel informed instead of overwhelmed by your emotions?*

When a memory, thought, or belief keeps coming up and every time you experience it you feel as though you were right back in the original event as though it is happening right now, your body has the same chemical reactions as it did the first time you had the experience. *Your body doesn't know the difference between whether it's really happening or whether you're just thinking about it happening!* Either way, it releases stress hormones, one of the main ones being cortisol, which in excess, depletes the body and has numerous negative effects on your health.

The most common reaction during a traumatic event is to shut down or "freeze," in effect stopping the natural flow of the emotional chemicals released by the body. So, if you have experienced trauma (big or small), and you have not cleared that emotion out of your system, these chemicals of emotion can become "stuck" in the body, and whenever you think of the event or the person or trauma, you feel it all over again. *How stressful is that?*

Most of the time when I am working with someone around her fears (usually being more visible, speaking her Truth, owning her gifts and talents, sales conversations, public speaking, etc.), it ties back to some experience she had as a child (before ages seven or eight).

These emotional charges affect our everyday lives, business, and especially our intimate relationships, and you'll experience them every time you have the same argument or conversation you've had a million times. It seems like you just keep rehashing the same problems without getting anywhere. It never ceases to amaze me how often my clients and I start treating a specific issue, fear, or miscommunication and long-forgotten issues come up. The best part is that we can then work with those issues that were long-gone in the conscious mind, but still fresh in the subconscious mind, and reduce or eliminate those negative emotions from running the show. It's so cool and humbling to witness this process and to have experienced it myself. When the negative charge is gone, there's lots more space, lots more freedom, and lots more energy to do fun, interesting activities!

Once again, we turn to techniques that calm the amygdala. A long-term practice of meditation and breathing is very beneficial, as are relaxation techniques, visualization, hypnotherapy, etc. I recommend all of these, and with each, the effects are cumulative. For rapid relief, I turn to meridian tapping and other energy psychology methods (like EFT, as I mentioned before), and I teach them to my clients. When you are in a panic, sitting to meditate simply doesn't work—unless you've been practicing regularly for a significant period of time.

Furthermore, when your limbic system is firing, the cerebral cortex, or logic and learning part of the brain, doesn't get as much blood, and therefore, it functions at a deficit—so trying to learn a calming technique when you're in the midst of emotional upheaval is challenging at best and can actually have the opposite reaction you intend. (Think of someone saying, "Relax!" when you are fired up; does it work?)

Just as you observe how certain foods and drinks affect your energy and physical wellbeing, watch whom you spend time with and the activities you engage in. Observe your reactions to people, situations, thoughts, and experiences. You may begin to see patterns of emotions that are clues as to what are "safe" activities and people for you to engage in and be around. Naturally, you'll want to avoid those people who set you off, but what if you can't? There's help for this too, and my clients and I address these situations much as we address fears and other anxieties.

REDUCING AN EMOTIONAL CHARGE

It takes about ninety seconds for the chemical reactions of an emotion to flow through the body—isn't that comforting to know? So what you want to do is learn how to reduce quickly that emotional charge, rather than engaging in some activity that just covers it up or shoves the emotion down. The problem is that most of us during that ninety seconds do one or more of the following:

• take action from this place and do or say something we later regret

• try to stuff the feeling with food, alcohol, drugs, or some other "comforting" activity that just covers it up

• analyze the feeling and try to make sense of it from a logical perspective and make leaps of logic that are way off base

• start ruminating about all the other times we felt this way

All of these tactics only serve to "lock-in" the emotion even more firmly and create a looping mechanism that keeps the emotion firing, especially if your "buttons" get pushed. When you begin to experience an emotional reaction, or notice you're in the throes of one, take a few deep breaths, ground yourself like you learned in the first key element, and allow the emotion to flow out the soles of your feet as you exhale. Do this for at least ninety seconds. The world and others can wait for you to calm down. After you feel calm, then you can think clearly and take action or speak from a centered place, or even make sense of what just happened.

There are really only two basic emotions, upon which all other feelings are derived or experienced: Love & fear. Love is a cohesive force; it unites, coalesces, brings together, connects, inspires growth, and is anabolic, or building, energy. Love's opposite, fear, is a destructive force; it breaks apart, dissolves, entropies, and destroys. It is catabolic, or destructive, energy. Both are necessary in a dualistic world.[12]

The determining factor in how we will perceive or experience the world around us is to what extent our everyday, moment-to-moment thoughts

---

12 Adapted from *Energy Leadership*.

elicit feelings of love and cohesiveness vs. thinking thoughts that tear-down or break apart us or others.

Feelings that are closer to love: appreciation, contentment, faith, excitement, joy.

Feelings that are closer to fear: anger, resentment, hatred, guilt, shame.

Hawkins' describes a *Map of Consciousness* in his book *Power vs. Force*. In the map, the following emotions are calibrated to the corresponding energy level as noted with a number. The numbers are logarithmic progression, versus an arithmetic progression. For instance, while fear has a vibrational level of 100 and courage has a level of 200, it doesn't mean courage is twice the vibration of fear. Fear is 10 to the 100th power (10^{10}), while courage is 10 to the 200th power (10^{20}). Shame has an energy level of 20, guilt = 30, fear = 100, courage = 200, acceptance = 350, love = 500, joy = 540, and so on. What this means is that as you move up the energetic scale, even a slight shift toward a positive emotional vibration can have a powerful healing or nullifying effect on the lower vibration emotional states. Even a little spark of light and love in a dark situation can light the way, and *lighten* the way!

In Schneider's *Energetic Self-Perception Chart*, in his book *Energy Leadership*, leading from a level four or higher is leading more from the heart with the emotion of compassion than the three levels below, which are apathy (level one), anger (level two), and forgiveness (level three). When you can discern which energy level (or emotional level) you are leading from, you can see why you are getting the results you're getting, and begin to make shifts toward a higher vibrational emotional state, and lead from there. The impact it has on yourself, others, and the overall result is powerful, and often it is only a small shift within that makes it happen!

When you no longer feel a charge around people, places, and experiences, you come to realize that "safety" is relative, and in the eye of the beholder. You get to determine whom you want to spend time with and what activities you want to do, not because you feel emotionally obligated or wanting to avoid something altogether, but because you are following your own desires and Truth. That's emotional freedom, and very much in alignment with your Inner Voice.

In the Human Design chart, we see that some people are designed to experience all the waves of emotions, the highest of highs and the lowest of lows. These people have their emotion center "defined" and, as such, experience the world emotionally. Their emotions are also the key to their inner authority, and seeking clarity amid the often tumultuous waves of emotion is how they will best lead their lives. Other people, like myself, have the emotional center undefined, which means we don't get caught up in every emotion; however, we are more susceptible to taking on the emotions of others who are in our vicinity. In either case, discernment about what emotion is present, and whom it belongs to, and then how to observe it without being overwhelmed by it, is a big part of the work of we human beings no matter what centers we have defined.

A discussion of what triggers us emotionally wouldn't be complete without mentioning value. Specifically, how we value ourselves and our "substance" because the beliefs around our personal value and the value of what we offer the world are so often deeply emotionally charged.

VALUE

"Offer your substance where it can do most good."

— Raymond Holliwell

"Your substance is your genius, services, talents, gifts, time, energy, insights, and intuitions. It's your advice, feedback, and for better or worse, your opinions." ~ Kris Prochaska

Seeing ourselves clearly also consists of valuing our unique talents and gifts (our "substance") and not allowing oneself to shortchange any of that, just to make peace, or make a buck. If we allow our energy to be drained by working with people who do not honor us, value us, or celebrate what we have to offer, then we quietly shut down our joy and enthusiasm and we don't do our best work. That's being out of alignment with our truth and is not very attractive at all.

One of the ways that we can oh-so-subtly get caught in a value-trap is through listening to the little voices who "should" us about being *responsible*. Responsibility tugs at our heartstrings, but not that higher vibrational level of our heart, rather the lower conflicted, wounded heart. It leads us to making decisions and doing things from an emotional state, a state that tends to devalue self and others.

RESPONSIBILITY TO VS. RESPONSIBILITY FOR

I had a client a few years back say to me "I want to be successful and make a lot of money and get back to the level of success I had years ago—and it's your job to get me there." Yikes! No pressure, right? *Right.* There was none because I was clear—it's not my responsibility to make sure she's successful. I responded by saying, "It's my job to offer you tools and processes that remove whatever blocks you may have to taking action or receiving money and resources, and it's my job to help you be accountable, but it's your responsibility to do the work, not mine." Interestingly, just the day before I had been talking with my coach about this very thing. I had been feeling responsible *for* my clients versus *to* them, and so I used the tools I have to "clear" the beliefs, emotions, and the energy around this before going to bed, and *voilà*—the next day I had a great opportunity to be tested and see whether I was indeed seeing the world and my role as a coach from a new perspective—and I was.

How much of the time do we as mothers, as businesswomen, as wives, girlfriends, partners, daughters, sisters, friends, etc. take responsibility for others—for their outcomes, for their results, for their successes or failures, for their happiness or lack of it, and actually think that we are doing them a favor? How much time do we spend taking responsibility because it makes us feel indispensable? How many of us feel that if we "help" others feel better or do things for them, then we have value and cannot be set aside?

When we get a sense of ourselves as valuable—or stop judging ourselves as valuable based on what we can *do* for others versus knowing that our being, our essence, is valuable, period, we begin to let go of the need to be responsible for others. We trust that they can handle it themselves, that they are sovereign beings and can deal with the results that they create. We let go of the need to control and fix because we realize there is nothing to control, or fix—it's both a lie and futile. We stop justifying ourselves through over-explaining or trying to look good to others so they will like us.

When our children are very young, we are indeed responsible for them—to a certain extent. We are responsible for what and whom we expose them to, what we feed them, what we allow them access to (i.e., is it physically, emotionally, spiritually empowering, and honoring of them?), where we live, how we deal with our stress, and the level of responsibility we take for ourselves. This one is tricky because really *in order to be responsible to our kids (or clients!), we have to be responsible for ourselves first,* and that is easier said than done. Most of us are quite shocked when we become parents and realize that we need to clean up our act because the "Do as I say, not as I do" myth gets mirrored back to us daily by our kids who call us out and give us the opportunity to make different choices constantly.

When we are responsible *for* ourselves, for our thoughts, feelings, actions, words, etc., we are able to be responsible *to* our kids (and our clients/customers and everyone else in our world) through the clarity that responsibility for ourselves brings. The clarity of whose stuff is whose, and what are our own needs and wants, and what are their needs and wants, and what is their responsibility and not ours, all brings in the space clearly and confidently to be, say, and do what comes from a place of wholeness and expansion.

Okay, before you start thinking that I've got this perfectly dialed in and don't slip up, I'll just nip that in the bud right here. I joke that I have a therapy jar for my kids so that all the things I've done that I set out to do with the best intentions and ended up doing with the lowest vibrational habits can be healed when they are ready for it. It's awareness and practice and owning my stuff, and the willingness to do better next time.

How do we take responsibility for others and not even know it? More importantly, how do we stop this habit?

One way is to notice when we are feeling the urge to "fix" others, control the situation, or otherwise judge others as incapable of helping themselves, or judge the world (or others) as somehow faulty and it's our job to fix it. Another way is to notice when we feel the need to justify ourselves, our decisions, our services and offerings, our place in the world. This one is particularly close to home for me! When I finally saw the pattern, it was like a huge lightbulb went off! Seeing the pattern isn't enough, though; we actually have to *be* different, take different action, and manage all the emotions that arise in our urge to justify, explain, take responsibility for, or fix others. Not a particularly fun process, but a totally freeing one!

Karen Lynn's story of listening to her Inner Voice when she suspected her son was in trouble twenty years ago really shows how responsibility plays out. She had to learn to trust her instincts, with no evidence, and against the opinion of her therapist, make a call that would surely change the outcome of her son's life. Through the process, she learned about responsibility.

Karen Lynn: When I think about my Inner Voice, I view that as the voice of God. That's how I think of that, as the overall sort of guiding force in my life. I hear, literally hear, my voice. In my thinking, I don't hear a different—it's not a different sound, like auditory sound.

[Here's a time] where I felt like I did listen to my Inner Voice really well and then the result around that. About twenty years ago I put my son—he was fifteen years old, and I put him in a residential drug and alcohol treatment program in Florida. It was an eighteen-month program. It actually was going to take as long as it took, but he was there for eighteen months.

I knew something had to happen, that he was going down. I was watching it. He was going to end up in jail or dead, and I didn't exactly know what was going on, although one day it hit me that, "Oh, he's involved with drugs." I didn't have any solid evidence about that beyond his behavior.

So I trusted that...and did what I needed to do. Set up an intervention, pulled people together, all that, and put him there. Actually—and all of the little small voices, the little nagging self—and I call them self-doubt...said that that was all wrong. Even my therapist at the time told me, "You shouldn't do that. He will interpret it as you abandoning him."

Kris: Even your therapist wasn't supportive?

Karen Lynn: Even my therapist. Who had been kind of with me during all this and I started questioning, "Well, maybe I'm just trying to get rid of him because it would make life easier." It came down to knowing, "This is saving his life. I need to do this."

I only know twenty years later, that it was without any doubt, without any questioning, without any little tiny voices going off in my head, I know it was the right thing to do.

Kris: Yeah.

Karen Lynn: Because he's just out of the second time out of treatment and in resolution and relationship with him, now knowing the whole story about twenty years ago and what he's now shared with me about what was going on.

Kris: Did he perceive it as you were abandoning him? I'm just curious, twenty years later.

Karen Lynn: He does not now feel like—he understands my rationale for it and he knows that he was going down. He might feel like I abandoned him. He hasn't really said that, but he knows it was the right thing to do because he gets where he was.

Kris: Right. So even though you didn't have any evidence, you trusted a knowing that you had, even at the risk of losing him or him thinking or feeling that you were going to abandon him and against what your therapist was telling you and other people and the voices of self-doubt in your head. Wow!

Karen Lynn: Right. I did listen for a while. But yeah. The only evidence I had was his behavior and my interpretation of his behavior because when I would confront it, ask, and just get lies. What he said and what I saw didn't—weren't aligned, so I just went with that. That's pretty crazy making.

Kris: Oh, yeah.

Karen Lynn: That was a time where I followed that, and like I said, I have a peace about it now that I've never had before. It's been twenty years of kind of living with some turmoil about it. It would be more turmoil when he would get mad at me. He'd say, "Well, you did this. When I wasn't straight, it just messed up my life. This is when I started feeling anxiety and all that stuff." But now I get it. All of this anxiety and stuff that he would refer to [meant] he was back using again.

Kris: I think what really strikes me about this story is that it ended up having a positive outcome, at least right now, currently, based on what you've told me—outside of this interview based on what you've told me, that you could never have known that and if you had known what you'd have to go through to get to this place twenty years later, would you have done the same thing?

Karen Lynn: Oh, absolutely. Yeah, because I literally believed it saved his life. He wouldn't be here or he'd be in jail, which, to me, is a death.

Kris: Right.

Karen Lynn: He believed it, too. So yes, I would do it again. I'd take his butt to treatment again like I did earlier in the year. I would do it in a heartbeat. To me, that's not abandoning somebody.

Karen Lynn took responsibility for her emotions and the intuitive hits she got about her son, and she acted on them. However, she didn't (and it was a process!) take responsibility for his getting better; that was his, not her responsibility. While it took work on her part to practice letting go, she still did it and their relationship is better than ever. That's prosperity and wealth you cannot buy.

OWNING AND MANAGING OUR VALUE

One of the ways we can own and manage our value is through time. Time is the only thing we have equal measure of relative to everyone else, and it is the least expensive commodity, as far as our capital investments in our business go, with the greatest amount of return. That is, provided we invest our time wisely.

As with all valuable lessons, I learned this one the hard way, and it relates to the need to justify above. As embarrassing as this is to share, it was such a turning point for me that I share it because it really had to get this bad for me to see exactly what I was valuing, and what my time is worth to me. I also got the valuable lesson of being reminded that people value what they pay for, just as I have learned and valued the most when I have made an investment myself to pay someone for his or her expertise. I hope this example will help you see where you may be giving your substance away and just how valuable your time and substance is as well.

I enthusiastically decided to "try out" a new offering by putting it out there to my email list. I offered a free energy session, a diagnostic session which I had done face-to-face, but not over the phone in this specific way. I wanted to gain practice and experience, and although it was something that I do in my office and get paid for, for some reason, I felt compelled to offer it for free this time. I had someone in another country enthusiastically take me up on the offer, and I set out preparing to serve her as I would any paying customer.

I spent about forty minutes preparing for our call, including scheduling, emailing her with questions, and doing an energetic assessment before-hand. I had the hit to set up the call on a free or low-cost teleseminar program I use, but it wasn't until I was actually dialing the phone to call across the world that I had that hit. It was strong, but I ignored it. At the time of this call, my hourly rate was $200. I spent ninety minutes in direct and indirect service to this woman, which I didn't consider as I was setting the whole appointment up. In my excitement, I just acted without any real consideration of the amount of time or value of the service I was offering. Positive emotions can trip us up as easily as negative emotions do!

That "free" call was a $300 value for this woman (strictly timewise, it didn't count the insight and healing energy transmitted during the call). And it was a $300 "cost" to me. That is not where this story ends though. Two days later, I received a text message from my phone carrier that said I had accumulated over $100 in international charges on my account! Holy Shit! When I contacted my carrier, I found out that the total charge for that call was actually $178.00. Double Holy Shit!

Did I go through the roof on that one! I was so mad at myself I could hardly believe it. Seriously, it took me at least forty-five minutes to calm myself down and reframe the whole situation. I missed a group coaching call with one of my coaches because of this upset. I couldn't focus. Why was I so upset? It wasn't just the money, or the time spent—that was the least of my concerns, despite the sting of embarrassment, and the pain of having to pay that bill (which I later got reduced!). The biggest pain was that I had completely gone against my own commitment to honor my substance and give it where it would do the most good. I knew when I hung up that this woman (despite the fact that she said she felt lighter and better than she had felt at the beginning of the call, and that my diagnosis was on target, as well as the energy routine I shared with her) would never do anything further with it. Why? Because she had invested nothing but her time. Time that she wasn't even valuing herself since she wasn't charging people for her services.

Ugh. The total value/cost of that lesson: $478.00, plus an hour of coaching with my coach, and the time spent cleaning it up with my phone carrier.

Was it a waste? Yes and No. It has the potential to be a waste if I allow myself to do it again. Did I learn something really valuable? You bet. The funny thing about this (funny ironic, not funny haha) is that I just got reminded, as I am writing this, that I also have a commitment to making things a lot harder than they need to be. I got to kill two commitments with one call on this one!

So, your turn. Where have you been devaluing yourself and your time? Where have you been making your lessons a lot harder than they need be?

Are you so distracted right now by the story I just told and all the judgments you have about me that you can't even answer this question? If so, good! Now you are one step closer to owning your own crap. Because I can tell you this, if you are judging me or having an emotional reaction to the story I just shared, it is wholly because you have not yet owned your own emotional charge, judgments, and miscalculations around your time, value, and fees you charge for your substance. Begin owning that and you will be free. Free from the judgment, and free from the need to justify or devalue yourself, or any of the other ways the pattern and commitment shows up for you.

VITALITY

Vitality is closely linked with value. When we value our time and substance, when we surround ourselves with people who also value their time, their substance, and who value ours as well, our vitality, or emotional joy, increases. When we engage in habits and thinking, listening to and speaking from our Inner Voice, we experience a vitality that carries us through any and all adversity and temporary setbacks. This vitality is what attracts others to us. It is the twinkle in our eyes and the lightness in our step. It is the way we show up in our body, fully taking up residence, and shining our light and radiance out into the world. Vitality is what gives juice to our vision. It's the result of, and the fuel for, taking action: committed, definite action on our goals and our vision, no matter what circumstances present themselves.

Vitality is life force, chi, prana, and inspiration. It is what we experience when we are in tune with the positive forces of nature and allow them to flow freely in us.

When we devalue others, we steal their vitality. When we devalue ourselves, we give away our vitality. Begin to notice where the way you speak and what you say steals others' vitality, and where you offer words and actions that build others' vitality. Know that, ultimately, we are all responsible for our own vitality, but we can definitely affect others' life forces, too, positively and negatively. Notice when how you speak to yourself robs you of your vitality, and all the habitual ways you try to get it back, which may temporarily give you the sensation of vitality, but in the long run drain it.

QUESTIONS TO FREE YOUR INNER VOICE

What increases your vitality? How can you bring or do more of that in your life?

Finish this statement: Successful people feel _____

How often do you feel that way?

What are the emotions that you have been tolerating:

In yourself?

In others around you?

Sometimes, and especially when we are very sensitive/empathic, we can take on the emotions of others and not even realize it.

Ask Yourself: "Whose is this?" (If you feel lighter, it's not yours. Send it back to the person with love and light attached to it.) No need to blame the other person; she didn't "make" you feel that way; you simply "picked up" the emotional charge in the field between you and took it on as your own.

The key is not only to protect yourself, but also to inquire what you get out of processing other people's stuff so they don't have to.

A few ways to manage strong emotions:

- Breathe into them. Remember, ninety seconds from the initial surge to when they begin to dissipate. Practice increasing your ability to sit with these emotions through the power of your breath.

- Yoga, Tai-Chi, Qi-Gong, any class where you have to pay attention to what the instructor is telling you to do (like Zumba, aerobics, dance, etc.) can all be helpful for anxiety. If you have to move your body and concentrate on what the person is saying, it will distract you from the anxiety as well as dissipate the anxious energy. Of course, if you are in class and cannot relax, then by all means do what you need to do to practice self-care! Sometimes walking or hiking can help too.

- If the anxiety or depression won't shift, then get in to see a therapist or healing practitioner who specializes in EMDR, EFT, or other mind-body techniques.

INFLUENCE

"The meeting of two personalities is like the contact of two chemical substances; if there is any reaction, both are transformed."

— Carl Gustav Jung

The third aspect of the Inner Voice, influence, has us really examine how we are influencing others and by what and whom we are being influenced externally and internally.

We tend to think of people of influence as having a lot of money. Influence is not just about making or having money, though. It's about making an impact. Sometimes that impact is made through taking a stand. I've said it's important for us to let go of judgment, especially of ourselves—mostly because it does us no good mentally, emotionally, spiritually, or physically. That being said, it doesn't mean that others won't judge us. And indeed, it's likely that because we judged someone else that we rejected something or accepted a new way of seeing something, we made distinctions and decisions based on those judgments—just as others will do with us.

POLARIZATION

"If you're not being judged, you're invisible."

— Seth Godin

The thing to recognize is that we cannot control how people will judge us, but we can influence them to polarize in some way. This polarization is not all bad! Even if people don't resonate with you, at least they'll potentially wake up and have an opinion. Maybe it will even inspire them to take some action, whether that's to work with you or your "competitor" or maybe even become your "competitor," either way, it's all in service. We can't please everyone, but we can influence many, if not most, and we do that through taking a stand.

Look at your relationships, whether in your family or your business. Where have you played both sides of the field in order to "keep the peace"? I was very good at keeping the peace. I learned how to stay safe by keeping my options and opinions open. There were times, however, when I spoke out and allowed what I truly felt and believed to be expressed, and I was always surprised by how appreciative people were when I did this. I loved to know I was making a difference in the world through speaking up and being authentic, but I was still scared to do it consistently throughout my life and relationships.

I'm not talking about just taking a stand to be obstinate or rebellious. I'm talking about daring to be fearlessly authentic. When I was younger, and even now, it seemed everyone dyed her hair random colors and got tattoos (I had some too) as a way of making a statement and expressing individuality. I used to laugh because my thought was, when everyone is doing it—

it's not a statement anymore; it's just another colorful hairstyle or tattoo among the masses.

I've often thought the real way to stand out and make a true statement in the world is actually to say what you think and mean what you say. It's a hell of a lot harder to do that from a heart-centered authentic place that's vulnerable and powerful than it is to wear a certain kind of clothing style, dye your hair, or pierce something (and I've tried those too, so I know).

Expressing anger and rebellion is easy. Taking a stand for what you believe in, not so much. Look at where you may be only half-invested in making a difference. If you are feeling, as I once did, that I wasn't fulfilled and that something was missing, consider it's because you may be playing only half-heartedly. When I slip back into that, it's as though I die a small death and I think thoughts like "What's the point anyway?" We have such a gift and opportunity in this lifetime. Truly we are alive at an incredibly special time in the evolution of humanity. It is not a mistake that you and I are alive right now. The questions we need to ask ourselves are: What will I do with this opportunity? How will I influence others in a positive way? Am I willing to piss some people off, even if only to wake them up to a new way of seeing things?

RESONANCE

"In everyone's life, at some time, our inner fire goes out.
It is then burst into flame by an encounter with
another human being."

— Albert Schweitzer

Dr. Dain Heer of *Access Consciousness*™ teaches about "entrainment" which is where folks vibrate and attune to the "lowest common denominator." Napoleon Hill in his book *Outwitting the Devil* also described this phenomenon. The message here: Watch out whom you're hanging around and being influenced by! Surround yourself with harmony and people who inspire you to be great. Seek harmony in your environment (house/work/business/ etc); seek out harmonious people—people who are positive and forward-thinking; surround yourself with things of beauty and meaning; explore new ideas that cause you to see the world differently and expand your perception; update your clothing and your look—not just your outlook (though this will help!).

Surrounding yourself with people who vibrate at a higher level is essential to creating a new vision of your Self and for yourself. When I first heard Dr. Heer say this, I thought he was just being "woo-woo." When I re-searched emotional entrainment, however, I found lots of information on the Internet. I liked the simplicity of this explanation by Daniel Goleman:

> Setting the emotional tone of an interaction is, in a sense, a sign of dominance at a deep and intimate level: it means driving the emo-tional state of the other person. This power to determine emotion is akin to what is called in biology a *zeitgeher* (literally, "time grab-ber"), process (such as the day-night cycle of the monthly phases of the moon) that entrains biological rhythms. For a couple dancing, the music is a bodily zeitgeber. When it comes to personal encounters, the person who has the more forceful expressivity—or the most power—is typically the one whose emotions entrain the other. Dominant part-ners talk more, while the subordinate partner watches the other's face more—a setup for the transmissions effect. By the same token, the forcefulness of a good speaker—a politician or an evangelist, say—works to entrain the emotions of the audience. That is what we mean by, "He had them in the palm of his hand." Emotional entrainment is the heart of influence.

Basically, the most powerful person in the room is the one whom people will entrain to emotionally. If that person is negative, and the rest of the folks are susceptible to being triggered by that negativity (I call it listening to and speaking from the little voices), then that's the emotional tone for the room.

In the Human Design system, we note that people who have their emotion centers defined, or fixed, meaning they experience all the waves of emotion, can and do influence others, especially those of us with open, or undefined, emotional centers. In other words, people who are more emotionally open and flexible, are susceptible to riding the waves of the emotions of others around them. Knowing this, and being able to discern between what is one's own emotional response to something or someone, and what is purely someone else's emotional experience is crucial.

IF MOMMA AIN'T HAPPY

"If momma ain't happy, ain't nobody happy." My husband doesn't like that saying, but you know it's true! If I'm having a rough day, or I'm distracted, ungrounded, or otherwise out of sorts, my kids bounce off the walls. They bicker more and whine *a lot* more. But when I'm grounded, and my energy is coherent—when my head and my heart are aligned—they listen better (of course, so do I!), they are calmer, and they get along with each other quite well. We all get along better in fact. This is where I learned how much our energy influences others—from being a parent. The things I do to get my energy back "online," as I like to say, are listed in the Appendix. When I'm feeling off, I spend about five minutes, sometimes less, getting my heart coherence flowing again and getting my energy flowing as well. It changes everything.

Everything.

Sometimes I have to put myself in a time-out. I tell my kids I'm going to reboot my "computer" at times; especially when they get home from school and have had a rough day, I'll do my energy routine in front of them *or with them*, and we'll all end up in a pile on the floor hugging and laughing—literally within two minutes.

That's influence and it works in business as well. When I'm feeling "off" and I go to a networking event, I don't have as much fun and I don't shine as brightly. That's not a stuck-up statement; that's an observation. When

I shine more brightly, I attract people who shine brightly, and I can reflect back to them their brightness as well. It's so much more fun and the flow is awesome. What do I do to get to that place? I do a quick energy routine (listed in the Appendix); I do Heart Coherence Breathing™ from the Heartmath Institute[13]; I exercise; and when I have time, I listen to recordings of people and music that positively influence my thinking, which affects my emotional state and my energy state as well. It all goes together.

Who do you listen to who boosts you?

Who or what do you listen to that brings you down?

You have a choice. Sometimes the people around us, especially if they are the negative influence, will not like it if we choose not to spend time with them. Natural consequences suck, don't they? AND it may be just what they need to move out of the rut they are in because I don't believe there are any people who are totally miserable who are unaware of that fact, though they may be unaware of how it is affecting others. Your setting clear limits with them by honoring yourself may be just the feedback they need finally to get some help. Or not. Either way, that's their choice, not yours!

I've noticed two things really help when it comes to "taking on" other people's energy. First, you must be willing to acknowledge that you are more psychic, intuitive, and energetically receptive than you think you are. We are spiritual beings having a human experience, and we communicate energetically first and foremost. You must be willing and open to the idea that what you are feeling is at its essence an energy, and that we are swimming in this energy all the time. By allowing this to be a perspective that you view the world and your experience through, you are more open to perceiving the subtle nuances inherent in the energy dynamic between you and others.

Second, when you are feeling heavy, dense, negative energy (which may feel like anxiety or sadness), ask yourself "Is this mine?" or "Who does

---

13 At the Heartmath Institute, a person can learn heart coherence breathing techniques to reduce stress and stabilize his or her heart rhythms.

this belong to?"[14] and wait for the answer. If it belongs to someone else, you will feel instantly lighter and will notice more space around you. Send that energy back to its rightful owner with love and consciousness attached to it. You may also get a hit about whose energy it was, and how you can interact with that person (or not!) in a way that acknowledges how he or she is feeling, without taking it on yourself and processing it as if it were your own "stuff" or feelings. (The person need not be present for you to be picking up on her emotions or energy, especially if you are very intuitive or empathic. That said, you will likely experience this more acutely when near the person. Time and space do not factor in when we are looking at this level of communication).

QUESTIONS TO FREE YOUR INNER VOICE

Who are you allowing to influence you and your moods?

What kinds of television are you watching, if at all? Notice what the story-line is. How much violence or drama is portrayed? How do you feel after you watch these shows? Just observe. That which is entertaining, can also be entraining.

The computer programming language GIGO—"Garbage in, Garbage out"—applies here. What is the "garbage" that you are allowing into your mind, body, environment, and relationships? Is there garbage you are spewing onto others that would be better taken care of through counseling or some other avenue (exercise even!). Remember, no judgment here—just observation. When I eat certain foods to which I have a reaction, I become irrationally grumpy. I then can spew that grumpiness on others, quite often my husband and kids. I have come to learn that there are certain foods that are not worth eating; they are like poison—garbage, in my body and create garbage coming out. Notice whether you have people, foods, beverages, thoughts, shows, music, places, clothing, or even certain chemicals that set

---

14 These tools are taken from Access Consciousness™

you off. If you find something, remove it for a while and see whether you feel differently.

Another aspect of influence is how we are influenced internally. We've already spent quite a bit of time looking at how we can be influenced negatively by the little voices; let's look at how we can level the playing field and align ourselves with the influence of our Inner Voice. We do that through listening to our inner authority. One of the most powerful and prevalent sources of connection to the Inner Voice (meaning most people are designed to use this built-in guidance system) is through our intuition.

I used to think everyone across the board accesses his or her Inner Voice through what is commonly called intuition or a gut instinct. Then I really had to look at what intuition is and how it's been defined and taught about because I think we call everything that is our inner knowing "intuition" and that can trip up some folks. It causes confusion because one person may feel it in her gut, while another "just knows," and still another may feel it in her heart or chest. What I love about Human Design is that it discerns between each of these "inner authorities"—what we've called intuition as a blanket statement—and helps us know which one we were designed to use to access our deepest truth and live in harmony with that.

Very briefly, Human Design describes six "Inner Authorities" or decision-making styles (and ways of accessing personal spiritual truth) based on what energy centers a person has defined in his or her Human Design chart:

1. **Emotional Authority:** A person may or may not get a "gut-feeling" or "intuitive hit" to explore something further. No matter what, a person with this inner authority style needs to get emotional clarity first before taking action. This can take moments, hours, days, or even months to do. This comes from the solar plexus.

2. **Sacral Authority:** The classic gut-response. Energetic information comes in, and the "gut" either opens up in response to it with an "uh-huh" (yes), or an "uh-uh" (no), or even no response or neutral response. It's felt low in the belly.

3. **Splenic Authority:** Instantaneous, intuitive, and instinctual "knowing" whether or not something is harmonious with us. This authority is not so much "felt" anywhere, as it is simply "knowing" instantaneously. For example, something "sounds" good/bad, or "smells" good/bad.

4. **Heart Authority:** This too, is an instantaneous "knowing" if something is in alignment with a person, but it is not based so much on a response to something as it is based on "This is what I want, desire, or value and I'm going for it." It's truly following the will of the heart and what a person wants.

5. **Self Authority:** A person's truth is held gently in the center of his or her chest, waiting to be invited to act. When the person is invited to participate in something or with someone, she will often experience this as an opening or expansion in her chest toward the opportunity or person offering the invitation if it's in alignment with her truth; if it's not, no expansion.

6. **Outer Authority:** This one is the rarest of all; only about 1 percent of the world's population have this authority. These people need to ask the most questions and get the most clarity through seeking information and feedback outside of themselves. They need lots of time and space to explore all possibilities before committing to something.

Most people fall into the first three authorities, which is why we tend to think of intuition as we do, as a feeling of emotional clarity, a felt sense of being drawn toward something or repelled by it, or just "knowing" something instantaneously. People with heart, self, and outer authorities are all more rare, generally speaking.

For this book's purposes, I'm going to lump these different inner authority descriptions together and call them all "intuition," both to keep things simple and because the reasons why people don't follow their intuition are pretty much the same, no matter what your inner authority style is.

INTUITION

"Trust in yourself. Your perceptions are often far more accurate than you are willing to believe."

— Claudia Black

You already possess it—we all do. It shows up differently for different folks, but it's there nonetheless. It's our way to connect to Source, to God, to our Higher-Self. Are you listening? If you are, then are you using the information you are given and acting on it? If you're not listening to your intuition, why not? A large part of my work with clients is teaching people how to listen to and follow, and communicate from their Inner Voice—the voice of God within them. As I mentioned before, we are so often listening to the "little voices" which are filled with fear. Your Inner Voice, is based in Love, and as such, it will NOT speak to you in images, thoughts, or feelings of fear. The pictures, thoughts, or "hits" you get may be scary or uncomfortable, but in my experience, they don't come with any feeling of fear. They are powerful and "neutral" in their emotional signatures.

People discount their intuitions for many reasons. I would say the most common reasons are:

- They simply *don't know what it is!* They get an uncomfortable "instant hit" or "gut-feeling" or "sensation in the chest" and dismiss it as a physical symptom of some unknown disease (really it's dis-ease they are feeling!). It can look like indigestion, muscle tightness or pain, headaches, stomach issues, joint problems—all of which have no underlying physical cause or trauma. Those physical symptoms *could be* your intuition speaking to you, telling you, "This is not a good fit; move on and leave this situation behind." On the other hand, people may feel drawn toward something or someone and discount it as a silly or childish fancy, or in the extreme, fear rejection or failure so much they just ignore the positive indications they are receiving to move toward that thing or person.

- They *learned not to trust themselves* at some point. Well-meaning parents, teachers, and other authority figures taught us to "think" before we act, or to use our mind. While some of us "see" things in our mind's eye, that's different than thinking and figuring something out with our minds. There is a lot of weight given to thoughts, which is kind of ironic given that most of them are mindless drivel anyway. The mind is not where the intuition resides; nor is it good for making decisions (as I've explained elsewhere in the book).

- They are afraid of what people will think; in other words, it's *socially inconvenient* to follow their intuition because they may upset someone or have to make a choice that others won't like. Folks discount their intuition because, frankly, it's a hell of a lot easier than rocking the boat. Our intuitive hits are telling us what's best for us (and at times, what's best for others, especially when we're parents), and often they are socially awkward because we may be guided to do something that most social constructs would say is totally irrational or rude. (It may even cost us a lot of money to undo a decision if we don't listen to our intuition and then suddenly clue in after the ink is dry. I can't tell you how many times and how much money I've spent doing this!)

BENEFIT OF THE DOUBT: HOW THIS UNDERMINES OUR INTUITION

"The first time someone shows you who they are, believe them."

— Maya Angelou

How many times have you had the hit about someone, perhaps you met the person face-to-face, perhaps not. And you thought or felt "something is not quite right, but I can't put my finger on it." Maybe it was just a fleeting feeling, or perhaps even a nagging pit in your stomach—which you quickly attributed to something you ate, or just being "off" that day (especially if you didn't want to offend anyone). Perhaps you told yourself, or someone told you, to "give him the benefit of the doubt." I was talking with a friend and fellow therapist about this. She and I both felt that "benefit of the doubt" can be dangerous, not just to women, but to men as well.

In my opinion, benefit of the doubt is *not* the following scenarios: when you're with a child or someone who is learning a new skill and you're not sure of his or her abilities—*and your uncertainty is not a safety issue*—then I see it as letting go of the need to control and giving the kid space to see what he/she can do. Or, and I've had this happen with my own kids and others' kids as well, intuiting the outcome (literally getting a hit about how it's going to turn out) and simply *choosing* to know the *potential* outcome (intuitive hit), but letting the child try anyway to see how he or she will deal with the situation as it unfolds. How many times have you said, "I just knew that was going to happen"?

Do I believe that giving someone the benefit of the doubt is wrong? No. Do I believe that we are asked to do that categorically, and if we don't, it means we are judgmental jerks or bitches? Yes. It's subtle, but expected—because that's what "good" people do. The times when I naturally gave someone the benefit of the doubt were the times that I genuinely did so, not because I was asked to, but because I intuitively knew that whatever the person was showing up as or with that day wasn't her "A" game and it wasn't indicative of who she potentially could be. In other words—when I feel called to give someone the benefit of the doubt, it's typically been because I knew on some level it was in the highest and best good to do so. When I felt I *should* give someone the benefit of the doubt because others were doing it, or because I was asked to do so against my inner knowing...well, I can't think of any time it worked out well.

A couple of years ago, I went to get a mani-pedi. The place I wanted to go to was booked and I had limited time before I had to pick up my kids from school. I drove up to a strip mall in my town and saw a man smoking outside the nail salon. I knew he was either an owner or worked there, and my gut reaction was to turn around and leave because his energy was "off," but I dismissed my initial reaction to keep driving and go home. I parked my car and nodded to him as I walked past him into the shop.

He didn't help me; another woman did. It wasn't the last I saw of him, though. That evening my toe began hurting and swelling and burning, and, by morning, it was on fire and too painful to walk on. Long story short, I had a staph infection in my toe. I went and had it cultured and tested at a local emergency clinic. I got a prescription for ten days of antibiotic, and I promptly went back to the shop to ask for my money back.

I went in there clear in my purpose: To ask for my money back without creating a scene. He tried to tell me it wasn't their fault, and he questioned the cleanliness of my house—implying I got the infection at home. He refused to apologize or even refund my money. There were other women in there at the time. Prior to this, I was deliberately being discreet since this situation is apparently a big issue in the world of nail salons—or so I read on the Internet when I Googled "infection after pedicure." I ended up creating a scene, which is not something I intended nor like doing. And during our interaction, looking into that man's eyes...let's just say, my original hit about him was spot on. He was very dark. I had overridden my intuitive doubt and I'll never forget that. I had given him the benefit of the doubt instead of listening to my inner knowing. I eventually came to a place of appreciating the whole experience because I got more validation for my intuition and practice speaking my truth—without attachment to the outcome. (Was I scared for my health and angry about the situation? Heck, yeah! I spent some time using energy techniques for clearing the anger, frustration, and fear, and I managed to get over it quite quickly. I think my toe healed so fast because of the emotional energy work I did to let it go.)

If you do listen to your intuition, are you able to live your intuitions in a meaningful way? Are you following them and heeding their call, or are you still setting them aside because they may rock the boat, or be impolite, or make someone angry or upset? Are you still ignoring your hits because you want that guy/job/friend to work out so badly that you can't imagine your life without him/her/it? Or because you want a mani-pedi and can't wait....

GOING WITH THE FLOW...
EVEN WHEN IT'S A STRUGGLE

"Trust your own instinct. Your mistakes might as well be your own, instead of someone else's."

— Billy Wilder

Going with the flow is often thought of as an admirable trait. Being easygoing and not letting life get us down is one thing, but staying in the boat, though we were pretty sure on some level our boat was on the wrong river, is another thing altogether. We don't want to rock the boat, especially if it seems like it's a good thing or "sure thing" that leaves the easygoing person treading water and struggling when her intuition tells her it's time to jump ship, or she's forced to walk the plank, as in a layoff situation! It's so much easier to stay in the pain that we know and are comfortable with than to branch out, take a risk, and dust off our dreams and goals and swim in uncharted waters.

One of my clients shared with me that she had pretty much spent her adult life and career "going with the flow." She followed a trajectory in her career that by all counts to everyone else was successful. And she even acknowledged her success climbing that proverbial corporate ladder. But she also realized that once she was out of that "flow," she saw just how much it was someone else's "flow" and not necessarily her own. She didn't consciously choose what she wanted at each juncture of her career; she went with what was showing up, and when she was out of that environment and looking at her life and what she consciously wanted to create from here on out, it was evident the difference between following some trajectory that was "easy" and following a path that was more challenging, but also infinitely more rewarding.

Other ways we'll "go with the flow" and not listen to our intuition or consciously choose what we want in our life:

- Allowing someone access to our personal space, even when it didn't feel right or good to do so.

- Staying in a job that's unsatisfactory.

- Staying in a relationship that we are no longer interested in or committed to.

- Living in an environment that doesn't sustain us because we don't want the hassle of moving.

- Keeping friends that drag us down with their negativity.

- Playing small when we really want to live big.

Feeling drained by relationships and activities is a big clue that something needs to shift. We get out of alignment and can't understand why we're doing the same thing over and over again when what we really need to do is stop being easygoing and take a stand on something.

There is a difference between going with the flow and Being in the Flow. The first is drifting with the little voices; the second is being in alignment with the Inner Voice and heeding its messages and directives, then taking immediate action. When you are clear what you want to create and are listening to your Inner Voice and are following the path of greatest ease because you're in alignment with it, and it with you, that's being in the flow. It doesn't mean you won't be challenged or have opportunities for growth; it just means it's your path, and not someone else's.

Being in the flow strengthens your belief in yourself and in your ability to maneuver your boat when the waves get really churning! Finally, it just feels good and "right."

DIFFERENT STOKES FOR DIFFERENT FOLKS

How do we stoke the flames of our intuition? Intuition can literally light our way through the darkness. And because we are different, we get our intuitive hits in different ways.

In Myers-Briggs' terms, I am an "N" or "intuitive type": (I'm an INFP in case you want to know). I get huge chunks of information downloaded all at once. I see pictures or hear sounds (often a "Ding! Ding! Ding!" as in "We have a winner! That's it!"), or I just know, without knowing how I know. I'm also empathic, so I get a lot of information through emotions. In my Human Design, I have a sacral authority (gut knowing) with the spleen defined, which means I get an instant knowing as well as a gut sensation. My emotion center is undefined, so I can "read" people's emotions pretty darn clearly.

My husband, Mike, is an "S" or sensing type. (He's an ISTJ.) He also gets a clear "knowing" at times, but for him, he really uses his body to receive and follow guidance. In Myers-Briggs terminology, he's not described or labeled as intuitive. However, his scalp tingles, he feels electricity in his body, and his stomach may turn or have butterflies. He describes a sense of knowing which direction to go by perceiving resistance or flow. For example, when hiking, or racing, or even driving to a new location, he senses whether or not the route he is on is correct by noting whether it feels "alive" or "dead" as in a dead end. He knows whether it's the right way because it feels lighter, or because there is a flow and ease to the movement (aka a lack of resistance). He too has his sacral center defined, but he's an emotional authority because he has the emotion center defined, which is why he "feels" his way through things, even after getting the initial "gut" read on it.

As I am writing this, my son Eli shared with me the different forms of energy he's learning about in third grade science: Heat, light, motion, electricity, and sound. They describe what Mike experiences perfectly: Is the trail warm or cold? Does it seem lighter or darker? Is there movement or resistance? Does he feel a tingling sensation or not? How does the trail sound? His gut says, "Uh-huh," or "Uh-uh." It's all energy, and our ability to listen to its subtle messages will lead us where we need to go. Once again, no matter what you've believed or been told about your type or intuition in general (that it's woo-woo, only for women, or you don't roll that way) you absolutely have access to it, and it's literally there to guide you and help you live your most fulfilled life.

Here is an experiment for you to try around listening to your body and it's messages or intuition. No matter what your inner authority style, this can be helpful for everyone as it embodies the most common denominator between all of us human beings: emotions.

LOVE/HATE & FELT SENSE

Sit quietly for a few moments. Inhale and exhale deeply, without straining for a count of 4-6 on the inhalation and 5-7 on the exhalation. Take at least three breaths this way to get yourself centered. If this causes tension or strain, stop and simply breathe normally. Sit comfortably erect and relax your shoulders away from your ears. Take a minute or so to scan your body; notice what you notice. There is nothing to change here; you are simply noticing so you can get a baseline, so you know what you're feeling before you begin the exercise. Take another deep breath and let that scanning go. Now think of something or someone (could be a person, place, thing) that you love. Pick something that has no other charge for you than love—for instance, don't pick your favorite puppy whom you love, but he just piddled on your couch and now you're angry with him; pick someone or something for whom it is easy for you to feel love, appreciation, gratitude—especially love.

Say to yourself "I love_____." Really get in touch with that love you have for this something or somebody. Now notice the following: How does your body feel? How about your chest? And your belly, how does it feel? What do you notice about your posture? How about your breathing?

When you're done noticing, let that image go and go back to breathing normally; take a few deep breaths again and think about something neutral, anything that sort of clears the palette, if you will. Now think about that *same something or someone you just felt love for* and instead say, "I hate_____." Notice what happens to your posture, breathing, how your body feels.

To finish on a positive note, just go back to loving that someone or something, and send him/her/it some love for good measure.

Practice this until you have a good idea of how your body talks to you when you are in alignment with your conscious thoughts and when you aren't.

If you begin to look for the signs that your body gives you when you are feeling good about something or someone, then when you're in alignment with those things, you'll be able to take this information into your conversations, and when people say and/or do things that overstep your boundaries, you can know unequivocally, "Okay, that's the line—and they just crossed it."

My friend and intuitive coach, Nadhira, from Down Under, shares how important discerning the Inner Voice really is:

Nadhira: I just want to let people know that they can trust that Inner Voice no matter how illogical the situation seems or what it's trying to tell them. I feel like if there's one thing you can learn, if you can learn how to discern between the two voices, how one speaks to you versus how the other speaks to you, then that's the greatest gift you can give yourself as well.

I did invest in even learning how to tune into that Inner Voice more and more...I feel like that's my natural way of being. Why not get really good at discerning between the voices? I almost feel like when the little voice talks to me I feel a lot of pressure and a lot of, "You should do this." Or justify making a decision whereas when my Inner Voice speaks, it's just a much more sort of calm— it doesn't have to say much, very quiet.

Kris: Yeah.

Nadhira: It's almost like that little nudge and that's all I need. Also knowing in my body where it comes from. For me, personally, it's in my gut when something feels right, but I feel like everyone will have their own way of tapping into that, that if you can learn that and be really tuned into that, then yeah, that will be so helpful with any decisions you make.

Kris: Yes. Is it your experience that when you get psychic or intuitive hits, do you have a lot of emotion around them? I tend not to. I tend to just have—it's like a flash and there's not a lot of drama around it.

Nadhira: Exactly. That's true. That's true for me as well. It's just like, "Okay. Yeah, okay, cool. I'll do this." I think because there's so much certainty in there. And it's funny...it's certainty, but if anyone from the outside looking in is looking at how you made that decision, they would go, "How are you even making that decision?"

Kris: Yeah, right.

Nadhira: Everyone around you now—that doesn't seem like the right thing, but you just know it just feels right. You can't—no amount of words that you can come up with to try and tell the other person why. You just have to say, "Well, it just feels right."

Kris: Yep, yep.

Nadhira: Yeah, that was a good question. No drama.

How does your Inner Voice communicate with you? What about those little voices?

Learn to discern....

CHAPTER EIGHT

Key Element #4: Align With Spirit—Choice

*"Love takes off the mask that we fear we cannot live without
and we know we cannot live within."*

—James Baldwin

*"Angels descending, bring from above,
Echoes of mercy, whispers of love."*

— Fanny J. Crosby

I love angels. They help so much—when I remember to ask. I often felt when I was working in research at the UW that there was an element missing in therapy—it was Spirit. And when I went into private practice, it was with the intention of acknowledging something bigger than myself, or my client, in the room. I wasn't sure how that would look because I want to be honoring of all perspectives and spiritual preferences, regardless of my personal beliefs, but I knew it had to be there. I also knew there was something more to it than just talking; I could sense the energy as I wrote about before, but I had to learn to trust what I was seeing, sensing, and perceiving, and be willing to have a different viewpoint about it all. A viewpoint that we are not alone and we have support and guidance, and at our essence, we are whole and complete as we are.

TURNING TOWARD THE LIGHT

*"Sometimes, as practice for trying to convince myself that God exists,
I try to convince my shadow that the sun exists."*

— Robert Brault

Sometimes it feels like we are in a dark tunnel and we can't see the end. We don't notice there is light all around us because our head is down and we are only seeing the evidence around us of the darkness we feel inside and the thoughts we think about ourselves, others, and the situations we find ourselves in. The truth is that there is always light—all-ways light. But we must look up, look within, and look without for it. It's in our hearts. It's in the world around us. It's in the sun and the moon and even in a rainbow after days of rain. It's where you least expect it and when you need it the most.

Sometime we push and push in the process of "birthing" our vision, not realizing that in between pushes there is a time for resting—for relaxing, for putting our head up, looking around and seeing the help and support that is always there. Maybe it's another person, maybe it's spiritual help, a message, a "sign," an idea or insight; maybe it's simply the sun coming out when it's been gray for five days straight, and it seems to shine just for you because you needed it to so badly.

What you put your focus on grows. If you are in the darkness and you are trying any way you can to get out of it, to alleviate the discomfort of it, this frantic searching will only cause the darkness to perpetuate. But if you relax into it, open your eyes and take in your surroundings, the light will show itself to you. It will illuminate the way out of your distress, but you must choose to do this.

Many years ago, a friend of mine was getting trained as a river rafting guide. As part of her "final," she had to guide a group of people downriver. She asked me to go and I said, "Yes," and as soon as I did, I had a feeling in my gut and a knowingness that something was going to happen on that trip that would be significant. I had a feeling I would be swimming, but I knew I *had* to go anyway—I was *supposed* to go.

The river was swift, and the waves were pretty big; it was still early in the season. It was a sunny day, but Northwest chilly and the water was cold snowmelt. I was on the starboard side of the boat nearest the bow and having fun paddling through the rapids. We got to a part of the river called "the eye" and saw the big hole created by a large rock that was sucking water backwards into an eddy. We paddled furiously to avoid the eye, but we didn't make it. Our trajectory was too fixed—we hit the eye and the left side of the boat went under, and, I recall, as my side of the boat went up into the air, thinking, "I knew this was going to happen." I felt both scared and strangely calm because it was simply part of the plan. I hit the water still holding my paddle, and popped up feet down toward the bottom of the river, paddle behind my head and holding on for dear life. All the calmness of the slow motion fall on top of my boat mate into the cold churning water was gone. I was terrified and moving fast downriver through the rapids.

I tried to remember what I was told: to get my feet up, lay on my back, feet first downriver. The paddle was not necessary, but still I clutched it, and it was dragging me down because my arm was over my head and behind my head so it kept pulling my head under and I couldn't get a breath; I was sucking in a lot of water.

I recall thinking, "If I don't do something different, I'm going to die." I really felt that way. I really thought and felt like I was going to die, and it was the strange calmness of knowing it was a distinct possibility that kept me so aware and made time go both quickly and slowly at the same time.

I looked up at the sky and saw how beautiful and blue it was. I thought, "Well, if I'm going to die, I might as well enjoy it," and, immediately, I had the clarity and opportunity to pull the oar up over my head and place it in front of me across my stomach; then I somehow got my feet up to the surface and facing downriver, and the peace that overcame me was amazing. I got a few breaths of air without drinking river water, and I lay back and surveyed the sky. It was crystal blue, a few clouds, sunlight, warmth on my face, and voices yelling at me to swim to the shore.

To this day, I think that was one of those opportunities, those choice points we each get in our lives, to choose life and to become aware and conscious of what's really happening around us.

Love is recognizing there are two main forces in the universe, Love & Fear. It's about choosing love over fear. Asking for help, letting go of the need to control it—turning it over to a Higher Power. It's about choosing to be and seeing the light whenever things get scary or rough.

CROSSING THE LINE

"Sunbeams out of the clouds. Faith out of all my doubt."

— Terri Guillemets

Early on at my first Mastermind retreat, our coach asked us to stand outside the meeting room. She asked us to choose consciously to make the commitment to build our businesses, and when we felt ready to make that commitment, to cross over the threshold into the meeting room. I closed my eyes and really asked myself whether I was ready to do this, because I didn't want to take this lightly. I knew it was a promise I was making myself, and I was done making quick promises that I didn't follow through on. I also knew that in making this commitment I would be called to face my fears. I wanted to be sure I was ready for this, and, intuitively, I knew it was a soul-level decision. When I opened my eyes finally, I saw my coach patiently waiting for me. Everyone else had returned to the room. I stepped into the room and took my seat.

Everything was fine that first morning, but as the afternoon wore on, I could feel my fears coming up. By the third and final morning, I was a wreck.

I felt lost and scared in the dark. I went for a swim in the morning in the ocean—something I had never done before. The water was churning so it was murky and cloudy and a lot of stuff was floating in it. During the afternoon before, the water had been clear blue and beautiful; now it was like being in a washing machine with my son's clothes after he rode in a mud puddle with his bike. I kept moving out into the waves, allowing them to crash into me, and feeling so small and scared, like any one of those waves could just knock me over and under and I wouldn't get back up—and I was feeling so low that I didn't actually care if this happened! I knew I had to be in the water for some reason, so I stayed in it.

As I stood in the waves that morning, wanting to cry, but not able to do so, letting the salty ocean splash my face instead, I decided to allow myself to really be in it. To really feel how dark and scary this place was. I turned my back to the waves for a few moments because they were big and I was avoiding getting a mouthful of water, and when I turned back around, the sun was just coming up over the horizon. Another wave came, and just before it crashed into me, I noticed at the very top, where the water was much thinner, the top of the wave glowed! The sun was shining through the wave, and it sparkled and danced like the most beautiful jewel I had ever seen! I knew I wasn't alone, and that God was saying, "I am always here. Turn to the light; find the light and you will always find your way out of the darkness." It was all I needed to snap out of the fear, and to begin to access the faith and courage I needed to keep going. Interestingly, that same evening, on the plane ride back to Seattle, the basis for this book was "downloaded"—I had a flood of ideas and began outlining the chapters. I felt totally revitalized and full of light.

I was talking with a client shortly after this experience about breakdowns and the light, and she said she felt like she was in a fog. I asked her to close her eyes and really get into her body and notice in what position or posture her body was in her mind's eye. She said she was curled up in a ball with her head down. Of course, it's hard to see the light when your head is down and your eyes are closed, right? So I asked her to imagine opening up and to look around her and see where the smallest glimmer of light was that she could see. She saw a little piece of glitter on the floor catch the light. It was enough for her to snap out of the fog at least for a moment so we could find a way to clear it more fully.

Sometimes that's all that's needed—a glimmer (or glitter!) of hope that breaks through the darkness and allows us to see the way out.

If and when you find yourself in this dark place, look around you. Literally, open your eyes and look for some light. Look for some evidence that all is not doom and darkness. Perhaps it's a lit candle; maybe it's the sun through the clouds; maybe it's the light in your child's eyes, or reflections of moonlight on a puddle. Maybe it's literally turning on all the lights in your house for a few hours during the dark days of winter. What you focus on grows... so focus on the light.

Something else that I've found is that when it's very dark and I'm feeling resistant, it's usually because something wants to come through me and be "born," and I am pushing it back instead of allowing it to be revealed. Sort of like the ring-of-fire when giving birth. Hurts like hell and the urge is to retreat, but the body says "Push!" and then the baby comes...sweet relief.

IT'S DARKEST BEFORE THE DAWN

I was listening to a recording of Dr. Michael Bernard Beckwith talking about Spiritual Liberation the other night. What's really interesting is that I had heard this recording repeatedly a few years ago when I bought it for my husband. I had totally forgotten about it until I heard him speak, and it was funny because I had experienced two huge breakdowns or "dark nights of the soul" in my business since the first time I listened to him speak and had forgotten all about what he said when I was in those breakdowns—it didn't even register. I think it was because I hadn't experienced them yet, and so I had no context for them when I heard him speak originally. This time, listening to him speak, I knew exactly what he was talking about, and I had an even deeper appreciation for the breakdowns I had experienced and the gifts I received as a result of going through them.

Beckwith describes three kinds of darkness. There is the darkness of *gestation*, when a seed of inspiration is beginning to grow and it needs the darkness to sprout and gestate, to take root and begin to grow. There is the darkness of *cleansing*, where we release what no longer serves us, and a darkness is there until we fill the void with something that is of a higher vibration and more beneficial to us. Finally, there is the darkness that comes with *spiritual blindness*, or being blinded by the light of our own Divinity, and because we are habitually seeing through the eyes of our ego, which cannot stand to look at a light so bright as the Light of Source, we go blind—literally, and figuratively. It is a temporary blindness, but terrifying nonetheless.

Breakdowns can happen in gestation when we try to force the seed of inspiration to pop before it is ready, before we are ready. We resist the process, and so it is painful and drags on unnecessarily.

Breakdowns happen in the cleansing phase when we resist letting go of that which no longer serves us. When we try to hold on to old, outdated ways of thinking and feeling, we experience the fear of darkness and the growing pains that happen when we are moving forward, but our mind and body are trying to stay put.Finally, the breakdown of blindness occurs when we see and touch possibility, when we have a glimpse of who we *truly* are, and what we can be and do in this lifetime, and it's so eff'n scary that we just shut our eyes and say, "NO WAY! I'm not ready!"What is a breakdown? It's where your whole world (and your business) gets thrown up in the air because you made a deeper commitment to yourself really to step into what's possible in your life and in your business, so every part of your being freaks out and tries to sabotage the whole thing. When we are in the throes of a breakdown, it sucks. Afterwards, it's awesome—provided we didn't quit or run the other way completely! It can feel like the surge of adrenaline, endorphins, and feel-good hormones you get after surviving labor pains to give birth.If you've ever tried to do something really different than you ever have done before, or listened to your inner wisdom and made decisions that were radically going to change your life or the lives of others, you've likely experienced breakdown.Some signs that you may be in breakdown or one of the stages of darkness that Beckwith describes are:

- It feels like the solid ground you were standing on just got ripped out from under you.

- You may have the sensation of floating or falling in space and never knowing when, where, *or if* you'll land.

- You may start trying to rationalize *everything* in order to gain some sense of control.

- There is nowhere to hide. All the "comforts" that used to work to help soothe, whether that's food, drink, TV, or some other drug of choice (chocolate anyone?) no longer work the way they used to. You are face-to-face with yourself, and there's no more hiding or kidding yourself. (This, by the way, is a very good sign and worth every moment when you move through it without getting stuck!)

- Crying…lots of crying. Or being on the verge of tears until you have a good cry.You or your family may start experiencing all kinds of disruptions, illness, lack of sleep, accidents, or things not working out the way you thought they would—hitting "dead-ends" or even having several things break down in a short period of time. It's like "all hell breaks loose" and you need to spend a lot of time "cleaning up" or taking care of yourself, your family, or the drama that's going on around you, and nothing gets decided.

How do you move from the breakdown to the breakthrough? Through the most simple and powerful gift we possess as human beings: Choice.

CHOICE

"When an inner situation is not made conscious,
it appears outside as fate."

— C.G. Jung

This is the fourth aspect of the Inner VOICE and it is related to spirit because it is the one thing that sets us apart from all other animals, and because when we exercise choice, we have the ability to be free and truly feel our connection to Spirit.

After a talk I gave where I was sharing how we humans possess the ability to choose as part of our make-up, a woman approached me and told me I better read an article in *Scientific American* about how neurobiology and physics determine our free will as human beings and that we may have less choice than we think. In this article,[15] Christof Koch describes all the science that points to evidence that we don't, in fact, necessarily have free will or choice. That science has shown through studies of the brain and quantum physics that there are things we don't seem to have any control over, let alone choice in the matter. What I love about the article is that, just as I was questioning whether I actually have any sort of control in my life whatsoever, he ends the article saying that the one thing we do have choice in is knowing ourselves, and that knowing ourselves better is how we can exercise choice more consciously, instead of being ruled by the unconscious parts of ourselves. Amen, Brother.

Apparently, we do have choice after all.

This article helped me to understand even more clearly how beautifully spiritual science truly is as it keeps proving the existence of a force greater than us, even if unintentionally. I say this because when I think of the article in terms of Human Design, yes, it's true, there are certain "defined"

---

15 You can read the article at: http://www.scientificamerican.com/article.cfm?id=finding-free-will&WT.mc_id=SA_emailfriend

ways of being in the world that we are both consciously aware of and that we inherited from our ancestors and are not conscious of. It's all in our design from the moment of birth. (Actually from conception, but we typically don't have that specific information to create a chart from!) Those defined ways of being in the world are energetic signatures that determine how we interact with others and the world. Where choice comes in is when we know how we were designed in this lifetime to express spirit, and we *choose consciously* to live in alignment with our unique design; then we are naturally living in alignment with God (with our Inner Voice), and we experience ease and a greater sense of purpose and joy. When we choose, either consciously or unconsciously (i.e., out of ignorance), to live contrary to our design, we are in effect living at odds with God and our unique expression.

The choice begins with being awake and aware that there is even a choice to make in the first place. The ultimate choice we have to make is whether we are going to live our truth and live in harmony, or live someone else's truth and experience pain, struggle, burnout, and disconnection from Source.

It's this self-knowledge and awareness that helps us truly know God. Not self-awareness from the stance of the little voices or ego, but from our Inner Voice, from...Love.

When I first read Yann Martel's novel *Life of Pi*, I didn't get it. Recently, I watched the movie and it made more sense. I finally understood what Pi meant when he found God out in the open seas on that life raft. At least I understood it from my perspective in a way that makes sense to me! He made peace with the animalistic "evil" or fierce parts of himself, and he received the beauty and grace available to him through God's love. He learned that he is all of it, and he owned that. Through this awareness and ownership he had choice: The choice to express that which he wanted to express, to express that which helped him feel closer to God versus farther from God. When we own everything—the things we like and dislike about others (which are really the things we like and dislike about ourselves), the things we abhor and the things we adore, the horrific and the grace-filled, the bad and the good, the ugly, the beautiful, when we own that we are both the victim and the perpetrator, the hero and the villain, the beauty and the beast, when we can own all of that—then we have access to a full range of choices. We can say, "Yes I can see how a person would act that way, or say that horrible thing; I've thought that or said that myself (even if only in my head), AND I choose not to express it." That's freedom.

Here's what has worked for me to help me own everything: Find a trusted companion/coach/colleague, the kind who helps you hold the vision you have for yourself and who knows what you're going through. I do not recommend talking with someone who will only commiserate with you, or who has no idea what the hell you're going through because that person is either totally stuck in her own stuff or she has some vested interest in keeping you small. These are folks who haven't looked at their own darkness or shadow selves and they aren't able yet to allow you to see your own. (You know who I mean, right?) There is nothing "wrong" with this (or them); it is a process after all and everyone is in a different place in the process. That said, it will not serve you to open up to someone who is in a judgmental or fearful place about her own stuff.

Recognize that when you find yourself in breakdown, it's often in the face of making a decision. This decision or choice is often one that has you being called forth by your Inner Voice, and those little voices are putting up quite a fight. This is why it's so important to talk with someone who will listen to you from her Inner Voice, not the voices of her egoistic fears and limitations, because that's when you are most susceptible to being drawn back to the status quo by them!

If you don't have someone with whom you can talk, then try the following: Take a break. Play. Exercise—just move! Let the decision or whatever it is take care of itself for a while. You gotta get your rational mind out of the way and let the process unfold somewhat. When you're playing or exercising or simply moving, it will help you feel better, distract you, and let the answers come more easily through your inner authority.

Jacqueline, a hypnotherapist and personal coach, shared with me what she did when she was feeling this darkness of gestation and having her life on hold. She bought flowers! She was guided to go get these fabulous orange roses, and what she learned from that bouquet led to some big aha's, especially around the subject of choice:

Kris: Is there some event or something that happened where you just said, "I've got to do this or I'm going to die, or I'll die doing it"?

Jacqueline: I think that part is a process, and I can remember when I was back living in Vancouver and I was just—it felt like my whole life was on hold while I was waiting to get my papers, waiting for my approval to come and join my husband in the States. I felt like my life was on hold. I didn't want to start business-building in Vancouver, so I was working with some people online and I remember sitting and writing a blog post and...I had gone out and bought myself this big, huge bouquet of orange roses and they had just hit perfection, and I looked at them and it's like, there is part of me—I wrote this whole blog about it—there's part of me that is so frightened that if I completely bloom, then the only thing to do is die afterward. It's like you come out and go, "Ta-da, I'm here. I'm a big rose, full in bloom. I'm absolutely gorgeous," and I knew within the next two days the petals would start dropping on the dresser. I had never, ever considered that I was holding myself back because I was frightened of what happens once you've peaked.

That was a turning point for me in [understanding] that's how life is supposed to be; it is a circle. You're never going to bloom; you're just going to be one of those little unopened buds—like sometimes you buy roses and they never open? You're never going to open because you're going to die, so you're just going to slowly die anyway. That, for me, that is something that I occasionally come back to, and then the journey becomes how to bloom. My recent Aha was when I was asked what is it that I do for people, which is the never-ending question and has been so, so difficult to answer over the years. I've always talked about what I do, and this coach I was working with just happened to phrase it in a way that I heard it differently. She stopped me when I was saying, "I have the School of Complementary Therapies and I do this and that," and she said, "No, that's what you've *been* doing. What do people get out of it?" I found myself going, this little voice, I said, "This is really silly. This sounds silly as I say it. But I just make people happy." And she went, "Bingo," and it was such an Aha that felt like I had been—honestly, Kris, it feels like it took me twenty years to get to that moment where it went, "Oh."

Kris: Isn't that amazing?

Jacqueline: I make people happy. Then what comes in after that is that is just my natural state of being, so isn't everybody like this? What's it worth? I was in a group coaching thing where a kid expressed that and someone came back and said, "Do you know how much money Adam Sandler makes?" A different tact of doing it, but this thing, of course it's valuable, people want to be happy. Whatever tools I use, that's the end product and then it becomes that exposing yourself, which I think is the blooming, where you become very vulnerable instead of hiding behind my previous incarnations, if you like. I was a doctor, a naturopath, and I am a licensed hypnotherapist and now it's like, what do you do? I make people happy. That's very vulnerable.

Kris: And highly attractive, too. I love what you were saying about how to bloom, that the journey becomes how to bloom because I wrote about being in the flow and being a flower. Are you a flower or basically are you a flow-er? And I too noticed that our energy, when we're dialed in and we're connected and we're grounded, we're in the flow, and as soon as we cut ourselves off, we start to wither, just like a cut flower starts to wither. But the thing is between us and a flower is that we have free will and choice, and so we can reground and replant ourselves at will where a cut flower can't.

Jacqueline: Isn't that nice?

Kris: One of the things that struck me when you were talking about the orange roses and how scary it is, like what if I bloom and then I die? I got this hint, but then because it's full circle, like you said, we get to bloom again and again and again, and each time we bloom, we can bloom a little different color, we have a different scent, we have a potency that grows, and it's like roses that have been hybrid, or over time, they're bred to be always more beautiful, luscious, and wonderful than the last.

Jacqueline: That's lovely. I really like that. That really speaks to me on so many levels because I absolutely adore roses and I do love the aroma as well as the look; everything about them. That really does appeal on so many levels, that we can blossom again. Why not? We have that choice.

Kris: Why not? But I love what you go through around looking at those roses, and it's such a powerful metaphor because really most people, I think, or many people, they cut themselves off when they're still a bud. And we do this ourselves; nobody comes and cuts us. We do. We either cut ourselves off when we're a tight little bud or when we're half open, and then we never get to fully open, or some people just go ahead and blaze. Maybe it's an infant who blazes and fully opens for six months, and then they pass because that was their life. You know what I mean? So many different ways to look at it. Maybe they're eighty and they're finally blazing—you know. It's interesting.

Jacqueline: Wow. I can picture in my mind, I wish I'd taken a photo. It was a big jug and it was a cheer me up thing, like I've got to go buy flowers. And I can picture them; it was in a rented, furnished apartment and there was a big jug on a dresser and I filled it with these roses and it's something—it's one of those pictures that is in my mind forever. It really was a moment of awareness that was so exciting and so scary.

Kris: It's so interesting because I think too what propelled you to buy those was you were feeling down and you wanted to bring some cheeriness, some life to the stuckness that you were feeling. The thoughts I'm having is that—personally on the outside looking in, this is my interpretation—is that God or Spirit or your higher self, Inner Voice, said, "Go get these flowers. There's a gift in them for you. Not just the beauty of the flower, but there's a gift there." You listened to it and you did it, and then because you listened to it, because you went and did this thing that didn't really make sense to logical people, like you're just going to go buy some flowers and that's going to make the whole difference, and you're [in the place of], "I'm stuck. I can't afford flowers. What am I thinking?" and then you get them and you have this really powerful experience.

Jacqueline: Yeah, that's it. I mean, we can talk ourselves out of these things so easily, but why would we when we can have these moments? I think that, for me, is when I'm grounded and in the flow I will just say, "Yes, let's. Let's do this," and not listen to those little voices that are saying, "No, no, no."

Kris: Getting grounded in the flow helps you to quell the little voices.

Jacqueline: Absolutely. When I feel myself grounded, when I feel myself in the flow, when I feel myself connected to spirit, the little negative Nellie voices are very easy to push aside. They just—they're not there for me. Or if they are, there I can just go, "You're not important." For me, it's very much that connection with Spirit and that's why I say the number of levels that that hits me on when you talk about the rose blooming again and again.

Kris: There's so many different levels too because it could be each bloom is a lifetime, each bloom is several "incarnations" within a lifetime, reinventing ourselves, or re-upleveling ourselves. There's lots of different ways that it can show up; it doesn't have to—because everything is—there's always that cycle of conception, birth, death; conception, birth, death; over and over and over again.

Jacqueline: It's empowering when you think of it in those terms. It makes sense of when people feel that they've failed, and I've certainly done that umpteen times in my life, and it isn't a failure; you've just bloomed, had that, and then you start the process to bloom again.

If you are still in breakdown after all this, know it is nothing more than second-guessing yourself and not following through with the decision you made. This is where people get really stuck and stay in relationships, jobs, business models, etc. that don't work, and then they become depressed, anxious, and have all sorts of other health challenges. It feels like hell and it really is that!

Often, we have to dig deep and draw from a strength we didn't know we possessed. There are places where things seem to flow and times where everything stalls and we feel stuck. There is an ebb and a flow. The more we can relax into this ebb, the more easily we can regain the flow. It's when we resist and struggle that it gets hard, and that's when we suffer the most. Where are you in the birth-bloom-fade process? Life and business cycles are not something to avoid or dread. When the bloom is full of life, celebrate it! Choose to own all of it by *being in it* as much as you can. And prepare for the next phase of the cycle. It will die out, and then you'll bloom again... provided you don't cut yourself off first.

HAVING FAITH

"Living is a form of not being sure, not knowing what next or how. The moment you know how, you begin to die a little. The artist never entirely knows. We guess. We may be wrong, but we take leap after leap in the dark."

— Agnes De Mille

Creation itself is an act of faith. When God created the world, God did not hesitate, doubt, or question anything. Any question as to whether or not something was viable, or even a good idea, was, and still is, taken care of in the evolutionary process. As human beings, we have the same power to create our world, yet so often we lack the faith. With faith, we can commit ourselves and actually follow through with that commitment more easily. The Inner Voice holds all the faith we need. When we are in alignment with this Voice, we create miracles. We create a new world, a new way of Being. We evolve. We allow those things that have played themselves out, and which cannot be sustained, to go. We allow them to become extinct. And it is good!

We take the energy generated by the release of the old and use it to create new—NOW. Without doubt, regret, fear, grief, self-judgment, or criticism, we go on creating as God does, fearlessly with faith. As we open to being a creative channel for faith to work through us, as we take action: putting pen to paper, fingers to keyboard, mouth to microphone, walking in the dark by following our own Inner Light, that's when we prosper—and not only ourselves but the world as well.

In order to create, we must be willing to destroy. We must be willing to destroy and release the energy held in what no longer serves us, what we no longer need. Destruction and death are inherent in the creation process and absolutely necessary. What holds most people back is the unwillingness to die to the old (outdated and limiting beliefs, fears, experiences, environments, etc.).

Acting in faith during creation is truly being willing to take a canvas that you've been working on for years and trashing it to start anew. My friend and colleague, Roma, psychologist and energy psychology practitioner, did just that. She listened to her Inner Voice and did what she was inspired to do—she let go of the "typical trajectory" of uninspiring job interviews post-graduation and simply chose to follow the quiet voice with a big feeling:

When I was about to receive my Ph.D., I found myself driving back to graduate school in Illinois from a job interview in Ohio. It was in a dreary-seeming large city that just didn't feel right for me. I also knew I didn't want to go back East where I grew up because the practice of psychology there felt conservative, stodgy, and uninspiring. My next job interview was to be in Lubbock, Texas, and without ever having seen it, I felt that working there would just be killing time till I found a more exciting place to live.

As I drove along the highway, I heard myself thinking, "Or, I could just load up my car and move to Seattle." Suddenly, I really *heard* what I was thinking and realized I had been having that thought in the back of my head for quite a while. Now, it was in the front of my mind and seemed, not only do-able, but inevitable. Several of my friends in grad school were from Seattle, and it sounded like a great place to live. I would have that component of my existence in place, and I could put my attention on building my life in other ways. I knew one colleague in town who was willing to help me get started, and I could begin a new life, totally on my own terms.

So, a few weeks later, I loaded up my car and moved to Seattle, never having been there before, but feeling as if I were home from the moment I arrived. From that daring move has flowed an incredible chain of blessings—not just my practice and my professional colleagues, but my husband and stepdaughter, our home, our grandchildren, and even our poodles.

It seems as if one can connect with every opportunity in the world here in Seattle. Over the years, I have followed many interests until I discovered Energy Medicine and then Energy Psychology, an incredibly exciting and effective way of practicing that draws on my intuition and artistry as a therapist and feels, in its own way, like coming home. I love that it helps me to relieve suffering quickly and gently, making it easier on both my clients and myself. I don't believe I would ever have found Energy Psychology if I had not been bold enough to transplant myself here based solely on a feeling, a quiet voice knocking on the back of my brain till I opened a door and let it be heard. Then all I had to do was listen.

Two more aspects of choice are important for really understanding how much practical faith and choosing to align with your Inner Voice is a *conscious* choice. Those two aspects are commitment and action.

COMMITMENT

"Unless commitment is made, there are only promises and hopes; but no plans."

— Peter F. Drucker

The results we are getting will show us what we are committed to. If we want new results, we need to commit to something else. We must recognize that whether or not we like it, we are leaders in our own lives and businesses. Most of us, though, and I'll willingly acknowledge that I've also been guilty of this, are followers in our own lives. We are like backseat drivers yelling at everyone else to drive differently when, in reality, we're the ones who abdicated the driver's seat. What do you spend money on? That will very quickly show you what you are committed to. People put their money where their commitment is. What I've learned in business is if you want someone to invest money with you as a coach, therapist, or other service professional, you need to be doing the same elsewhere. It shows you believe the work is valuable, not only to offer it, but also to receive it. Leaders are committed to something, something quite big, and much bigger than themselves. Whether it's a dream, a vision, a cause, or simply a belief, they are committed and take actions that are in alignment with that commitment. Great leaders are committed to what's possible; their commitment lies in heading toward some greater vision, not just avoiding some pain or fighting against something in the moment to avoid a temporary consequence, but rather making choices that have the end goal in mind.

"Illness is the most heeded of doctors: to goodness and wisdom we only make promises; pain we obey."

— Marcel Proust

Most of us make decisions and choices based on avoiding pain or trying to limit the pain we think we may experience. We have "concealed commitments" that rule our lives from the realm of the subconscious, and even with the best of intentions, we continue to make choices based on these underground commitments. This is the opposite of choosing based in faith by the way!

Some examples of concealed or subconscious commitments are: the urge to play it safe, to please others, to "fix" others or ourselves and the world, to control others, to hide our true self from others, and to get revenge on others. Through exploring the results my clients and I are currently getting, and through applied kinesiology (a fancy term for muscle or energy testing), we explore both objective results and facts, and subjective or subconscious commitments in order to shift them.

Fear of commitment is a huge issue for many people, often due to seeing ourselves as less than perfect or ready. Faith is the remedy for fear of commitment. Sometimes faith comes when we see others practicing it. I met Megan online while in a training group for speakers and entrepreneurs. Her story shows how she allowed herself to receive, and own, the power of faith and commitment to her life's purpose through experiencing the conviction and commitment of another person:

Kris: Where in your life or business, because it all intertwines…where have you either listened to your inner-voice and what happened, or didn't listen to it and what happened?

Megan: You want me to give you a specific example?

Kris: Yes. Or it could be where were you listening to the little voices so much that it really held you back? What happened, and what did you do to break through that?

Megan: When I started my coaching business, I was…I just turned thirty two weeks ago.

Kris: Happy Birthday.

Megan: Thanks. I was in my twenties when I started, and I look young for my age. People guess that I'm twenty-five or twenty-six, so my little voice was, "You're not old enough. You don't have enough experience to be doing this. Why would anyone who's forty or fifty listen to what you have to say?"   So the two big ones for me were, "You're not old enough to be doing this. You're not old enough to be sharing this type of information with people who are ten and twenty years older than you." The second one was, "You don't have the kind of experience to be sharing this type of information with people who have owned businesses for ten or twenty years, who have gained so much more life experiences than you have because they've been around a lot longer." Those are my big pieces that held me back. More so in the beginning; I still hear that now a little bit, but I did some…I'm sure you're familiar with EFT and tapping.

Kris: Oh, yes. That's one of the things that I do with people.

Megan: I did a little bit of that. I think I only had to do it three times, and I pretty much got over that. In the beginning, that was really big for me. It was preventing me from moving forward really at all, I think, and just deciding to…it was really holding me back from deciding to 100 percent commit; to commit to the business, to commit to growing it, to commit to setting the goals and taking the small steps that were going to get me to my big vision.

One of the things that really clicked for me is a book that was written by actually a friend of ours. He went to high school with my husband. My husband is from West Palm Beach, Florida, and my husband is actually ten years older than me, so this guy is a little bit younger than my husband; I think he's thirty-seven or thirty-eight.

He had a horrible childhood upbringing. He was an alcoholic and smoked three packs of cigarettes a day by the time he was twelve years old. He barely graduated high school. He ended up going into the military, and he became one of the men on the Delta Force. He was a Green Beret. He was the guy…one of those guys that does the scariest stuff that nobody else wants to do.

He was in the military for, I think, seventeen years. He quit two or three years before he was supposed to retire. I didn't know him at this time. He quit because he wanted to start a business and write a book. Everybody told him he was crazy.

He had a Facebook page that was dedicated to his book, and my husband had been following him because he knew him. At this point, I didn't know who he was or that he even existed.

He was creating these short, webcam videos of himself sitting in his office about getting out of his comfort zone. The first video he posted was about how scared he was to do this video; he was getting out of his comfort zone, and he was sharing a little bit of what he was writing in his book. At this point, his book wasn't published.

I think my husband said to me after Scot had…Scot is the name of the guy that we know who wrote the book…I think he had done about four videos and posted them on his Facebook page about his book. One day my husband said to me, "I think you should listen to this guy. I think this may be something that you need to hear. Maybe you need to connect with him." I was like, "Yeah, whatever."

I was really not in a good place at this point. This was last year in the fall. I listened and watched his videos, and there was something about him, what he was going through himself, or what he was talking about that really clicked with me, and I emailed him. I didn't know him at all.

He and my husband really hadn't reconnected; my husband was just paying attention to him. So I emailed him. I knew that he had already written his manuscript, but I also knew it was unedited. Obviously, his book hadn't been published.

I reached out to him and literally wrote two long paragraphs about my sob story or wherever I was stuck at that point in my life with my business and my life. I asked if he would send me his manuscript, and he did.

I stayed up one night until two in the morning and read it. I think I cried half the time I was reading it. The name of the book is *Your Life*. He wrote the book about his own life, but he wrote examples from his own life, teaching you about getting out of your comfort zone or getting rid of the negative people in your life, and not being that mediocre and normal person.

Every chapter was about some lesson that he had learned throughout his entire life that's allowed him to start this incredible business. Now he's a consultant for business owners, huge Fortune 500 companies, just in the last year and a half.

I read the book, and I think it was the whole book, itself. It was just knowing that here's this guy who barely graduated from high school who was such a decorated military guy. He has no education to even be writing this book or consulting other business owners, and he's doing it because he simply believes in himself.

He has a goal, a vision, and a message to share, and he's not afraid to share it. Why am I sitting here feeling sorry for myself, when this guy is out there doing it?

I actually then contacted him, have met him, and have spent a little bit of time with him. He sent me lots of his books. It was when I read that book, I was like, "I need to stop feeling sorry for myself. I need to get over this. I need to stop being normal and being okay with the life that I'm living."

I have something to share with people. It doesn't matter if I don't have experience, or if I'm speaking to someone twenty years older than me who's had a business for twenty years. I have something unique to share, and I'm going to go out there and share it. It was that book that did it for me.

Kris: Wow. What I get is that for a while you were listening to the little voices that said, "I'm not old enough. I don't have enough experience," and "Who's going to listen to me?" and "No one's going to want to listen to what I have to say, especially people that are older than me and have more experience." Then through connecting with someone who obviously you really resonated with, he influenced you in such a way that you went for it. Plus the tapping. I totally get that, because of my background as an energy therapist, I do that kind of work with people as well as coaching; it's very powerful.

You got over some of those fears, but then really resonated with someone who had been doing his own personal work There was something in there that clicked for you in that. That's so powerful. That's influence!

Megan: Yes. That's so funny, because I grew up in a very all-American family. I had the perfect little family. My brother and I played sports. We were competitive tennis and baseball players. Here's this guy who did not grow up the way I did, so I definitely didn't resonate with the way he grew up and his upbringing. I guess I really resonated with—he didn't have experience in what he was now teaching people. He didn't have experience as a business owner. He quit his job. He quit the military right before he was going to make retirement, and I quit my job; I quit my teaching job. I had a kid, and I quit. No money coming in. He quit his military job. Had no money coming in, and literally set out to write this book with no money. He did it, and he's made it work. I think that's the piece that I resonated with more than he was an alcoholic, and he had a mom that was awful. I didn't connect with that, but I connected with a lot of the other pieces. And then it's his book; it was just like he talked about my life.

Kris: It's so interesting because what I got from what you just said is that what you resonated with was his Inner Voice, his true voice. Because it really spoke to your true voice, the part of you that knows, "I have something to offer." All that other stuff, the story around it, all the details of alcoholism, the military and all that, and your story growing up, your happy, healthy, household; that part didn't matter. What really mattered was that he was living his truth, and that inspired you and sparked you to live yours.

Megan: Yes, exactly.

Kris: That's so cool. Wow. What a gift, isn't it? I'm really getting that as I'm listening to people's stories, and I'm listening to your story, that it is so powerful when we have the courage to step into our truth and live it. It really makes a huge difference because look at all the people's lives you are touching and transforming, and that he will touch and transform because of that. It's really powerful.

Megan: It is. You have to get to this place, I call it a space, where you allow yourself to receive that. I think, really, my entire life until the last eighteen or twenty months of my life, I don't think I was ever doing that, I really don't. The way I live my life and the way that I see everything around me now is so different. I'm still the same person, but I see things a lot differently. I live my life a lot differently. I know that I can control my thoughts, and I am very open to receiving whatever opportunity I'm supposed to receive instead of closing that off. I allow myself to have connections with people. With me and Scot Spooner, who wrote the book, I didn't know him from Adam and didn't connect with his life story, but I allowed myself to be so impacted by that Inner Voice, whatever that inner thing is inside of there. I really let that do work inside of me.

I love Megan's willingness to surrender the beliefs and stories she was telling herself and how she allowed herself to be influenced and inspired by someone else. She decided that she is enough, just as she is, and to go ahead and move forward no matter what, and that is what makes her so successful today. She shifted her subconscious "pain" button, so she is no longer obeying the pain to the detriment of that which she truly desires to actualize.

Marty, another fellow student and coaching colleague from online, has a story that shows the darker side of commitment and how through small choices over time, we can become committed to something, like money, and totally forget our once-heeded Inner Voice. But when we finally get the smack upside the head that wakes us up, we can change it all on a dime and recommit ourselves to living from our heart.

Kris: Where did you ignore your Inner Voice in your life and business and what were the results?

Marty: For a good part of my life, I was able to listen to the Inner Voice and be able to kind of follow along and have success. I've done everything from run a sailing school on the Hudson River to end up being a writer for a while up in the Adirondack Mountains. I just kept going where my heart led me, and then something happened to me.I was a successful broker in Annapolis, Maryland. I went to Miami where I was not successful. After that, I spent five years chasing the shiny thing. It was sort of like the dark night of my soul. The forty days and forty nights in the desert took me five years, where I was not listening to my heart. I was chasing the dollar bill. That cost me not only tens of thousands of dollars, but self-esteem, time in my life, and just took so much out of me, [and my] relationships. It just was not okay. So what happened is I finally—I kept saying, "God, stop pulling me through the eye of the needle here. What is it I'm supposed to get? What's going on here?"

Finally, I got it and I closed my five businesses. I was doing different networking businesses and real estate stuff. I finally one day got it and just—that's it. I closed all—came home, closed all five businesses, and that afternoon I began writing my book. I wrote for twelve hours straight. That's how hungry I was to be doing what I loved. That just awakened me, and then I started doing my coaching business in earnest. I had been doing that along with the other five businesses. That is where there was a big turnaround in my life, with finally listening to what I had denied.

It's interesting. We come into this world with everything. We have all our talents, gifts, and abilities. Then along the line— way—we get squooshed. People don't mean to do things, but we get squooshed along the way. We lock away our talents, gifts, and abilities because we don't want anybody to steal them away from us, what we've got left.

One of the things that happened to me was inadvertently my mother threw out a book I had written when I was ten years old. She didn't know. She didn't mean to do that, but somewhere that made an impression on me. I was finally allowing myself to realize the writer that had been waiting to be expressed and actually publishing—that was listening to that voice.

Kris: Wow! Wow. What was it? What happened—because you said in one day that you came home, you had five businesses. You closed the ones that were like, "I'm done." Was there something that happened or had it just been building up and you finally said 'enough'? Was there an "aha" moment or was it sort of a quiet building up…because that's pretty big!

Marty: Yeah. Yeah, it was a twenty-four-hour battle. It felt like I was with Muhammad Ali in the ring. I was with a real estate company and I've done real estate and been successful in real estate, but I bought into this program because it was going to be the magic wonder, million dollar, instant program. Right, one of those. I was desperate and not listening to myself, so I bought it.

There I was and I realized I was out of integrity with myself. But what happened that triggered it was that I couldn't get the program to work. There was a special program that I had to do a certain way to get the documents to work so that I could take care of my clients. Of course, I care about people, so I wanted to make sure that they were getting service. I couldn't get it to work.

I mean I was gnashing my teeth and just every possible negative thing I could think of to call myself I was doing it. I felt abandoned by the person that was supposed to help me. Everything from childhood, I guess, got triggered. Whatever got triggered, but just feeling abandoned when I needed someone most.

It was really just that final—I mean I was gnashing my teeth a lot during those five years, but this was the final battle. When I stopped long enough and stopped forcing it, I thought of a friend who understood Mac and he wrote me a one-line answer for what I needed to do, and I did it, and the program worked.

It was just like—I just knew how out of integrity I was with myself and the other businesses were in my estimation, some were actually out of integrity, and others were just out of integrity for me.

It was just sort of the tipping point. I said, "Okay, that's it. I cannot do this." I cried all the way to the mailbox, and I cried all the way home. Then I said, "That's it." Then said, "I'm going to do what I love." Of course, we've been told, "If you do what you love, money will follow," and I finally said, "Okay, I'm going to believe it." That's where I began.

Kris: Wow. That is really powerful. What I'm so struck by in that is that sometimes it really is like that. It's this battle between, "I made a decision to do it this way. I'm going to do it this way, dammit! It's going to work." We just bang our heads against a wall and then if we stop just banging our head against the wall long enough to get some little hint, an inspiration is all it takes, this little tiny glimmer, a little tiny window to open the whole thing up.

Marty: Yes.

Kris: If we choose it, because the other piece of it is that you, at that point, you said, "Just wait a minute. What have I been doing?"

Marty: Right. Well, it's also what I find with the clients I work with as well is we abandon ourselves right at the moment we need to give ourselves the most love. Right in the moment when I'm frustrated and I've done it fourteen times the way they're telling me to do it, but it didn't work on a Mac, which is what the issue was. It wasn't that I wasn't doing it right. It was that it didn't—there was one thing I didn't do so it didn't work because a Mac is different.

Instead of loving me and calming down, as you were saying, and taking a deep breath, what I did is I beat myself up more and more, thinking, "If I just try harder and harder, it's going to work." I think we do that in our lives, that we find people that we just push and push and push and push and if we just work harder, if we just work harder, and that's not it.

When it doesn't work, we need to listen to the Universe and stop. But the stop sign was there. It was saying, "Stop," and I kept pushing harder. "No, I can't. No, I can't." So what we resist persists. What we are saying we don't want to have happen is what happens in our life over and over like *Groundhog Day*, as I call it, the movie.

Until we stop and really see where we need to align with ourselves and be gentle with ourselves and love ourselves and say, "In this moment, wow, you need support, Marty. What can you do for yourself to give yourself some support?" That's when I could breathe. When I breathed and thought that, then I thought of this man that had been—he's always available. He's right there. He's always answered my questions about Macs, but I couldn't think of him for twenty-four hours while I was beating myself up. Yeah, it's just important that we take care of ourselves and love ourselves and not abandon ourselves in that very moment that we need the most care and support.

When we are as committed to giving ourselves the care and support we need, and listening to our Inner Truth as we are to money, success, fame, and looking good for others, everything turns around—in an instant. Quantum leaps can happen, and they can happen really quickly, but what most people don't share, and what I love about Marty's story because it shows this so well, is that there is a lot of internal work and action that leads up to those "quantum leaps" that make them look like they happened suddenly.

JUST DO IT!: GETTING INTO ACTION: PRACTICE FAITH

"Face your fears and the fear of death is certain. Thinking may not overcome fear, but action will."

— Dan Zadra

Action is simply the fastest way to get results. But let's not forget that taking a whole bunch of action without some intention behind it can be more draining and ineffective than taking inspired and intentional action from a higher vibrational place. In other words, being in a higher vibrational mindset and taking small (or large!) but consistent actions is far better than just being busy and trying to "keep up" or "stay ahead of the eight-ball." Doing for doing's sake is not what we are talking about here. When I worked at the University of Washington at the Behavioral Research & Therapy Clinic, a friend and I were discussing what made people change. He was a behaviorist and focused more on what people do. At the time, I was much more into the philosophical and analytic approach that favored insight and understanding internal experiences—the why behind what we do. He said something that really ticked me off at the time because it challenged my thinking, and at the time, I really was more interested in being "right" versus being open to seeing other ways of looking at things. He said, "Insight doesn't equal change." For some of you, that may make total sense, and you already have been living that way for years. However, the number of self-help books lining shelves that explain the "why" of things so you can have insight is huge, but once you have insight, it doesn't always equal change! (If it did, people would change, right?) I still believe insight is hugely helpful; otherwise, I wouldn't have written this book, but it must be put into action or else it's not very useful.

"An ounce of action is worth a ton of theory."

— Ralph Waldo Emerson

Throughout this book, I offer you tips, techniques, and things to do so you can get a new result as you gain insight through reading the stories. I believe the energy techniques I use in my practice are a huge part of what supports people in making big changes relatively easily. But the biggest thing I want to say here is that there are lots of books out there on setting goals and taking action, but if you are not actually taking the action, then you will not get the results. The same goes for the techniques herein. If you don't do them, they won't work. Period. When you are called to take some action, and it's in alignment with what you want (to have, to be, or to do), and it doesn't violate anyone else's rights or dignity, and having or doing the thing will get you closer to your objectives, then by all means ACT! Take the leap!Beth Buelow, The Introvert Entrepreneur, shares her story of when she just leapt, against her typical "nature."

Beth: The second time I listened [to my Inner Voice] and the consequences were good was when I discovered my calling to be a coach. This was back in 2007 and 2008, and my husband and I had just moved to a new community and I was kind of depressed. We had agreed to make the move, but I came without a job. I came at the beginning of winter. I didn't know anybody. So I was home a lot by myself while my husband was off at work. I felt lost.I finally found a job that I was really interested in. I applied. I came in second and I was just devastated. Somewhere in that space, I let the [Inner] Voice pop in that said, "Hey, wait a minute. You have something and you have always been interested and curious about coaching. Why don't you take a look? Maybe this is that opportunity."So I followed it. Within two weeks, I was enrolled in a coach training program and off and running.

Kris: Wow!

Beth: Yeah. It was not necessarily my M.O. [*modus operandi*]. Usually, while my personality type or my Myers-Briggs is INFJ, I think the J combined with (if you put any stock in astrological signs), I'm a Virgo. So apparently my keywords are I analyze, which I find very true for me. Combine that with my J tendencies, which like to have structure and information and process, [and] it's kind of surprising that I just moved. I didn't do a ton of research. Didn't spend a lot of time on it. I went up, did an info session, said, "Yes, this is for me," and boom! There it was. I definitely credit some inner knowing with bringing that to me.

Kris: What I love about this story—it's so clear that your Inner Voice just knows. There's no typical "J" nature of doubting, of questioning, of wondering and having to know, "How's this going to go? What's going to happen? Where are the details?" It's noise. It becomes extraneous information we don't need, and the decision is very easy.

Beth: As an introvert, you know as well as I do, it's kind of part of our fabric to listen to that internal voice, whether it's coming from fear or it's coming from our truth. For me, at least, that's where my wisdom comes from. It's not from external sources necessarily, even though I like to have my information, and I'd like to do my research. Ultimately, it's kind of what does my Inner Voice tell me?Learning to trust it and listen to it has been really important. I would say it also led me to figuring out, "Okay, within coaching, who am I called to serve?" That was another instance of listening to that Inner Voice, that inner truth and not needing to rush back and do a bunch of research and call a bunch of people and do a focus group or market research. It was just, "No, this is it and I know it and I trust it."

Beth's story illustrates the quiet simplicity of the Inner Voice, and how, no matter what your personality type is, or how you receive and process those intuitive hits from within, you can trust them and move on them. That said, sometimes we get the nudges to do this or that, and we still don't do what we know we need to do. I used to think I had to analyze it all and figure out all the reasons for my resistance and clear it before taking action. This is not always true. When you're so paralyzed you can't or won't take the action, then yes—it's helpful to clear some baggage out of the way. But frankly, just saying, "Yes" will drop so much baggage you won't believe it.If you are not taking action that you know you need to, the best thing to do is: *Make a decision—then act*. Take some action that reinforces what you just learned or decided. Big action creates big results and those ever-enticing and often elusive "quantum leaps." And...there is something you should know about quantum leaps....

QUANTUM LEAPS ARE BULLSHIT

I'm going to let you in on a little secret. Quantum Leaps are one of the coaching industry's biggest myths. I see it all over the place: "I made a quantum leap in my business," "My income increased 300 percent overnight!" "I went to one class and was totally different afterwards." Here's the cold, hard, unsexy truth that no one wants to tell you, and that you likely don't want to hear: Transformation takes time. Quantum leaps are a result of lots of decisions that lead up to a person being ready, internally and externally, to make that one decision that sets a cascade of results in motion that appear to have happened "overnight."

Technically speaking, a quantum leap means that a subatomic particle moves from one location in space and time to another location without passing through any other locations in between. While it is possible for a person to make this leap from one mindset or belief system to another, where she doesn't have to go through every step of the process in between, the fact is that the information or experience most often is preceded by lots of internal work. This internal work (often years in the process) is the reason a person is finally ready to have that "leap" happen when she is exposed to someone or some experience that causes the internal shift actually to "stick" in the new paradigm without slipping backwards to the old belief paradigm. I have attended so many trainings, retreats, seminars, and workshops that promised "quantum leaps" and "radical shifts" in mindset and income as a result of attending. And in some of those, I experienced pretty big changes, as did other people. However, most of the time, I'd make a series of smaller shifts, one after another. I'd feel badly because I couldn't understand why other people seemed to be making such huge shifts when I wasn't. I thought there must be something wrong with me. I felt ashamed and incapable of changing. (Recognize the little voice feelings and thoughts?)

When I finally understood that change is a process that happens over time (because we live in the dimension that includes space and time), I started to see that what really creates a quantum leap (so to speak) is creating an internal and external environment through making decisions that are in alignment with one's truth and taking action one step at a time. How do you speed up this process and prepare yourself to transform more quickly? Surrender.

Give up the notion that you are in control or need to be in control. Let go of the need to look good, stay safe, or fit in. Let go of any feeling that you should be anywhere other than where you are right now.

Learn to discern between the Inner Voice and little voices of fear that can, and usually do, come in and try to scare you back to where you began. They will either keep you from making a clear decision and taking action on it, or have you second-guessing that decision and pulling yourself back like a rubber band to where you were before you were stretched by the decision.

Give yourself a break and allow yourself to be wherever you are in the process. Recognize that old habits die hard.

Use your inner authority to make decisions that are in alignment for you.

Get accountability and someone who can see your truth when you can't.

You will get more powerful results all around, including deeper healing, more profound transformation in your life and business if you *decide first, take action, and process the fear later.*

Energetically, our system needs to catch up as well. Our physical and energetic system needs to shift and accommodate our bigger reality and paradigm. We have to drop the energetic resistance or blocks (like a detox) to help us adjust to our new reality. Sometimes that's dropping behaviors or doing new ones; sometimes it's letting people go, sometimes it's teaching people how to treat you differently based on your new paradigm. These are all decisions and actions that take time. Nobody likes to talk about this though in their copy writing or marketing. It would freak people out.

Here's the thing, though: Once you make the decision and start taking action, it gets easier. It really does. As someone who loves a good processing session, it's taken a long time for me really to get this. God can't help you until you make a decision. And when you do decide, all manner of grace, support, and resources can—and will—show up.Breakdowns happen, and losing our focus happens, often because we need to make a decision and take action, and we are not letting ourselves know what we need to do, let alone do it. We are afraid people won't play along or they'll judge us. Remember all the different ways we access our inner authority and the reasons why we don't? That's what shows up here as confusion and resistance. I was just sharing with someone that when I was feeling called to upgrade the level of financial and time commitment I was doing with my coach, I went into an electrical storm. I literally could not drive our VW bus; it would just die on me (my husband could drive it fine the same day); I burned out the light fixture in our bedroom; my cell phone went on the fritz; and I kept running into walls. When I finally just made the decision my Inner Voice was guiding me to do, everything was fine and working again (except for the light fixture; we had to replace that!). I could have easily said that I was in a storm, and that means I shouldn't do it because my ego was so damn scared; it KNEW its days were numbered! But the storm was really the resistance I was experiencing to making that commitment.

Resistance is futile. It's also no fun.

ACT TO FIND YOUR WAY

"I learn by going where I have to go."

— Theodore Roethke

We also need to take some action so we can calibrate our future efforts. If we don't know where we stand relative to our target or goal, we won't be able to get there. It reminds me of my GPS on my phone. I can plot my destination and see my current location. I can even follow a little dot right on the blue pathway that highlights my route to my end destination. (Don't you wish life were really like that?) Sometimes, though, I get off track. I miss a turn, or the route option isn't working and all I can see is the red dot that says where my endpoint is and the green dot that shows from where I started. If I stay put and don't move, I won't be able to tell whether I'm heading in the right direction. But if I keep moving, I am able to make adjustments along the way. And it's fun to see how close I can get to the mark in as few turns as possible.By the way, the decision/action dyad happens throughout the day, constantly. When you are in the flow, the decisions and actions you take are congruent with one another; things flow and you are in integrity. Resources, like time and money and helpful people, show up more easily and quickly as well. It's easier to course correct when you're moving than when standing still. Like a car with power steering, when the car is off, you can't turn the wheel, but when it's moving, you can turn it with ease and steer with a light touch.Julie, a friend and gifted healer, and I discuss this "easy" aspect of the Inner Voice, and the fact that while there is greater ease, you still have to push through the fear and resistance. She was telling me about a recent trip to the States from her current home in Australia to receive coaching:

Julie: ....I knew, "I've got to go to this." It was just so clear. So I went to that event and I ended up, again, changing my plane flight, staying with my brother for like six weeks in Minnesota so that I could come back for Ann's coaching program in September. It was like I was away for ten weeks. But it was just so clear. Actually it was easy to do.

Kris: Easy. That, I think, is—tell me more about that, because it's interesting. I've had some times where it's been really easy, absolutely. Then there have been times where for myself it was the right thing to do, but it wasn't easy. What do you think? What's your opinion on that? Do you think when we're just totally dialed in, it's easy; when we're not, that's when we're listening to the little voices a bit more?

Julie: Yeah. We've got that resistance still. That's one of the things I guess that has been my focus in the last few months is that I know this can be easy. I know there are all those little voices in my head saying, "Yes but," and "What if," and all this sort of stuff, but I know this doesn't have to be hard. I spend—I don't know, I do a lot of different things, but with [energy work], I spend probably at least a half an hour a day probably releasing stuff. I actually noticed in the last couple of days I just had a lot of stuff shift. What happened? I don't know.

Kris: I definitely get that.

Julie: And then there are those hard times when you just have to push through it. Or at least that's what it feels like. You know it's right and you have to do this.

Kris: I think that's really true because having given birth a couple times and seeing what happens there, it really is an effort. There is belief and surrender and relaxing; you have to do all those things. But there are times when you have to push, and actually, you can't *not* push; it's actually more painful not to push when in labor. So it's really fascinating finding that rhythm of it. Not the harmony, not the balance of it, but the *rhythm* of it, because it's really more that. Sometimes we do simply have to push through because that is that place where the breakthrough will happen, and if we don't push against it a little bit, it's just not going to happen.

Julie: And it's usually at that critical point, just before the seedling pops through the earth, it's just like if only I'd taken that one more step, I would have been there. All the "if only's." It's where we keep coming up to that one barrier that keeps showing up at the same time: when the money gets to a certain point, when the relationship gets to a certain point, and then at that point we keep backing off, and that's the point where we actually need to move through. That's probably the hardest point. It's recognizing the pattern and, like you say, the rhythm. There is a rhythm to it. You get to that point and you back off, and you get to that point again and you back off. What would happen if I actually stepped through this time?

Kris: Exactly. That's a really good point, and I think that it's interesting the way you say that because maybe that's why when we go to do some of these weekend workshops and everything, they're like, "Just step through, just step through," that once you do that, you'll have this huge breakthrough. And certainly, I have had the experience of that where I did; I said, "Yes" and I had huge breakthroughs. And then there have been times when I resisted the heck out of it and just stayed stuck where I was. At the same time, I think that sometimes in the marketing and messaging out there it's like we have to do that—if we do it just once and we find that one that we have to break through, then it'll be fine, we'll be good and there won't really be another one to do. Sometimes I find that really a little frustrating because it's like, "I did that and then I had a huge breakdown and now I've got the next part."

Julie: And there's more.

Kris: Right. Or I think I must not have done it right. And then I guess as I'm saying that out loud those are just the little voices that are saying, "You didn't do it right. You didn't actually fully do it." You still have some way out; you found some way out.

Julie: When Suzanne was coaching with David Neagle, she said, "You never told me that you had more than one meltdown." It's like, well I know what's going to happen next time when I double my prices, for example. Then I have all those issues to go through again, but at least you know what to expect.

Kris: Exactly.

Julie: But yeah it is—I just find it interesting how—and we don't even see what's going on in our heads or in our lives. We get to that point and we back off, we get to that point and we back off. It's like, I've done this before. When did I do that? Oh yes, I can remember as a child at age such and such that happened, and from then on, it's like I said, "No way. I can't do it," or somebody said,

"You can't do it. Who are you to think that you can do something like that?"

Kris: For you, would you say that what's been most helpful for you, at least until now, has been the little voices when they're coming up, working on healing them?

Julie: Yeah. Even accepting them.

Kris: Sure. Accepting them, healing them.

Julie: Which is healing them. It's like, "Oh great, why aren't I moving, doing this? Oh, that's why." It's made me grateful for the little voices that actually come up to be healed. It's like, you can either support me or you can go away. Which one? I just find it fascinating working with myself, as well as clients, what comes up, and how just about all of it is childhood. You'd know that anyway. In the first seven to ten years where we just download stuff and we take on everybody else's beliefs and then we have to work out ours as we grow up. Yeah, I just actually love the whole journey of it. Yes, it can be frustrating and, "When are you guys ever going to stop?" but yeah, it's—I don't think that it does stop if we keep up-leveling our lives and going that next step.

Kris: It sounds like what really matters is which voice are you going to listen to. It's like, how do we in that moment access what I call our Inner Voice? Because we have all the clamoring of the little voices begging for their attention and they're telling us, "Go this way, don't do that, do this, don't do that," and it's very confusing. What has been, if you have any tips or anything that has worked for you—how have you reconnected to your Inner Voice then? What have you needed to do or done? What helps you connect to what's really true in your inner guidance?

Julie: First of all, just recognizing the voice. Like we said, it's there and it's—because we're numbed to what's actually there a lot of the time, so just to take a breath and stop right where you are and actually listen to what's going on in your head and be open to recognizing the voices. You know if there's fear or anything like that in the voice, that's not your true voice. It's like, your true Inner Voice is the one that's supportive. You may have heard the thing where you've got two wolves in you—which one are you going to feed? You can feed the drama wolf or you can feed the loving wolf. Am I going to worry about what all these people say, or am I actually going to look and step into what I really enjoy doing? Stop living your life for other people and now make a choice to live your life for you. [Immediately you hear] "Oh, how selfish." As soon as you make a decision, stuff comes up. Just be aware that every time you make a choice, stuff is going to come up, and where are you going to look? What are you going to listen to? Make up your mind beforehand and just—it's empowering just to know that stuff is going to come up; the doubts, the fears, the what ifs. Be ready for it: "Oh yeah, that's right, they said you guys were going to show up. Thanks very much, this is where I'm going." For me, that's probably been my biggest Aha—first of all stopping and realizing the voices going on in the head. For me, Emotion Code [an emotional energy healing technique] has been brilliant for that....The programmed tapes that are running in our head, to be able to release those, reprogram them, that kind of thing. It's just chains falling off you when you get through some of the stuff. You just feel so much freer and lighter.

Julie said, "Accept the little voices and heal them." It's true! They are a part of us, and they have valuable information and lessons to share, but mostly, they are there for protection, not necessarily guidance. They tend to "guide" through avoidance of pain or wanting to feel pleasure versus guiding and acting from pure Love. Accepting them and hearing them out from a detached place can be a form of healing. They feel heard and welcomed, and we don't have to buy into their drama or do what they say to do in order to heal them.

Just so we are clear about the difference between easy and "ease" when it comes to listening to and acting from our intuition or Inner Voice: When we follow our inner authority, we experience more ease and being in the flow; however, this is not always easy! Danielle LaPorte points out the myth of listening to our intuition in New Age thought and how it all sounds so easy and flowing, but in reality, it isn't always that way. Yes, I believe that life flows more easily when we heed our Inner Voice, but I'll be the first to say it's been some of the hardest work I've ever done, or avoided doing in my life! Danielle says it best:

> Following your intuition ain't always an act of grace—it can be a total grind. You will have to burn things. You might sweat, toil and dig dig dig to do what you know must be done. Following your intuition might call on you to do the hardest thing you've ever done in your life.[16]

As a person who has chronically doubted her decisions and second-guessed her intuitive hits—especially if they were socially inconvenient or might upset others or the status quo, I've had to learn to make every decision "right." This is not always easy. But I will say the times I listened to my Inner Voice things opened up in a way, and there was less "work" as far as cleaning up lousy decisions goes!

Making every decision "right" means: make the decision, take action, learn from the results, recalibrate, and move on to the next decision. Spending a lot (or even a little!) time second-guessing yourself or beating yourself up for a "wrong" choice or decision is wasted, and low, vibrational energy. Look for the lesson and move on. This is "building the plane as you fly it." This can be especially hard for folks who like to be in control and who are perfectionistic (ahem). Sometimes the plane isn't going to look too good or feel very stable. Instead of judging the darn thing and trying to decide whether or not you're going to trash it at every turn, commit to making it fly no matter what.My husband does adventure races and orienteering. He describes to me how he both has to move quickly through the woods on the course, sometimes on foot, sometimes on bike, while often hearing other

---

16 Taken from http://www.daniellelaporte.com/inspiration-spirituality-articles/the-myth-about-following-your-intuition/

racers crashing through the bushes around him. He has to be able to pause long enough to take in his surroundings, read the map quickly, ignore the adrenaline pounding in his blood, access his intuitive hits, and then move in the direction of the next checkpoint at a breakneck pace in order to beat the other racers there. There isn't time to sit and think through all possible options and make sure he's recovered enough to move on. He course corrects *while moving.*

QUESTIONS TO FREE YOUR INNER VOICE

What do I know about _____ *that I'm not letting myself know*:

My relationships

My business

My health

My home

My kids

Other:

Based on the answers I wrote above, the action that *makes the most sense*, or is the *most logical choice* is: _____.

Based on the answers I wrote above, the action that *feels the best*, or *feels like the right thing for me to do* is: _____.

Are these two answers the same? If not, why not?

Based on the answers I wrote above, the action I know I need to take, but am avoiding taking is _____.

In order to take that action I need to _____.

On a scale of 0-10, where 0 is "not at all ready" and 10 is "Get the hell outta my way; I'm going to take action now!" my readiness to take action or make that change right now is _____.

In order for it to be an 8 or higher I need _____.

Based on that need, the next step is _____.

I commit to that next step now, and I will set this book down and do something to take action even if it's write myself a note and put it on top of my to-do list with top priority for action. Yes _____ No _____

If you check "No" above, call or email me. Or call your coach, therapist, or other trusted mentor and get clear on whatever story is holding you back from taking that action.

If you checked "Yes," go ahead and take that action.

Go ahead. I'll be here when you get back....

Nice work. That feels better, doesn't it?

Don't Quit

When things go wrong as they sometimes will,
When the road you're trudging seems all uphill,
When the funds are low and the debts are high,
And you want to smile, but you have to sigh,
When care is pressing down a bit—
Rest if you must, but don't you quit.

Success is failure turned inside out,
The silver tint of the clouds of doubt,
And you never can tell how close you are,
It may be near when it seems afar.
So, stick to the fight when you're hardest hit—
It's when things go wrong that you mustn't quit.

— Author Unknown

A PURPOSE-FULL LIFE

"There is a vitality, a life force, an energy, a quickening,
that is translated through you into action, and because there
is only one of you in all time, this expression is unique.
And if you block it, it will never exist through
any other medium and will be lost."

— Martha Graham

Are you feeling lost? Wondering why you're here and what to do with your life? Unsure what skills you possess and what makes you passionate and how to express these in a way that feels both fulfilling and puts food on the table? This is one of the most common reasons people don't take action—they just don't know how to orient themselves to the next step. You often won't get the whole outcome and all the steps at once. That would blow your mind and your circuits. But you can get a sense of the bigger picture and receive guidance about what to do next through getting quiet for a few moments. When I am working with my clients, we do many exercises so they can develop a working relationship with their Higher Self and intuition. Frankly, most often I'm innovating in the moment with each person based on what intuitive hits and visions I receive in that moment about what the person needs to hear to connect to her Inner Voice. That said, the brief meditation that follows is one that I've used many times with clients to help them get started. As our work progresses, my clients discover the unique way each one of them experiences her intuition and then hones that so she can go out and use it confidently in her life and business as a powerful guide.

Here are a few things to consider before I share the meditation with you:

- It's okay if you are not a visual person. Even if you cannot "see" this light, allow your other senses to kick in and experience it in your own unique way. Just know that energy follows thought, so even just setting the intention to receive a message from your Inner Voice as you let the following words direct your awareness and energy will be beneficial. There is a recording of this exercise on my website; you can listen to it there and follow along.

- Often the reason why people don't receive accurate or clear guidance from their Inner Voice is because they have all these desires and preferences, fears, and limitations on what they are willing to receive. Also called preconceived notions, bias, or filters, these all create resistance to receiving clear and accurate information. In graduate school, we were taught not to pretend we are a "blank slate" and just be open to whatever comes with our clients. Instead, we were taught first to acknowledge our own viewpoint, bias, and expectations, and consciously name them and set them aside so we could then be as clear as possible to hear and experience the person in front of us. This is essential in this meditation as well. I've observed with myself and with my clients that often we already "know" the answer, but for some reason, we are afraid to get real confirmation of what we already know—probably because we either think we aren't worthy enough to follow through on what our purpose is, or because we are afraid of the actions we will have to take to live out our purpose. We fear the risks we will have to take, the comfort zone we'll have to step out of, the people we might upset, etc. So, before you begin this meditation, I encourage you to make a quick list of the things that you suspect the answer might be, the things you "hope" it isn't, and any fears you may have about what receiving this truth and information from God (aka your Inner Voice) will mean. Remember, you get to choose whether or not you'll take action. You've always had that choice. Now you will be choosing consciously instead of avoiding or choosing out of fear and ignorance.

- When you are ready, the message will come. A helpful prayer a friend shared with me is "God, when I'm ready to see the big picture, will you show me?" Over time, as she felt more confident and took small steps along the way and felt more ready for the big picture to be revealed, she changed the prayer to "God, I'm ready to see the big picture. Please show me." She did this weekly as she drove to her radio show every Friday morning. One day, the big picture was revealed to her, clear as day. She shared it with a small group of confidants who can hold the space for that vision, and now she is holding the big vision while letting go of needing to know all the steps from where she is now to having the vision manifest, and doing what she is led to do, one day at a time as a walk in faith.

Connect to your Inner Voice and Receive Guidance on Your Purpose-Full Next Steps through the Inner Spark of Source:

Imagine a spark of light in your heart. Expand it, let it fill your whole heart, watch it glow brighter and brighter. Imagine it burning away all confusion, all worry, all sadness, all fear. Let it grow, filling your chest, your torso, arms, legs, and head. Radiating outward from the center of your chest, let it fill your body all the way to the edges of your skin. Almost like sunshine shining on your skin from within. Feel that warmth from your inner sun and savor it. Now gently expand this light to a few inches off your skin all around your body. Expand it some more until it's filling the space three, then five, then ten feet all around you. Feel this healing, protective light emanating from you and surrounding you—radiating your goodness and keeping you safe.

Leave that glowing light all around you and turn your awareness back to the source of the spark in your heart. Imagine it holds all the wisdom and answers you need. Imagine that if you wanted to, you could ask this spark anything and it would give you an answer. It may come right away, or later today, or next week; it may be a physical sensation, or an intuitive hit or a *knowing*; it could be an emotion that seemingly comes out of nowhere; it could be something you hear or see or sense. Trust it will come to you in your own secret language and connection to your inner authority and be open to the messages. Know you can come here anytime and ask any questions you desire. Let go of the need to know the answer so it can come. You may wish to state/ask:

- "Thank you God for showing me my purpose in this situation."

- "What do I need to learn in this situation?"

- "What am I resisting in this situation?"

- "What is the next best step for me?"

Ask and listen. You may "see" the answer as an image or a person's face that you need to connect with; you may hear a specific message or a name. You may just "know" instantly what to do next. You may get a feeling and nothing else—that feeling may be your clue to what to watch for as you move through the world meeting people, having experiences, and when you feel that feeling, you know you're on the right track.

When you get an answer (and it could be right there in the meditation, it could be hours, days, weeks later), take action, however big or small. Just like any conversation when you feel heard and when the other person feels heard, and some action to follow through on what is communicated in the interaction happens, the conversation keeps going. A trust and rapport is established and the connection grows stronger.

I believe that we are all born knowing our mission, our calling, or purpose. Most of us forgot or unlearned it through the conditioning of parents, teachers, grandparents, friends, media, etc. I've seen it over and over again in people's Human Design charts. Their purpose is right there, in the centers, channels, and gates they have defined. It's in the way they access their inner authority. That purpose is basically living true to their natural frequency and combining that with their desires and preferences of what lights them up. When we are connected to our purpose, and we know what our Inner Voice wants to express, our fear of failure and rejection falls away. Sure, we may still be a little nervous, but there is something greater than our little voices, than our ego, that wants to be expressed. When we know what that next step is, we can't help but take action and share it with others.

CHAPTER NINE

Key Element #5: Harmonize Your Energy— Embodiment

"Please be responsible for the energy you bring to this space."

—Jill Bolte-Taylor

Are you aware that you are more than just a bundle of skin and bones, thoughts and emotions? *You are pure energy manifest in physical form.* When your energy is out of harmony, it can affect the way you think, the way you feel, and your ability to attract what you desire to experience. We are like big magnets. We have a polarity, just like a magnet does. The earth is also a huge electromagnet; it has a polarity as well. It, too, has north and south poles, and it has an awesome gravitational pull that keeps us from floating off into space. What I have noticed in my own life, when I'm working with my clients, is that when our polarity is on, we feel calmer inside. We also think more clearly, have more energy, and our energy is flowing in a coherent manner. The same experience happens when we are grounded. Like an electrical current that needs to be grounded in order to flow properly, we too need to be grounded and have our polarity "on" so we can be in the flow and focus our energy in the direction of where we want to go and what we want to draw to us.

When our polarity is off and when we are not grounded, we don't think as clearly and we tend to default to what I call our "lowest vibrational habits." Then it's much harder to act and speak in a way that we desire—we easily slip back into old patterns and feelings. When we aren't grounded, we can feel spacey—it feels like we are floating off into space, and we'll often try to latch onto anyone or anything that will help us feel grounded again—instead of going to Source energy. By the way, when we try to get grounded through other people instead of grounding directly ourselves to Source energy, they can feel it—and they often run the other way, leaving us confused as to why it didn't work out, and them feeling like they were hooked in or slimed....

When we are plugged into the earth, when we are grounded, then we naturally draw to us what we need and desire in our lives. We have the clarity to choose what is beneficial to us and to remain in alignment with our Vision and how we want to act, speak, feel, think, etc. Think of grounding as being like a flower that needs to be grounded in order to bloom. As the flower's roots draw in nutrients from the soil and it receives sunlight and rain from above, it grows without judgment or comparison of itself to any other flower—it is in what I call a "Divine Flow."

As the flower blooms, it expresses its *voice* through color and scent. It uses its *voice* to attract what it needs in order to express itself fully, in order to share its message (its pollen) with the world. The flower attracts its ideal customers, bees and butterflies, through its unique scent and color. These ideal clients and customers help spread its message in the world, thereby fulfilling the flower's purpose, its *raison d'être* (reason for being). Furthermore, it needs to be alive and grounded to fulfill this purpose. Cut it off at the stem to put it into a container and its energy immediately begins to fade. It is the same with us. The difference between flowers and humans, though, is that we have free will. We have choice and we can choose to replant ourselves or reground whenever we want or need to.

Are you sensing a theme here? Twice now I've suggested ways to ground and why it's so important. This time I want you not only to ground, but to surround yourself with a bubble or ball of light, about 3-6 feet (1-2 meters) in all directions—even into the ground and behind you. Make it whatever color you wish—golden white or blue are both great options if you're not sure what you feel like choosing in the moment.

I call this process The Thought-Leader Creation (TLC) Turnaround. And it is the quickest way I know to clear your energy field and create harmony in your energy body, while protecting yourself from negative energetic influences outside yourself. You can do it anywhere, anytime, and in less than thirty seconds, you can feel much better!It takes only a few moments, literally less than a minute once you know the flow. If you'd like to spend more time playing with visualization, please do, but know it isn't necessary. What's needed is your *choice* to stop what you're doing, ground, surround yourself with Divine white light and a bubble of protection, set an intention based on how you'd like to feel and what your desired outcome is, and then take action from there.

I often find that when we start down a path and we are stuck in our habitual pattern, it can be really hard to stop it. Since our only point of power is here and now, right in this moment, then that's when we need to engage. The following exercise gets us right back on track, easily, quickly, and painlessly. No judgment, no shame, no long drawn-out process session needed—just a willingness to stop, ground, surround, and move on.

The Thought-Leader Creation (TLC) Turnaround:

- **Stop what you're doing:** *Feel your body.*

- **Ground:** Sitting or standing, feet flat on the floor, palms over your navel—Imagine you have cords (or roots) of energy coming out of the soles of your feet and going down into the center of the earth. Inhale through your nose, exhale through your mouth gently, and send those cords deep into the earth. *Feel that connection.*

- **Surround:** Picture a *large bubble around you* that surrounds you about three feet from your body in all directions. It is composed of beautiful golden white (or any color you choose) light. Now you may not feel or sense a thing and that's okay—not to worry; it still works, and over time as you awaken more and more to the energy *around you and in you,* you will begin to *perceive the vibrations* of things and people in a powerful way that is uniquely yours. Notice how soothing it is to be surrounded by this light, how safe it feels. *Feel held.*

- **Intend:** How do you want everything to turn out? Set an intention for how you want to feel moving forward. Listen for the inspired action to take. *Feel creative.*

- **Act:** Move back into your day, into your activity with intention and awareness. *Feel on purpose and aligned.* Go ahead. Try it right now....

COMMUNICATION

"Once a human being has arrived on this earth, communication is the largest single factor determining what kinds of relationships he makes with others and what happens to him."

— Virginia Satir

Everything is energy. Everything, from the chairs we're sitting on, to the food we eat, even our bodies, including the thoughts we think and the feelings we feel. In fact, scientists are now able to demonstrate through the study of quantum physics that it's the thoughts we think and the feelings we feel that inform the energy around us. In very simple terms, we are what we think, and we create our reality through the power of our thoughts and how we feel. What's really interesting to me is what we do *not* say and how much our internal dialogue influences others—at home and in business.

I've found that most miscommunication begins with us, meaning each one of us has a filter through which we are running other people's words and behaviors, and we think it's the other person's fault when we don't "get" them and they don't "get" us. This filter affects the way we feel and think, and it also affects our energy. Why is this last piece important? We affect other people with our energy. In fact, we communicate energetically first and foremost even before we've seen the person face-to-face or spoken on the phone. It even happens in the womb: We communicate through emotions which are biochemical (hormonal) secretions between mother and fetus, and we communicate psychically as well. Think about the last time you thought about someone, maybe even several times over a week, and you hadn't seen that person in years—suddenly he calls you…that is the kind of communication I'm talking about.

A couple of stories illustrate this energetic communication really well.

When my son, Eli, was about four years old, we were driving on I-90 from Issaquah to North Bend. He was in the backseat, his infant sister next to him sleeping, and I was daydreaming while I drove. It was very quiet in the car. I was thinking about a trip we had taken to Sedona, Arizona, about two years prior. During that trip, we had put down an offer to purchase a sporting goods store. My husband and I loved Sedona so much that we wanted to live there. Obviously, it didn't happen; we decided not to go through with it, but it was something I often wondered about. "What would our life be like if we were living in Sedona?" I was thinking those very thoughts when my son pipes up from the backseat: "Mom, where is Arizona?" My head whipped around and I looked at him and said, "What did you say?" I was shocked! He did that several times over the next few months, so I learned to "cloak" my thoughts, especially the ones that weren't very positive, or when I got bad news or read something negative in the paper because, obviously, I wasn't alone in my head!

Fast forward to autumn 2011 when I went on a retreat with my coach and mastermind group to Florida. After a long day of working indoors, we were told that our homework for the evening was to go outside and play on the beach and then draw a picture of our experience of playing. I built a sandcastle and then swam and played in the water with my friends. I swam more that weekend than I have in years, and just playing in the waves, I felt like a dolphin—so when I returned to my hotel room that night, I drew a picture of a big happy dolphin swimming in the waves with a bright sun with big rays. I didn't share my picture with anyone or tell my family about it when

I spoke to them that evening. When I got home I didn't see my kids until Wednesday morning, as my flight got in late Tuesday night. My daughter, Anja, who was three years old at the time, came into our room early in the morning and told me she had drawn me a picture while I was in Florida, and she wanted to show it to me. I was expecting typical three-year-old scribbles. My jaw dropped as she showed me her picture and told me about it: A big sun with rays all around it, waves, and a dolphin swimming. When I looked at my husband, he shrugged and said it was all her idea and she had drawn it first thing Tuesday morning when she woke up. Although 3,300 miles away, she had drawn the same thing I did twelve hours after I had drawn my picture.

I never again doubted that: 1) We are all connected, and 2) We communicate beyond the reaches of our voice and body language.

Rachel shares how her experience with equine therapy helped her to notice when her little voices had kicked in, and, as she made the choice to lead herself in the process, even though it was uncomfortable, that's when deep healing occurred with the horse and within herself and her Inner Voice. (From my understanding, equine therapy is based on the premise that the horse is communicating energetically with the client and is mirroring or reflecting back to the client what the person may not be consciously aware of. It's powerful work because, of course, a horse doesn't have an ego or filter so no need to be right or fix anything.)

Rachel: ...I thought about what is the most consistent thing my little voices have said to me. It's a great question when you think about this.

I realized what they say is "you can't do it your way. You have to do it this other way that you've been shown. You have to follow the rules. You have to do what somebody else says, or follow the path that's been laid before you. To not do so would be inappropriate, would be disrespectful. It's just not what people do. You'll do it wrong." That's the one that I think, probably, especially most recently that I keep coming up against and then I'm learning over and over—I have a story. Would it be better if I just talk?

Kris: Yeah, tell me the story. What happened?

Rachel: The one that really called it out for me was—because I've been in a lot of different learning experiences, and there's some ways in which I'm a great student and there's some ways in which I think I'm challenged as a student. This just totally eliminates that.

Somebody I know does horse coaching, like journeying into your work and your stuff using horses. She was training in it, so she asked me to come out and be a test session for her. She was newish at the time and she has me in the ring with her horse. Of course, I'm not a horse person necessarily. I haven't spent much time with them. They're these really big animals. If you haven't spent time around horses, they're much bigger than you.

Kris: Yeah, they're scary a little bit.

Rachel: Yeah. The part of me that doesn't want to startle them, worried about them startling and then trying to trample me or something. She had helped me steer toward an issue I wanted to work on, and then she instructed me to do something. She was like, "Okay, now walk around the ring and see what the horse does." I would walk around. For a while it was kind of like that was my process. Then she's like, "Okay, walk around again," and she had me doing things. I was doing them even though—she's like, "Oh, the horse is disconnecting."

Which seems almost like a judgment, like, "Oh, you're not being authentic," because with the horses when you're really in your emotional space and really being fully present, they're totally with you, they come and stand by you, they want to walk next to you or behind you or they'll do all kinds of stuff and when you're disconnected, they walk away. So it's a very visceral, tangible, visual demonstration of whether you're in your authenticity.

So she had me walking around the ring, and then she's like, "Oh [the horse], he's disconnecting. What's happening for you?" I had to do this a couple times before I finally went, "You know what; it doesn't feel natural to me to walk around the ring and be focusing on whatever. That's not where I'm at right now."

I was so trying to respect her process, her teaching, but I'm the client. It wasn't serving me. I was listening to the little voice that says, "No, just do it her way. Be obedient. Just follow along and I'm sure there will be some kind of benefit. But she knows what she's doing and you should respect that."

Of course, then I get all frustrated and tied up because other parts of me are like, "No, I don't want to be doing it this way." And oh, now the horse is walking away so there's some kind of judgment of me like, "Oh, look, you're disconnected." Well, I'm disconnected because I was trying to do it your way. Not my way.

Kris: Did you actually say that in the session or come to that in the session, or was that kind of an 'in retrospect' thought?

Rachel: No, I came to that in the session. I've done this enough and that's not the first time I've heard that message. So when I saw it, I was like, "Oh, there it is." I think that that was the first time I had said it out loud. So yeah, I said, "I really don't…" Parts of me felt apologetic and like, "Sorry, but doing it your way's not working for me. So I don't want to do that. I want to kind of wander around. I don't want to walk in a circle. I want to follow my own movement." She was like, "Oh, yeah. Great, of course."

Kris: What happened when you went ahead and wandered in your own way? What happened with you and the horse?

Rachel: The horse came to me. I just wandered around and the horse started—I think when I was walking before in the circle, the first time, the horse was kind of following me a little. But then when I was kind of wandering on my own, the horse went off for a little bit, but then came toward me.

Then we had this whole interaction where, what she said was that he was doing work with my chakras. He's standing right in front of me, like imagine a huge horse face, it's longer than your forearm, just the nose, above me, and he's standing to me and he's putting his third eye basically on my third eye, and he's like bowing down and kind of nibbling at my knee, like the jeans I was wearing at my knee, and putting that spot all over me. I'm standing there like, "Whoa." That all happened after I stopped following her process and just was with my own inquiry in my own way.

Also, my way tends to be not super-verbal, which can be challenging for coaches and things like that. Where it's like give me the space to just do it on my own and then later afterwards I can learn to translate that for you. But for me it's disruptive to keep being like, "Oh, I noticed this, that, and the other about this horse." Or, "I'm hearing this voice inside of me." I don't tend to partner with the person who's coaching me as much. When I do, I feel like I'm doing it for their benefit, not for mine, most of the time.

Kris: What a valuable lesson too, being a therapist and recognizing that what we think the techniques that we're taught or the modalities are everything, it's not the truth. And that when we can encourage our clients to listen to their truths, that's where the healing is, right?

Rachel: Absolutely. It's definitely great learning for me as a therapist. I tend to be pretty permissive already and very not dogmatic about any process or protocol. At the same time, I think more what I get

out of that is that I learn to notice when someone seems disconnected, kind of like the horse does, and to check in, "So what's
happening right now?"

A lot of times, people are doing the same thing, but they're not
verbalizing it. They're just struggling internally. "I'm trying to do
this thing you told me to do." "Okay, so you're having a challenge.
Let's talk about the challenge." You don't need to hide that from
me. It's really okay to bring it out. That acceptance of resistance
is really healing for a lot of people, especially in the population I
work with.

Kris: Especially because you work with "good girls", right? So they all
          have done it wrong or are afraid to do it wrong, right?

Rachel: They're really afraid to do it wrong. They're really afraid to be an
          inconvenience for people. Being good, part of it is being pleas-
          ing, participating in the way people want you to. That's been my
          challenge too. That's why when somebody says walk around the
          circle three times, I'm like, "Okay." I'll pretend like that's fine
          even though I don't want to.

Kris: Right. It's interesting because there's a difference between—you
          bring up a really good point, and maybe it's a discussion in the
          Inner Voice or not, I don't know. One is there's this feeling of you
          can't do it your own way. You have to follow the rules and you
          have to follow the pathway before you. In that respect there are
          times when we really should not be doing that, and you've dem-
          onstrated that. It really wasn't working, and so when you listen to
          that, you follow what you really need to be doing.

          Then there's this other path that says if you want to get some-
          where or you want to attain something that someone else has
          attained and they say here's [where] you kind of have to be, for
          lack of a better term, I can't come up with a word, a servant to
          it, a sub servant. You have to serve the higher purpose and let go

of your ego. You have to do what needs to be done based on the bigger picture—not on your own need to control or be in charge. You have to surrender to the process itself, right?

Rachel: Yeah.

Kris: There's this balance between saying, "I'm going to do it my way," and then, "But wow, what do I do here to surrender to this process and engage in it?" Can you talk about that a little bit? Has that ever happened?

Rachel: Oh yeah. That's part of the confusion—not knowing if that little voice is saying, "Just do it this way." It can be hard to determine if it's a little voice or if it's an appropriate voice, like an inner champion voice that's saying, "I know this is hard and some things just need to be gone through because that's the journey." So yeah, definitely. I have two master's degrees. I didn't get those by doing it all my own way.

Kris: Right, exactly.

Rachel: I had to jump through hoops and do certain things. So yeah, it's definitely a big gray area because there are ways that I still did make those my own path and did them my own way. Some things you're not going to know if it's okay until you ask.

So I think the key is, I guess, being able to find the space to listen and see whether the energy coming through with that voice that says, "No, just do it this way," if it's a supportive voice, like it's coming through and saying, "I know we don't want to, but this is going to be really good for us," versus a voice that's coming through with fear, "No, I have to do it this way. This is the way she's saying I'm supposed to and I don't want to upset her or disappoint anybody, or generally be a problem for people."

Over time I've learned that it's really okay for me to be a problem for people, because if I'm raising the problem systemically, other people were having that same issue, and it's okay to disrupt what was happening in order to address something that needed to be taken care of.

Kris: Yes, absolutely. So often I hear people say—it really comes up more in marketing and sales, actually, people go, "I don't want to talk about someone's pain. I don't want to make them feel bad." It's like shit, they already feel bad, pointing it out doesn't mean you caused it—it means you're paying attention.

Rachel: They already feel terrible, yeah. You might as well address it. They go, "Oh, you're talking to me, yea."

Kris: Yeah, exactly. Like, "Oh, you hear me? You understand me. You get me." That's very powerful. It's amazing how many of us don't want to call out what we see. I was talking to someone last week during one of these interviews, and I said, "Listening to our Inner Voice and our intuition is often really socially inconvenient."

Rachel: It really is. It totally is.

Kris: So what you were pointing out earlier with this woman, it would have been really convenient to say, "Huh, I don't want to question you or what you're doing here, but this doesn't feel right."

Rachel: Yeah. What I've learned just through different numbers of trainings is that no one is served by me pretending like it's fine because on some level inside everyone can feel when it's not right. You can just feel it. A lot of people don't know how to put a name to it or how to identify it.

This energetic connection and the proverbial "elephant in the room" happens in our businesses as well. Our thoughts and feelings precede us, and I'm telling you as a person who is sensitive to energy, it says a lot more than any words could ever say. When we have fears, negative self-image, shame, attachment to outcome, or needing people to say, "Yes" because we "need" their business—they can feel it. They may not consciously know it, but they can feel it.

So, not only is getting clear on what we want to say important, but also our alignment with it energetically, because that is also what is communicated, often first and foremost. Not only does our reputation precede us—so does our energy.

Beth Buelow, whom we heard from earlier, shares how the little voices affect her around envy of others and how people can pick up on our insecurity and mirror it back to us (remember the entrainment back in the chapter on emotion—here it is again):

Beth: [Listening to those little voices nowadays]...it kind of shows up as professional envy. It shows up as that and it shows up when I'm doing something that I admire other people for doing. Like I want to write a book or I want to create some great offering.

The little voice that shows up is, "Who are you to? Who are you to write a book? Who are you to think that you have something that other people are going to pay for? Who are you to think that people are going to volunteer their time to listen to you? What makes you think you're so special?"

It causes me to kind of—I question my worthiness. Usually that's the little voice inside me, although I have had a well-intentioned friend say after hearing me share something like, "Oh, I'm thinking about doing X." She said, "What qualifies you to do that?" I was like, "Oh, ouch!" I was feeling good in my head, but now that little voice is then reflected back to me by someone else.

Part of me thinks, and I'm actually just now thinking about this out loud, that somehow the niggling and little voice inside me was somehow getting projected, and she was just reflecting that back to me, probably not even knowing it, but that even though I was feeling confident and saying, "Yeah, I'm going to do this," sometimes you can tell when someone is not 100 percent there and there's something in their voice or a hesitation or the way they raise their tone at the end of their sentences. Like, "Yeah, I think I'm going to do this. Do you think I...?"

Kris: Right, yeah, yeah.

Beth: They kind of pick up on some insecurity even though we're trying to project confidence. Sometimes that's really the question that goes behind it, and even yesterday, I was giving a talk and somebody said, "So are you a psychiatrist?" It's like, "No, I'm a coach." I have to feel okay—I have to still know that it's not always about the qualification. It's not always about the degree or the letters after your name or whatever.

Kris: Exactly.

Beth: It's about how well you can share your spirit and how well you connect to people, and whether they feel like you have something you need to say, and how vulnerable you're allowing yourself to be.

Kris: Yes.

Beth: I have to be careful with that little voice when it's challenged. Or I should say, let that Inner Voice not become defensiveness. Like the, "Who do I think I am? I'm a coach." "No, I'm not [a psychiatrist]. I'm a *coach*." I can't be dismissive of myself and I can't make myself small.

Kris: Yeah! Yeah, "I'm just a...."

Beth: "I'm just a..." exactly. Our words have so much power. It's remembering, "Actually, I'm a coach. I'm a professional coach."

Kris: Yeah, who's been studying introverts and business and working in this field far more than most people—like I have a degree in psychology, but I didn't study this. You know way more about this than I do. Just because I have the letters and I find it interesting that doesn't mean I know more than someone who doesn't have the letters behind her name. We've talked about this before, but something that I came to a realization of recently was that I have used the letters LMHC [Licensed Mental Health Counselor] to justify myself, just like you were saying. Like, "Who am I?"

When I caught that, it was like, "Oh, do I want to keep them and my license because I need to justify myself or keep them because it helps me—because it's who I am? It's part of my past. It's part of what I bring to the table. It's not a justification nor does it devalue anybody else if they don't have them. That was a big "aha" for me.

Beth: Yes. We don't want to overanalyze things, but at the same time, it behooves us to question our motives about certain things, especially when it comes to areas where we're feeling insecure.

When I'm with a group of coaches and everybody is going around the table and introducing themselves and one person says, "And I'm an ACC coach or whatever." There's something about it that triggers, at least me, and I think sometimes it triggers my colleagues because it's like, "Okay, so what's your intention for sharing that?" Is it confidence or is it insecurity? Is it because you believe in credentialing in the profession, or is it because you feel like you have to justify or prove yourself in some way that you are worthy of sitting here at this table?

Kris: Right.

Beth: I think those are our little voices at work. It can either be a little voice or it can be an Inner Voice that's saying, "My truth is that I am proud of the work I've done. I believe in promoting my profession through licensing and credentialing, and I want to stand as a role model to encourage others to rise to that level." Whatever.

Kris: Yeah, yeah, you bring up a good point and that is that I think
           when we question or if we look at our motives there, because I'm
           all about energy too. The energy of communication, which we
           talked about earlier, our hesitation, our energy, or that insecurity
           gets reflected back to us. I think that when we, in this example of
           introducing ourselves as an ACC coach or something is if we're
           coming from that place of, as you just described, "I'm all about
           the profession and I feel good. I'm proud. It's not that I'm prov-
           ing, but I'm just excited about it."

Beth: Yeah.

Kris: Then I think it comes—there's something that happens in that
           that comes across positively. But if we're coming from that mo-
           tivation of, "I don't feel like I'm worthy to be here," or, "I need
           to show that I'm better than you because I'm certified and you're
           not," if it comes from that little voice, what happens is I think
           that the little voices can get triggered in other people. I think our
           little voices get triggered a lot anyway, but I think it's more likely
           that they get triggered when we speak from our little voice.

Beth: Mm-hmm. I think you're right.

Kris: Does that make sense?

Beth: Yeah, it's contagious.

Kris: It's contagious, exactly!

Beth: It's contagious. If we come from little voice, we will spread little
           voice. If we come from Inner Voice, that's what we will perpetu-
           ate, and we will embolden others to be able to trust and speak to
           their truth.

The evening after Beth and I did this interview (which was over a year
before publishing this book), we were both at the same networking event
for women. Out of the thirty people who were there, twenty-two of them
were therapists or coaches of some sort. As we took turns introducing our-

selves around the circle, I noticed an interesting phenomenon. We were supposed to have sixty seconds to share our name, what we do, or our business, and some quirky thing about ourselves. At first, it went smoothly— the first few people stayed on track and under a minute, but as soon as one or two people shared their credentials and started to say a little more about who they worked with and their specialties, the subsequent introductions got longer, more rambling and vague, and had a vibe of "justification" and wanting to stand apart from everyone else. Pretty soon, the introductions were ninety seconds, and by the end, they were nearly two minutes long. I was near the middle, and I, too, was affected by the little voice contagion, even though I was aware it was happening! I listened to myself express that I had my degree and license (only two other people in the room did as well), and I wanted to show how I was different in this sea of mediocre messaging. I was not immune. My message wasn't clear, and it was before I was clear about who I am, whom I serve, and what I stand for. It was such a perfect example and experiential confirmation of how quickly those little voices can influence and derail us, especially in a group where most people are not aware nor clear about which voices they are speaking from and the energy they are bringing to their communication.

Next time you are sharing your elevator speech, or talking about what you do with another person, notice your energy level. Notice what thoughts automatically pop into your head when you say something out loud. Are there naysayers in your mind? If so, is there something you need to do to bring yourself into integrity where what you say and what you believe is in alignment? Or is it a matter of telling those voices to be quiet because they are just scared?

Notice if you feel the urge to justify yourself or get triggered by someone else: You may just be picking up on the other person's insecurity—it's not yours at all!

Looking at the example of insecurity I just mentioned, sometimes it is yours because:

- The current situation is bringing it up and it makes sense because you're not prepared; or

- It's energy you've been carrying around with you for years and the current situation is validating the insecurity; or

- It may even be an energy or belief that you took on from your parents or other ancestors and are now expressing as if it's your own, when in reality, it's not yours at all.

Thoughts and emotions can become "stuck" energy in a person's auric or energy field. Vows and cords, while most of us can't see them with our eyes, are very real and palpable ways that energy can become fixed. They affect a person's actions and emotions through both the subconscious programming received when a vow is made and the physical and emotional feeling of being drained when cords are created between oneself and another person. If you notice patterns that do not seem to break no matter what you do, or no matter whom you're with, you have likely made some vow or you may have some energy cords that are blocking your full expression and intention for healing. Here's how to break those vows and cords.

VOW/PROMISES

A vow is a powerful soul-level promise. It is a promise that we make consciously or subconsciously because of two basic reasons. We either want to experience *more* of something because it brings us more of what we want and it is coming from a place of love and abundance. Or we create that vow because we don't want to experience something anymore. It is created with the energy of fear.

We could even have a vow that on the outside looks like a positive thing, but it's actually fueled by a negative energy or fear. Recall that there are really only two forces in the world: Love and Fear. Love connects us; it creates a connection to Source—something bigger than ourselves. And fear disintegrates things, which destroys our sense of connection to Source. Our vows, when they are created out of love and promises to ourselves and to others, or to God in the service of Love, do serve us and expand our world;

they expand our experience. However, when we make a promise or a vow from the place of fear, then we experience something that is an aberration of what we desire. It becomes a disfigured or dislocated experience. It shows up in an ugly way or keeps us farther from what we truly desire.

For example, let's say you made a decision to marry someone. During the marriage ceremony you make a vow "'til death do us part," but the reason you're making that vow is not because it's truly from a place of love and connection, or desire for this other person to be successful and for yourself to be successful, and that you're going to choose consciously to honor yourself and this person for the rest of your days together, but rather from a place of "I don't want to be alone." So the feeling or fuel behind the vow has a huge impact on how the vow will play out in your life.

When we plan to break vows, we are looking for: How did it get created? Why was it created? Was it created out of love or out of fear? I would venture to say that most vows are created out of the energy of fear with something akin to "I will never experience that again," or "I will never let myself or others experience that again," or "I vow revenge."

Look at vows of poverty—I mean *really*, making a vow of poverty to God? That is so counter to what God wants for us. It is a perfect example of negative, fearful energy and a negative feeling with negative results. But it's made with the desire for a positive outcome—to be closer to God. "I want to be closer to God; therefore, I will take a vow of poverty so I never have to deal with money so I can be closer to God." It's misdirected and coming from the place of thinking that it's more spiritual to be poor than it is to have money and to have resources available to you, which you can use to carry out God's purposes.

Vows are very powerful because they are created with a strong feeling behind them. It is the feeling of love or the feeling of fear that locks them into our energy system. It locks them into our chakras and into our experience, and they are so powerful that they can get passed on from our ancestors, through DNA or our energy bodies, and even what some call past life experiences. We can even pass them on to our own children.

Vows are statements and decisions that I would say are really made at a soul level because they are so powerful. There are times where people will make vows and not realize it—it's done subconsciously, or said in a fit of passion, and then quickly forgotten. Most people do not understand just how powerful our words are. If our thoughts and the emotions behind them create our reality (which many spiritual teachers in many different cultures and religions have shown us), speaking those thoughts with great feeling just anchors them even more.When we clear these vows and consciously choose to break them and the energy behind them, seemingly miraculous things begin to happen. I found I had unconsciously made the vow of "I'm all alone and I'm the only responsible one, I can't trust others, and so I've got to do it all on my own." This vow showed up literally everywhere in my life. I had no idea why I kept feeling overwhelmed and all alone, and why I couldn't seem to stop not only feeling this way, but creating situations in my life where I would *keep* feeling this way. When I discovered this vow through following the thread of an emotion (for me it was guilt), I was able to go back to when I originally made the vow and undo it. My life began rearranging that very day. I began making choices from a different place, and I could ask for the help I needed. My family life changed too; I felt more connected to my kids and husband and part of a greater whole, where before I only felt like a stranger in my life on the outside looking in.

I once heard David Neagle say that if we aren't getting the results we want in our lives, it's often because we're "doing the wrong things in the right direction, or the right things in the wrong direction." Often, we simply need to shift our thinking and actions a few degrees in either direction to get us on a course of success. But if you've tried everything else and still can't figure out why you're getting the same old results despite all the changes you've made, explore the possibility that you created a vow somewhere in your past that is determining the direction of your actions and decisions today.

Here is a sample script for breaking a vow. It is closely based on a vow-breaking script that a healing practitioner gave me several years back. I do not know the author's name. I've changed it somewhat based on my own personal work and work with my clients.

Breaking Vows

By Divine Decree, in the name of my God Presence, my Inner Voice, and under the law of Grace, Karma, Forgiveness, Love and Divinity, I now break all vows I have made in relationship to_____. I break this vow to/of _____ in all directions, all dimensions, all lifetimes, all space, and all time. I break it on behalf of my ancestors and on behalf of my descendents and future descendants. I break it on all levels of my awareness and consciousness and on the behalf of all parts of myself. I break it in service to the highest and best good of all, including God, and all those involved or impacted by this vow, including myself. All consequences of this vow both potentially and possibly are now fading and a new possibility is opening up to me. It is now being written in my Master Records. It is done—so it is!

There is no "right" way to do this. I encourage you to explore some rituals around using the above statement for breaking vows yourself. When I get clear what the vow is that I, or my client, have made (or what it *likely* is), then I explore it some so that I make sure I really have the energetic signature of the vow. I like to write where it's showing up, or just let my mind wander and "see" all the places where the vow has affected me, my sense of connection, happiness, relationships, finances, etc. When I feel like the energy of the vow is really present for me, I light a candle (or not!) and speak the vow-breaking script above out loud with conviction. Then I take a few minutes and think about what I would like to create instead. In other words, if I want to create a more positive vow, I get clear what that is, and I'm sure to create it from a place and energy of love and service to God and the Universe so that I'm not creating yet another reactionary vow from a fear place. If you do meridian tapping or other energy techniques, including chakra balancing, you can incorporate those techniques as you break the vows for even more energetic clearing. (It's not necessary, but is very powerful!) Do not underestimate the power of this or the cord cutting process. I have seen amazing things happen when someone (including myself) breaks a vow. Sometimes it's subtle and noticed over time—sometimes immediate and dramatic.

CUTTING THE CORDS

"All people absorb and take over, either consciously or unconsciously, the thought-habits of those with whom they associate closely."

— Napoleon Hill

Energy cords are interesting things. The majority of us can't see them, but if we are sensitive enough, we can feel them and their effects. Think about the original cord that we all had as a fetus. That cord gave us nourishment and information from our mothers. We got a tremendous amount of energy from and through those cords, and they were necessary to our survival before we left the womb. Energy cords are also ways we gain energy, or give energy to others, and while they are not physical like an umbilical cord, they are nonetheless powerful.If you are feeling drained, it is likely you have cords between you and one or more people. Honestly, if you have never done a cord clearing and you are human (which I assume you are if you're reading this!), then you have cords running between you and others. Remember, I said that we communicate energetically first and foremost, and we are just beginning to understand what that really means. Cords are one way that we communicate and get something from others—information or energy.

I have literally had the experience of "processing" or feeling another person's negative emotions. When I "cut" the cords energetically and "sent" the energy of the emotions back to that person and sealed up my own biofield (aura), the emotions I was experiencing were gone instantaneously. I've also felt extremely drained at times, but after cutting cords, I regained both energy and clarity and the feeling I was sovereign in my own body and aura. We can create cords between ourselves and our parents, kids, siblings, spouses or partners, extended family, ancestors, clients, customers, co-workers, bosses, friends, acquaintances, famous people, strangers...hmm? Did I leave anyone out? Those people too. Possibly even animals—though someone who knows more about that could tell you for sure. Feeling that "They hooked me in" would be indicative of a cording situation. So would parroting the beliefs and habits and people close to you, feeling everything they feel, even when you're not in close proximity to them and trying to get something from the person—an answer, attention, love, forgiveness—all of these are indicative of cording.

Here's the thing about cording and connection. *We are all always interconnected.* We cannot not be connected. We all come from the same Source, and we are made of the same stuff of Source. When we ground ourselves, literally and metaphorically, into the Earth and tap into, or make consciously aware our connection to Source, from above and below, then we feel how connected we are to each other. We have no need to send cords to others to try to get something from them, like connection, love, acceptance, attention, or a myriad of other things we desire and feel are lacking in ourselves.

I had an energy healer say to me once, when my son was about three years old, "Your son is pinging you" (like a dolphin would). I totally got what he was saying because I could feel my son reaching out to me psychically at times. When I was aware of it, I would send him a little acknowledgment back as if to say, "I feel you; you're not alone." I know this sounds counter to what I said above about grounding ourselves, but until our kids are older and we can teach them how to do it for themselves, we often need to give them this reassurance.

Cords can be created when we are sending energy to others or when we are trying to get energy or something from them. Either way, unless we are sending them pure love and light with no attachment, it can be a pretty invasive way to communicate.

If you are a doctor, healer, massage or physical therapist, energy healer, coach, therapist, or are in the public eye, such as a public speaker, then you will want to practice releasing the cords that get created between you and the people with whom you are working or speaking. There is more information out there about this topic, so I invite you to explore it if you find it interesting. But the cord cutting technique below will be just fine for now. By the way, sometimes we need to cut the cords between us and things, places, or ideas as well.

Cutting the cords is simple and easy, takes just moments to do (or longer if you wish to make it so), and is highly beneficial. Here is a simple version of cord cutting that has worked well for me and for my clients:

Imagine in your mind's eye the person, place, or experience (in this case a person) you wish to cut cords with. Take either your right or left arm, whichever you prefer, and make a large sweeping or chopping motion, as if you were clearing a cobweb or chopping a tree branch, in front of your body, starting just above your head and ending mid-thigh. Make several of these sweeping, cutting motions in front of your face, torso, arms, legs, and even your back (as best you can). Just set the intention for the cords to be cut, even in the places where you can't reach. As you "cut" the cords, actually say something to that effect like "I now cut all cords that are not of 100 percent pure Love and Light, and I ask Archangel Michael to assist me with his sword of Truth." You can even ask him to cut all the cords for you on your behalf!

Next, ask Archangel Michael to gather up all your own energy and bring it back into your body. Imagine all the energy that you either sent to others or that they tried to get from you, gathering together and funneling back into your body and going wherever it needs to go. Send the other person or persons' energy back to them, with blessings attached. Then ask Archangel Raphael to seal up your aura and all the places where the cords were attached to you and to fill up your body and your aura with Love and Light. *Voilà!* Done.

Another variation I learned from my colleague, Stephanie Eldringhoff, is to do a more elaborate cord cutting between yourself and another person at the level of each of the chakras. I've done this between myself and another person as well as with clients and people in their lives. Both people need not be present. We test each chakra to see whether there is a cord there, to determine where it started from, and whether it goes both ways, or in just one direction. What we are seeking to establish is a flow, which looks like a figure eight between each chakra of the parties involved. Unhealthy, or draining cords, will be a direct connection and look like a cord that is "plugged in" to the other person. As I said, it can go both ways, meaning it's a mutual cording, or in only one direction. Either way, cutting the cords and re-establishing a harmonious flow is highly beneficial.

I will say a word of not necessarily caution, but more of awareness: This is a very powerful exercise. The other person may feel you trying to pull away and send even more cords your way, so just know that you may have to go through this process more than once. Also, if you have sent cords the other person's way in order to get some need met from him or her, you may sub-consciously do so again, so be aware of that. If you deal with the needs that you are trying to get met through this person, the need to cord the person will no longer be present.If you are not familiar with chakras, muscle-test-ing, or don't feel comfortable doing this latter cord cutting exercise, then just practice the first version and do some figure eights between yourself and the people you suspect you were corded to. You can see examples of this on my website. The nice thing about the first version is it is a general cord cutting and it's not necessary to know who you're cutting cords with in order for it to be effective.

When your energy is clear, unencumbered by your own fears and blocks, and you're not taking on other people's stuff, which just weighs you down too, it's much easier to come to the fifth and final aspect of the Inner VOICE: Embodiment.

EMBODIMENT

"Your Life is your message to the world. Make it Inspiring."

— Lorrin L. Lee

It is the place where we see clarity, courage, conviction, and commitment come to life! At this point, you have aligned your vision of yourself with your greater vision or goal (**Vision**); you have owned not only the places where you have room to grow but also the places where you are a genius (**Ownership**); you are present to the influences—both internal and external—that are affecting your thoughts and emotions (**Influence**); and you are practicing faith through choice and action (**Choice**). You are **E**mbodying the Inner Voice more and more of the time. You are leading energy and thought.

The signature energy of thought leader embodiment is *enthusiasm.*

"Enthusiasm is the mother of effort, and without it nothing great was ever achieved."

— Ralph Waldo Emerson

Enthusiasm comes from a Greek word that means "God within." Much of the time when we think of someone being enthusiastic, we think of him or her being like a cheerleader or excited and bubbling over with emotion. In the true definition of the word, it's more about allowing the joy and freedom and energy of God to well up within us and to flow through us. It becomes who we are, versus something that we *do.*

This natural wellspring of energy, when I see it in my mind's eye, is like a fountain. It gives life and nourishment to us and it flows (when we both open to receive it and allow it to flow through us without trying to hold onto it). It's also like an energy vortex that creates synergy between what you want, or who you want to work with, and yourself—it's a magnetic and attractive, as well as nourishing, flow. It's acceptance, appreciation, gratitude, allowance, and joy all at once. It may be expressed by some as a "Rah Rah!" energy, but from what I've read and experienced in the Siddha Yoga tradition, it is more like an emanation, an energy that radiates and permeates everything.

In my lifetime, I've met a few people who have this kind of energy, and it is truly an amazing experience to be with them. They literally are so clear that when you are near them or hear them speak, they pluck at the strings of your soul and wake it up. They are like a clear bell that vibrates and shakes the very foundation of your heart and all the walls start to crumble just a little bit—in a very pleasant way. They resonate with Truth so much that just being in their presence awakens that Truth in you and everyone they come into contact with. For some, the awakening is like a beautiful song; for others, it is painful because their hearts are so closed off to everything that it all hurts.

Thought leaders possess an inner alignment and enthusiasm that is palpable. What dampens enthusiasm faster than anything else? Our *inner critic*. Countless times throughout writing this book, or getting ready to launch something, preparing for a talk, or even feeling inspired to reach out to a friend or my child or my husband and share from my heart, I've talked myself out of it. I've cut it off. Cut off enthusiasm because of fear of what others would think of me or the way it could be received—if at all. I've come to recognize this inner critic more quickly—to hear its subtle but derisive whispers that sound like "You're a fake, a fraud, not worthy." You're making it all up and you just think you're connected, but really you're not." This voice sucks, and it's there for a purpose.

What purpose could that possibly be? Very often, it's to keep us safe. Our inner critic has this very ass-backwards way of beating us up so we don't get hurt by others. Funny thing is, no one hurts us worse than our inner critic does, so we are stuck, some of us, in our own private dodgeball court, with no protection and balls coming at us from all directions—all thrown by none other than...part of us.

So, next time you're feeling dialed in, connected, and filled with the joy and enthusiasm of Source, and you feel inspired to create something, or share this Love and inspiration with others, then suddenly find yourself afraid, doubting it all, including your sanity—just know it's your inner critic lobbing balls at you fast and furious, trying to keep you in your small self, trying to keep you safe.

You can work with this inner critic in a couple of different ways. One way to shut the inner critic down is by catching the balls and having a conversation with this inner critic. Find out what she is scared of. Find out what she is protecting you, or others, from. If there is something there that is valid, and you need to check yourself, then do so. If not, then thank your inner critic for trying to protect you and take action anyway.

Another way, and this can really take some help because the inner critic can be sneaky, is to bypass the inner critic and the other little voices altogether and go directly to the Inner Voice.One way to do this is by asking, "What's right about this?" or "What's right about me?" The inner critic hates that question because it's outside her domain. She and the other little voices can't answer that question because that's not how they process the world, so the Inner Voice steps in and takes over.

Marty, whom we met earlier, describes another way to deal with the inner critic, and I especially love this way because it's engaging the creative process, which is really the opposite energy of the critic:

Marty: The inner [critic], the "not good enough, never going to make it," voice can pop up, as I always said. My sister used to rent—used a slot in the top—she had a sheet in my head. She would be there talking to me and telling me that I'm not going to make it. I'm not a writer and all those things that sisters can do. Not really; I think in her heart she was thinking she was going to protect me from being disappointed by my not having people buy my book or something, so she would tell me things like that. That was her way of meaning to do well and then not being very supportive in that area.

What I found to do to quiet those voices is to ask them to leave, and then to keep them because nature, of course, is a vacuum. If I don't fill that space with something, they'll come back in. What I've found to do is to do something creative in that moment.

When a voice comes in, what I do is I say, "Thank you, but you can leave now." Then I say, "What, in this moment, can I do that's creative?" By taking a physical action, filling myself up with myself and my creativity and honoring and valuing my talents, my abilities, and gifts, I'm filling me with me. Then the voice is silent because now I'm busy filling myself up with something that I love to do, and I'd say, "Well, I think I'll go downstairs and write another piece of my book." Or, "I know. I have that fun program I wanted to work on and develop for my client."

Then I would go and I would do that.

When I can be consistent with that, there are no voices. They used to be every—like all the time. Now it's only occasional. It doesn't take long. It took me about a week when it first happened so that I could consistently whenever I would hear it—sometimes I'd forget and she's talking for a while. Then I'd go, "Oh, yeah, there it is. That's what that noise is." But once I remembered, I'd wake up. Then I can say, "What can I do creative in this moment?"

It can be go for a walk. It could be read a book. It could be put some pictures in the photo album, just anything to fill me up with me. That's how I can strengthen my belief in myself and my confidence.

Sometimes, the process is not as easy as Marty describes it; believe me, I get it. As I'm writing this section, my inner critic is having a fit! It can be helpful to get some support, especially with someone who understands how to work with parts and the inner critic in a powerful and gentle way. Powerful questions, energy therapy techniques, NLP, hypnosis, all can be beneficial, as can a great workout or hike in nature. Sometimes I use a combination of all of them!

Ultimately, enthusiasm is why it's important to speak our truth, to speak freely, to share our genius with the world. It's why you and I, and all of us, came here. When we heed our calling and authentically share it with others, we give voice to something much bigger than any of us. It is Divine. We are Divine. Finding our voice becomes something more than a way to increase our sales or be a better leader, manager, or business woman. Finding our voice becomes more than speaking out against atrocities and expressing pent-up anger and other negative emotions. It becomes a way of relating to others, parenting our children, transforming the world, and leading the edge of creation with the energy of love and expansion. It's literally experiencing "God-within" and letting that be our primary expression.

Choosing to embody this high vibrational energy changes you. It transforms your physical, mental, emotional, and even your spiritual being. It's not about "fixing" anything. There's nothing to fix, remember? It's about choosing to step into and owning the energy state and level of consciousness you want to experience over and over and over again that is more natural to you than the blockages and fear until through force of habit and "hypnotic rhythm," it becomes who you're being all the time, without effort. You live in the flow, consistently.

MARY KAY

In her autobiography, *Mary Kay: The Success Story of America's Most Dynamic Businesswoman*, Mary Kay Ash devoted an entire chapter to enthusiasm. She talked about how some people just had it, and how it carried her and many of the women on her sales force through what most would call impossible circumstances. Another word that speaks to the enthusiasm as Mary Kay described it is *zest*. Isn't that a fun word? Feels good to say too!

When I searched for more about "zest" I found the following definition at Wikipedia: "In Positive Psychology, **zest** is one of the 24 strengths possessed by humanity. As a component of the virtue of courage, zest is defined as living life with a sense of excitement, anticipation, and energy. Approaching life as an adventure; such that one has "motivation in challenging situations or tasks." Zest is essentially a concept of courage and involves acquiring the motivation to complete challenging situations and tasks. Those who have zest exude excitement and energy while approaching tasks in life. Hence, the concept of zest involves performing tasks wholeheartedly, whilst also being adventurous, vivacious, and energetic."

How can you tap into your inner zest in seemingly impossible circumstances? What would a sense of adventure look like in your relationships, parenting, and day-to-day business?Look for people in your world, and the world at large, who exude zest, and watch how they move, what they say, what they do. If you can, you may even ask them how they think and what they do to tap into that energy on a daily basis. Then figure out how you can do the same for yourself. Connect with your why. Tap into your vision, and into something bigger than yourself. Take action from this place.

And something that I have to remind myself of often: If it isn't fun and doesn't light you up and make your heart sing, don't do it. Without zest, you're not your best.

ENTHUSIASM FEEDS ENROLLMENT

Enrolling others in your vision is what helps it to grow. Enrolling is a conversation about what's possible, not about what's wrong, or what happened in the past, or what could happen wrong in the future. It's literally a conversation from one Inner Voice to another about passion, possibility, and expansion.

When we want to do something that is totally out there and we need some help or support to do so, we need to have an enrollment conversation—especially with our spouse. I've tried it both ways, and the "asking permission conversation" versus the "enrolling in possibility conversation" are radically different, and get different results.Most women—and I'll speak to women here because men do it too, but up until more recently, men have traditionally been the breadwinners so the wife has been dependent on her husband financially—if they have an idea to start a business or make an investment in their business will go to their husbands in the "Can I have some money for...?" space. Yuck. I'm sure if you've done it, you know how disempowering it is for both of you. (By the way, if your spouse gets off on you having to ask, and it feels really empowering for him to have you in this position, you may want to look at that. How does it feel? And no, it's not normal or healthy.)

Instead of coming from this place of lack, because while you may not have the money part yet, you have an idea, and you have energy, and you have some inkling of belief that can grow and grow, you are not coming to the table empty-handed. You are coming with a vision, and many people would pay good money to have a vision that they can hang their dreams on.Approach your spouse with energy based in enthusiasm, determination, and belief. What if you don't have that kind of energy? Get connected to your Inner Voice. If this is really what you are feeling called to do, you will know it in your bones. If you have had negative conversations with your spouse in the past and they haven't gone well, just know this: When you enroll your spouse in your vision, and you share how you'd like him to be a contribution to it, or how he is part of it in your mind (not telling him he will have jobs to do, without asking whether he really wants them, but instead showing that you have taken him and his contribution into careful consideration), then you can have an enrolling conversation.Your spouse may not believe you. He may not be supportive of you. He may say "No." No matter what, it is important that you did not make yourself small or belittle your vision just because he can't see it with you. Our spouse is often our hardest sale, as well as our staunchest supporter. If you meet with rejection or obstacles at home, by all means find support elsewhere. Hire a coach, or find some friends who believe in you. You deserve it and the world deserves to have you share your enthusiasm as well!

Enrollment is not about manipulation. It is about first getting clear what you need and are asking for. It's about knowing when is the best time to have this conversation, and not try to squeeze in a half-assed conversation between soccer and gymnastics practice and trading kids at drop off times!

It's not about hiding certain details or hiding yourself and your dreams and desires. And it is not the time to play small. I have had many conversations with my husband over the last twelve-plus years. Some were enrolling; many of them were not. The enrolling ones went well. The other kinds of conversation tended to flop. Clarity about the whole picture is helpful, but not essential. Why? Because you may not have all the details; you just have a clear knowing that this is what you are meant to do. Then all it takes is courage and conviction, both of which come from the Inner Voice.

If you have come to a place of clarity either through accessing your inner authority style based on your Human Design, or because you just "know" this is your next step, great! You are ready to have that enrolling conversation. But what if you're not so sure? What if you're going back and forth and doing the waffling dance? It's likely that you are trying to use your mind to make the decision, and recall that the mind is lousy at that! What the mind is good for, however, is asking yourself and others clarifying questions.

QUESTIONS TO FREE YOUR INNER VOICE

Really get clear on your intentions and the energy of the decision you are making. Is it coming from fear or from love? Love feels lighter; fear feels heavier. Although, I know there are times when we can make a decision from fear because it feels lighter to back off from our dreams; our ego often freaks out if it knows it's going to be challenged. So spend a little time getting clear on the following:

•   Am I saying yes to this because I want to go toward it (love)?

•   Or yes because it takes me away from something I'm afraid of (fear, and often fear of losing something)?

Also ask yourself:

•   Am I saying no because I'm afraid of what I'll lose or sacrifice (fear)?

•   Or no because it's not the right thing for me to do (love)?

List all the reasons to say "Yes" or "No" in each of those questions relative to the decision you're making, and whichever one has the most pull for you will be your answer. If it's a "Yes," trust it, and go enroll someone in the vision from that place.

Remember, the voices are contagious. Are you enrolling people from enthusiastic, God-embodied energy, or from the lower vibrational little voices? One brings prosperity, the other suffering. It is a choice. Your choice.

SECTION 3

*Bringing It All Together:
The Aligndset™ Map*

CHAPTER TEN

Design Your Vision

Creating your own physical Aligndset™ Map is a way to get clear on your vision and set yourself up to create both an internal and external environment that is in alignment with that vision and any specific goals or intentions related to it.

As you are designing your map, your focus should be on the way you desire to FEEL as you are taking action to fulfill the goal or live your intentions. If you can't find a specific image or wording that is exactly what you desire, pick an image that is meaningful for you and evokes the feeling you wish to embody.

Since we have been discussing how to live in alignment with your Inner Voice, I invite you to begin with an Inner Voice Aligndset™ Map.[17] You'll want to choose for your map any images that inspire or remind you how it feels when you listen, speak, and create from your Inner Voice in each of the five key elements and Inner VOICE aspects. What's cool about creating this kind of map is that it will help you make decisions more clearly because, as you look at the images and the feelings that help you feel in alignment with your Inner Voice, you'll be better able to discern choices that come up in your day-to-day life, both personally or profes-

---

17 You can see a picture of my Inner Voice Aligndset™ Map on my website.

sionally, because you'll be reminded of what those elements and aspects look and feel like for you.

After you have made your Inner Voice Map, you can also choose to create a map based on your larger vision or purpose and allow it to unfold as you bring yourself into alignment with that larger vision (by adding images and words to it organically). Alternatively, you can choose to do a separate map for each specific goal that you wish to BE, DO, HAVE, or EXPERIENCE with all the Five Key Elements depicted. You'll want large pieces of poster-board on which to create each of your maps.

Let's say you choose to map out a goal to create your ideal business. In the center of the large circle, you would place an image or images that inspire you and that remind you in some way of what you are creating. They can be literal or figurative. Either way, they remind you of the vision or some image you have in your mind of how your business looks and *feels* and maybe even some components of it that are unique to what you are creating. Maybe it's a specific location or pictures of people. Maybe it's your product or your book that you want to share with the world. Maybe it's pictures of lots of people. Use words if there are no photos or diagrams that really fit for what you're creating because they haven't been formed yet. In either case, you'll especially want to *focus on the feeling the images and words evoke* and the meaning they have for you personally. (This map only has to make sense to you and no one else!)

In the five circles that surround the larger circle, you will place images that correspond to each of the following key elements of Aligndset™: body, mind, emotions, spirit, energy.

Instead of trying to fit the images into a little circle, which is frustrating, just put the images in the general area of the map where the smaller circles are located. Use the whole page if you wish, or leave lots of space. Again, it's yours and there is no "right" way—only what speaks to you.

QUESTIONS TO FREE YOUR INNER VOICE

Here are some thoughts and questions to guide your choices of images and words:

- How will your body look and feel *when you are living and embodying this vision?*

- What kinds of activities will you be doing and what foods will you be consuming that are in alignment with your vision?

- What will your environment look like when your vision is manifested?

- Where will you be living, working, playing?

- Who will be there?

- What kinds of things will you be doing with others?

- What thoughts and beliefs will you choose to hold that are in alignment with your vision? What are words that inspire you and the make you think positively?

- Who is someone who has the clarity, courage, conviction and/or commitment you desire to have? Put images of that person in any part of the circle that makes sense to you. You can draw on his or her strength and wisdom.

- Emotionally, how will you feel and show up in the world when you are living your big vision?

- Spiritually, what inspires you to stay connected to this vision?

- Energetically, what will you have in place or how will your energy feel when you are living your vision? Place these images in their respective circles.

- How will the Five Key Elements feed and influence one another? Play with the placement so that you can see and feel the flow between each element.

Bring your circle to life!

Hang it on your wall and focus upon it daily. Add images as you see fit, and take away ones that aren't quite "it" as you grow into your vision.

Here is an alternative way to do your Aligndset™ Map. I call it a *Blessing and Releasing Map*. The inside of the circle closest to your vision reflects your internal world, how you see yourself relative to your goal/vision, and the things you wish to change or feel need to change in order to be in alignment with your goal or vision. The outside of the circle pertains to the external world. You're going to build a map that represents all the things you would like to release or change in yourself and your environment. These may simply be images of things that are representative of something you wish to release in your life, like a relationship, or a way of being that no longer resonates for you.

For instance, let's say your goal is to lose weight. In the body circle, you'll place images of people, food, activities, etc., that either make you feel bad about yourself, or that block you from choosing healthier, more optimal foods and activities for your physical health. If there are people or things in your external environment that are blocking you from reaching your goal, place those images outside the larger circle. You may put images of overweight or unhealthy people, images of junk food, or the kinds of food that you crave and want to stop indulging in. You may want to put images of a TV if that's what you do every night with a pint of Ben & Jerry's™. In the mind circle, you may put words or other images that remind you of the tapes you hear in your head: "I'm so fat" or whatever it is you chronically and habitually think regarding yourself and your weight. Perhaps you feel others are making fun of you or you have people in your life who say unsupportive or cruel things to you regarding your weight; place words or images here that remind you of these people. Emotionally, put images that remind you or evoke the feelings you experience around your current weight. Spiritually, if you are feeling disconnected or ashamed (which is the furthest feeling from God or Spirit), put images and words here that remind you of your current state. Finally, how are you feeling energy-wise? Low, heavy, dark? Put some images here that reflect how you currently feel energetically.

Okay, here are some considerations when building this Blessing & Releasing Map:

- You may want to make the map of what you want to experience first. Especially if the topic, like weight loss, is very emotionally charged for you. It will help you to regain your focus quickly after you release the negative map.

- If you are very depressed or anxious and experiencing a lot of emotional or mental upset, I recommend you create this map with a trusted therapist or counselor.

- Make this map rather quickly. You need not spend a lot of time analyzing your pictures, or stewing in the feelings that the images and words bring up. Make this one based on your initial reaction to the images and words. If they have ANY charge at all for you, even if you're not sure what it is, put them on your map. Don't even worry about where you put them (i.e., does this fit in Body or Emotions?). Allow your intuition to place the images where they fit best.

- If you know how to do EFT (Emotional Freedom Technique) or other mind-body releasing, you may wish to do that as you gaze at the map. While it's not necessary, it can deepen the release and allow even more freedom and ease[18]. What's most important is to allow yourself really to acknowledge and forgive yourself for how you got to this place. Recognize that perhaps before this moment you hadn't fully owned your responsibility for your weight or any health issues related to it. Forgive yourself as you take ownership! Stay as present as you can to the feelings and images this map evokes. This process is not for the faint of heart! You may need a friend, coach, or trusted confidant to walk through the process with you. The key here is to get really present to the fact of where you are currently and that you have the power to change it through choosing a new Aligndset™, one that is aligned with how you want to look and feel. Bless every image and word on the map and then burn the sucker.

---

18 For more information on EFT or to find an EFT practitioner to help you, visit www.EFTUniverse.com.

- Intentionally feel the energy and "weight" of the whole thing (no pun intended), and burn it in a safe place. Break any vows you made to others consciously or subconsciously around your weight, cut any cords to the images or people you put on this map, let go of the beliefs and feelings that hold this weight in place. Make a conscious decision to move in the direction of your positive Aligndset™ Map. Again, it can be helpful to have the positive one already created so you can immediately, in the vacuum created by burning the other map, begin feeding your subconscious mind with new images and words that help you move in the direction you wish to go.

QUESTIONS TO FREE YOUR INNER VOICE

These questions are in regard to the vision you just created with your Aligndset™ Vision Map.

- Did you create an Aligndset™ Vision Map based on what you *truly* desire or what you think is likely, reasonable, or probable, or *safe*?

- What are all the perfectly reasonable reasons why you cannot live your big vision, let alone see it? List them. Don't hold back.

- Who or what is in your way? (Kids? Partner? Money? Time? Parents? Friends? Resources? Education?) *Are they really or is that part of the story you tell yourself?*

- Whose voice do you hear in your head when you begin to play with how you want to live your life? What does this voice say?

- What scares you the most about who you'd have to BE to have your life go the way you want it to go?

- What do you fear you'd have to give up in order to live your vision?

- What are you telling yourself will happen if you give it up? *Is that really true?*

- What might be possible if you gave it up? (i.e., what are the possible benefits of giving it up?)

• Complete the following statement: I'll know I'm living my purpose when I am _____ and I feel _____ and I'm doing ___ _____.

Share your Aligndset™ Map with a trusted friend, colleague, partner, or coach. This person is someone who is your champion, who has your back, who will hold you accountable to what you have put on your map—especially if there are things you know you need to change in order to realize your vision fully.

If you are part of an Inner Voice Circle, you may wish to share your maps with one another and ask another member to help you be accountable to some or all of the images on the map, especially the ones that could be most challenging for you to come into alignment with.

CHAPTER ELEVEN

Receiving It All So You Can Consciously Choose

Like you, your Aligndset™ Map is a living, breathing organism. I see it like a cell that breathes in oxygen and nutrients and releases carbon dioxide and other waste. Like us, it cycles through this inhalation and exhalation every day. The more we gaze and breathe in our map and the images on it, and breathe out any tension, worry, or dis-belief, the faster and more magical our results will be.

The little circles around the Map are the receptor sites between our internal and external environments. Like a big cell, with a nucleus that is centered in awareness of who we are at our core, our Inner Voice is aware of all our facets, and the receptor sites are the places where we take in and push out information between our internal and external environments. We are influenced by our outer environment, and our outer environment is influenced by us.

Looking at each small circle, you can see that it is halfway inside the larger circle and halfway outside of the circle. The half that's inside the circle is what you believe or allow yourself to see about yourself. These are the things you've deemed "okay" to own or acknowledge about yourself and others. The half that is outside the circle is what you have pushed away or disowned about yourself and others. Ultimately, we are aiming for everything to be incorporated into the larger circle, with no boundaries between any of the circles, or between the smaller elemental circles and the larger circle. In other words, the goal is to bring that which you have disowned into the larger circle, and allow it to be there with its polar opposite so you have the ability to choose consciously how you want to feel or act in any given situation.

A fully integrated Map looks like little circles with no dividing line or a large circle with all the circles overlapping inside and all the lines dotted to show the unimpeded flow of energy and lack of boundaries that denote oneness. We bring the "little circle" (little voices) into the big circle (which encompasses everything; i.e., the Inner Voice).

Those little voices, like all polarities in this dualistic world, exist on the flip-side of our Inner Voice, and they give us valuable information about our genius and the way we serve our clients, customers, and even our loved ones. We can no more get rid of the little voices than get rid of our DNA; they are a part of being human. They are like small children who need to be heard, and if we don't hear them, they will throw tantrums. But there are specific ways to allow them to speak and share their own wisdom with us, and, sometimes, we have to focus more on the Inner Voice and have it grow so it can embrace the little voices, like a loving parent holding a child who is upset.

Debbie Whitlock shares her experience of how she has learned to let her Inner Voice become like an understanding parent to the little voices:

Debbie: …There's some days that little Debbie Downer shows up. This has been part of my work with [my coach]. Instead of wanting to slap duct tape on her mouth, tie her up, and throw her in the trunk of my car and just leave her there, I just say, "Okay, you know what, just come on in. Come on in. Obviously you have something that you want to share, so come on in with it."

When I even listen to that little "eenie-ni-ni-ni-ni" voice, it sometimes becomes a reminder of how far I've come. I think sometimes that's why she shows up—just to affirm that I've made and continue to make huge progress. So instead of fighting her and trying to shut her up, I just invite her in. Come to the party.

You know when you get invited somewhere and you don't really want to go, you're kind of in a crappy mood, and you don't want your crappiness to spread all over everyone else, but you go anyhow and you think, "Oh, I just don't even want to be here, but I'm going to go because I feel compelled," or obligated or whatever my word is that makes me want to be there. Then when you get there, you find yourself kind of sucked into the energy in a good way. You find yourself pulled into the energy of that group and all of a sudden frowny, crappy, grumpy you is now happy having a good time you.

It's sort of the same thing that happens when that little negative voice comes in and we invite her in instead of trying to keep her out. It doesn't take long before she kind of shifts. She served a purpose for a long time. She was my gift. She was my gift that helped me grow and become the person that I am, and I don't ever want to get rid of her. And, oh by the way, she still does add some value, but she's not as loud as she used to be.

Kris: Absolutely. She really gave you your genius, how you are doing what you're supposed to be doing. Part of it is that intersection between the Inner Voice and those little voices because the little voices have even their genius; you have so many experiences and so much wisdom gained from the businesses and the experiences that you had coming from ego. You just never would have gotten all of that. Some of that wisdom you just kind of had to play that game for a while so you could see what it's like both ways.

Debbie: Exactly.

Kris: That really formed who you are and how you can help people and how you can be in the world of finances and all of that, straddling both. If you hadn't had that experience you wouldn't be able to do it the way that you uniquely do it.

Debbie: That's right.

Kris: I love that. Really it is about inviting them to the party and saying, "Look, you can engage. But if you're going to engage, we're going to positive town here. You're welcome; you're always welcome." That's really true because they are. They're trying to protect us or help us get something, and now we need to retrain them that there's a new way to get love, a new way to get security, self-esteem, all of that.

Debbie: Yep. Help me look out for—be my watcher. Be the part of me that looks to see if there's a pitfall ahead. Then let's run it through the filter. Let's run it through the filter. No, not valid. No, not real. Oh yep, that's a real one. Thank you. Thank you. Okay, good. Got it. Well done. Hi-five, see you next week. That's sort of it. They get to be scout. And I love, love, love that they get to be scout with me now instead of [keeping me from doing things I could have been doing sooner]. It was just the power that I gave it. When you don't let that much power go to that side of you, everything in your world changes.

We need all the voices within us; they all have a job and purpose. That said, some bring success and freedom, while others keep us small and constricted. Neither is right, neither is wrong. It has to do with what your intentions and expectations of life and success are and what you will allow yourself to receive and perceive about the world and your place in it. As the discussion with Debbie shows above, when she was able to allow her "little voice" of "Debbie Downer" in and actually have a voice, that's when she was really able to get her power back as well as get clear on why she's great at what she does. There's no "throwing the voices in the trunk," and because of that, she has more freedom, control, and peace in her life, as well as access to all parts of herself. *That which causes you pain is part of your little voice story. That which inspires you is your Inner Voice calling. Your genius is the intersection of the two.* It's your unique way of seeing the world, and the way you speak to and serve your ideal clients, which include both people in business and your family members, friends, and anyone you have a meaningful relationship with. In other words, the adversity you have experienced in your life, and the resulting little voices, are intricately enmeshed and inform your genius and your purpose. However, there is a caveat: They inform only if you will let go of the emotional attachment to the feelings of loss, failure, unforgiveness of yourself and others, and the judgment of self and others that those adversities brought upon you. As you welcome those adversities and feel gratitude and appreciation for them, you become whole. You have ultimate freedom because there is nothing to hide and nothing to fear "being found out about." As a bonus, when you come to this place within, you will know your purpose and the exact manner in which to speak to, and lead others out of, the hell in which you once found yourself.

THE TROUBLE WITH GRATITUDE

"If you concentrate on finding whatever is good in every situation, you will discover that your life will suddenly be filled with gratitude, a feeling that nurtures the soul."

— Rabbi Harold Kushner

Ever feel like it's really tough to feel gratitude for *all* areas of your life? Sure, there are those places where it's really easy to feel grateful and sometimes they seem kind of shallow. (No judgment there, huh?) For me, it's really easy to feel grateful for our warm bed in the morning. We have these beautiful soft sheets and comforters; they are so yummy and cozy, and in the morning, it's hard for me to get out of bed. I have no problem feeling grateful for those babies! Then there are the times when my kids are bickering, or my husband is working a lot and we both feel like there's not enough time...

well, period, and I'm feeling stretched in my business and experiencing writer's block—and it's really hard to feel gratitude for *any* of that. So, I end up writing something in my gratitude journal that I *should* feel grateful for, but don't really feel because I have too much of a negative charge around it, OR I just skip writing anything at all because gratitude is the furthest thing from my mind and heart. Ever feel like that? Am I the only one? It doesn't really get the gratitude flowing—that's for sure.

There are times, too, when I write what I feel grateful for and that feels good—but then I also feel sad because there are so many things I'd *like to feel grateful for* and I just don't. I judge myself for that—often harshly. Bet you never do that, huh?Recently, I began doing something different in my journal, based on a suggestion by Dr. Dain Heer, from Access Consciousness. He suggests writing three things you're grateful for (or more, but at least three) and then three things "*that you're not currently grateful for, but if you would or could somehow become grateful for would allow you to have gratitude for your life and living right now.*" During the dark rainy days in Seattle, it was easier to come up with the latter three than the first three, but by the end of the exercise, I was feeling gratitude for all of it—and much more.

After writing those things I'd like to feel grateful for, but currently don't, I ask myself some questions, "tools" from Access Consciousness, like: *What else is possible? How does it get any better than this? What would it take to change this?* and *What's right about this I'm not getting?* Whatever energy comes up around all of that I explore and journal about, and I use various energy techniques to clear the "charge" or heavy energy that those questions stir up.

How powerful is this process? A recurring block, literally the biggest block I kept coming up against in my business and life, was something I added to the "would like to be grateful for, but not currently there yet" list, and when I really sat with it, and explored the energy around it, I found a key link in my purpose, in my reason for doing what I do. I found a diamond in all that dark coal! Before that, I kept judging the coal, and myself, and I kept getting the same results—over and over again. I'll tell you that thirty-minute exploration of what I couldn't allow myself to feel grateful for, because I was so busy judging myself for it, was true gold.

The trouble with gratitude is that sometimes you have to explore what you're not grateful for in order to get the real gems and the deep gratitude that comes from the heart. Most of us are really uncomfortable with this darker exploration! I have several clients who want to skip right to the "feeling good" part and don't want to acknowledge any dark, mean, judgmental thoughts they are thinking because the process is so dark, mean, and nasty! But what I tell them is, "What you resist, persists," so go ahead and try to ignore it, but it'll just bite you in the ass again 'cause it's wanting your attention.

And not only that—*many of those thoughts and judgments you're experiencing are likely not even yours*—so that's a double whammy! You're thinking other people's thoughts and processing their emotions. I'm telling you, it's really hard to feel grateful when you're all bunged up with other people's baggage.

When we judge ourselves for having these thoughts and feelings, it only locks them in even more. Think about it: If you're not resisting anything through the habit of judging it, is there anything really there to resist? Play with that for a while.

Gratitude and appreciation for all the voices is the final piece of the puzzle. As you open to receive all of it through gratitude, then that which you have been seeking will be able to reach you. You open to receive prosperity through the practice of gratitude and acceptance.

Begin to notice your judgments; your thinking that says, "This is okay; that isn't." Notice where each judgment comes from and whether it's even yours. Often it's what society tells us to think, or some decision we made in the past, or that we learned from our family or teachers, and we decided that was the way it is, so there. This unwillingness to explore your judgments or let them go greatly limits what you can allow into your life. In all the work that I've done with clients, and personally, I have observed and found that there is always a gift in even the most horrific events, and when we begin to see with our spiritual eyes, instead of our ego-based human ones, the gift is revealed every time.

God judges nothing, accepts all, and the eyes of Spirit appreciate it all as well.

RADICAL ACCEPTANCE AND APPRECIATION

"Unless I accept my faults, I will most certainly doubt my virtues."

— Hugh Prather

One year for Christmas, I bought a bunch of blank journals for family and friends, and on the first page, I wrote ten things I appreciated about the person receiving the journal. I think I got the bigger gift that year because it was really hard to write ten things I appreciated about several of the people I had chosen. Others were easy!

But it was the ones who were a challenge that really opened my heart and had me blowing up the walls that keep my distance from them. I had to look for the jewels, and honestly, I found them every time. I was very careful not just to write something that I didn't really appreciate, but that others told me they appreciated about this person. I really sat with it, and in the process, I found that many of the things that I saw as faults were actually their strengths, and that realization pulled me out of my limited viewpoint of the person and into seeing him or her through the eyes of Spirit.

Accepting a person for who he is and appreciating him for it versus just being grateful for something he did, or something he did that had a positive effect in my life, was the key to it all. It was a celebration of the person and not a list of how I'm indebted to him. This practice allowed me to own some of those things about myself that I had either judged as not okay, or on the opposite end of the spectrum, didn't allow myself to celebrate because I felt it would be self-centered or egotistical to acknowledge these positive aspects of myself.

As a practice, make a list of all the things you have judged about yourself or others as not okay, or on the flip side, as desirable but unattainable or un-comfortable. Think of people you envy—what do they embody that you'd like to be more of? And the people who push your buttons...what is it that bugs you? Put all of those things on your list.

Make it a practice to say, "I am that" to all of the things on your list and see what happens. When you own it all, you have the power to choose.

And the power to choose is the power that creates worlds and the rest of your life as you want it to be.

Right here.

Right now.

CHAPTER TWELVE

A Life Well Spoken

"Speak a new language so that the world will be a new world."

— Rumi

In the yogic tradition, *OM* is the primordial sound from which all else evolves and manifests. It is a high vibrational, divine word and sound. In the Hindu tradition and ancient Sanskrit language, "The vibration of 'OM' symbolizes the manifestation of God in form ('sāguna brahman'). 'OM' is the reflection of the absolute reality, it is said to be 'Adi Anadi,' without beginning or end and embracing all that exists. The mantra 'OM' is the name of God, the vibration of the Supreme."[19]

What is your primordial sound, your beginning word? What is your OM? How often do you share it with others? How often do you muffle it with fear?

What do you really want? What did you come here to say that perhaps you shoved down—way down—because you were never validated or heard as a young child? What do your heart and your soul yearn for? Can you hear through the din of your little voices? You already know what

---

19 From Wikipedia: http://en.wikipedia.org/wiki/Om

you came here to do. Some part of you knows. Are you doing it? Are you *being* it? If not, when would be a good time to start?

If you are listening to and speaking from your Inner Voice, you are creating your world from the highest vibration. You are living and creating a life well spoken. You are chanting your OM.

What does a person experience when they are living a well spoken life? What three factors are necessary to cultivate?

CLARITY

A life well spoken is a life of *Clarity*. Clarity is the knowledge of who you really are. It's awareness of what you came here to do in this lifetime. It's knowing how you are designed as a human being to express God in your own unique way and living in alignment with that. It's being clear about your strengths, your genius, your gifts, and your relationship with God. It's being clear that you are more than the sum of your mistakes.

Clarity knows how to make decisions in alignment with your inner authority and knows what people, projects, and experiences to put your life-force energy into—and which to leave well enough alone. Clarity is the ability to discern from which voice you're speaking: The little voices of fear or your Inner Voice. Clarity knows your boundaries and limits, when to honor them as they are, and when to push them in order to grow.

Clarity knows it's not about perfection and that tomorrow is another day for gaining even more clarity, so it doesn't judge or compare oneself to others. It knows whose shit is whose and doesn't take on anyone else's baggage just to make others feel okay or keep the peace, or feel safe, loved, or worthy of being alive. Clarity is knowing what you believe, what your point of view is, and your personal truth, and when people don't agree with it, or even like it, clarity knows it's about them, not you.

COURAGE

A life well spoken is a *Courageous* life. A life that is fully present in the moment, because that is where courage happens, in the present moment. Fighting fear with willpower or just blindly taking action without clarity or courage behind it is what gets people in trouble, or causes more trouble. That is living life in the past or the future and is not allowing oneself to answer the call of what is being asked of her soul right here, right now. Courage literally means "from or of the heart," and it is at its essence about being vulnerable and receptive while in the energy field of the heart. It's being courageous enough to be in your body and to let down your defenses and let go of shame so you can be present with another person. Courage is sharing who you really are without holding back or making yourself small, invisible, or unheard. Courage is following your bliss, dreams, and what you are meant to do, no matter what others think you should do, or want you to do. Courage, however, is NOT following your bliss because you are under the influence of negative people or substances. It is not running away from responsibility or dropping the ball, just because you didn't feel like following through, or were scared.

Courage is totally surrendering your ego to God and letting go of ego when with another person. When we act and speak with courage, we create connection. Yes, maybe some people won't like what we say or do, but we always connect with our truth, our Soul, and with God through courageous acts. And I've found that ultimately we connect with those people who resonate with this truth as well, even as others are falling away. We are never alone and courage knows this. It is through acting with courage that we come to know this as well.

CONVICTION

A life well spoken is one that is simple, profound, and streamlined with *Conviction*. It is living by your inner authority. It is living in such resonance and harmony with Truth (one's own truth and Universal Truth) that your vibration is palpable when people are with you. You are so clear, you are vibrating with your primordial sound and people recognize this; it's appealing to them and it transforms everyone who hears it.

You are an instrument that is whole and perfectly designed for your purpose on Earth. Clarity is recognizing what kind of instrument you are, courage is choosing to be that instrument, and conviction is playing it as if no one else is listening or judging you. If you are a trumpet, you stop trying to be a trombone. If you are a tuba, you stop trying to be a piccolo. If you are a violin, you stop trying to be an electric guitar and you just *be* your instrument, making the music, the sound, the vibration, that you came here to make. No excuses. No apologies. No fear. No shame.

With conviction, you know without any doubt that you came here to make your sound. And you came here to be a part of this huge symphony and every single instrument has a place whether they are one cymbal crash and they're done, or one pluck on the string and they're no more, or whether they are the piano that is the foundation for the whole movement. Your instrument may be a little scarred, a little (or a lot) out of tune, but it can always be polished and tuned anytime, anywhere—but you have to choose to do this. When your instrument is tuned perfectly and played, it sounds "right" to people. It's harmonious and contributes to the whole symphony. There is no "convincing or justification" in conviction. It is simply living and vibrating to the tune of Universal Truth, your truth—your OM.

A life well spoken is experienced through caring for your instrument, loving your instrument, not judging your instrument, blessing your instrument, owning the brilliance of your instrument and tuning it to the highest vibration of God. Clarity about what your instrument is can be found in your Human Design. Courage to live true to your design can be found through coaching and accountability. Conviction comes when you are so in resonance and harmony with the instrument, the channel that you are designed to be, that you create a sound in the world like no other. This sound very often comes through your throat, which is the center of manifestation in Human Design. Often we think of our voice as the sound that comes out of our mouth, but "voice" is also your energy, body, and movement in space, emotional vibration, thought frequency, and spiritual connection. The Aligndset™ Map is a tool for tuning your instrument, your VOICE.

Conviction is a practice: When someone is out of key or out of resonance, you play your highest vibration even more instead of losing your tune and lowering your vibration to meet theirs. This practice is how you get even more clear, more courageous, and convicted. Let go of social niceties, fear, and constructs that were created by human beings and that are not designed to help you live in resonance with God. Let go of how your past defined you, and allow yourself to see and step into a greater possibility. Trusting in this process and the guidance you receive along the way is how conviction grows. My interview with Tabitha was perhaps the most revealing as far as clarity, courage, and conviction are concerned and letting go of her past so she could see her future:

Kris: …Where in your life or your business did you either spend a lot of time listening to the little voices and you got stuck and/ or where you listened to your Inner Voice? It might be that you didn't listen to it for a long time, and you had struggle, struggle, struggle, and then suddenly, you went, "Oh, my gosh. This is really what I need to be doing. This is what I'm called to do."

Tabitha: Well, that's exactly very much what I've actually gone through, which is why I wanted to share my story with you. I set out on this path, this journey, of becoming a heart-centered entrepreneur, going on three years in November. I can always remember the date because that was my first blog post that I did.

It has been this journey of listening to those little voices inside, because I also find when you're listening to those little voices inside, you're more prepared to take on others' opinions, even if they're an expert, because that's what you should be doing, because they know better than you.

Kris: Right.

Tabitha: That's what I'm seeing with this whole shift that I've just had, that I'm actually not about grief at all. I still want to help people who have been affected by life change or crisis, but it doesn't have to be the death of a loved one. It can be anything that is their most challenging moment to actually get them to that place of peace, passion, and purpose.

When I started coaching, and I was saying to my coach, "Well, it's something around life purpose, but I have all this experience, six years background in grief. I know that I want to help people in grief as well." I couldn't find a way to articulate really clearly what it was that I wanted to do. When I was listening to all the experts, it was like, "Well, your background will show you what you're supposed to be doing."

I was like, "Well, my background is grief, so I need to be staying in grief." I'd be speaking to people, and it was like, no, I do want the grief, because that's what people are saying. I had built up this whole identity as a grief coach. Even publishing my first book, I published the first book, and that was really therapeutic. I obviously had something to say on grief.

I'm realizing that the book is more than just about grief. It could have been used in a completely different context because there is a far more powerful message than just having attached to grief. But I went through this whole thing of building up, of connecting with people in my field. What I realized was that where I am within my own grief is that I have no grief, even with the death of my brother.

…there is no pain. It has been the biggest gift that I have ever had. I'm so grateful that my brother died because it really sent me on this path. I don't even miss him because I'm so strongly connected to him still in my present life. To hear someone say, "I really miss [so and so]," I'm like, "What do you mean you really miss them?" I can't resonate.

What I found is as I was going more and more into the grief, I was aware that, "Oh, gosh, if I say what I really think, I'm going to start alienating people." People have come back and said, "Oh, it's controversial. We disagree." I'd be connecting with other coaches in the field, and I'd be going, "God, nobody gets what I'm actually talking about."

There's just this general frustration and the knowledge that I'd been putting a lot of effort into this, but I wasn't getting the results I wanted. People weren't attracted to me. Then people would be saying, "Oh, yes, I know so and so. She's grieving. You should connect with her." Then I'd go, "Oh, actually, that's not the grief work that I'm actually about because she's not ready to take personal responsibility. She's not ready to move beyond it.

I'm very much like, "Well, you're in pain? That's awesome, because that shows that there's something that's going to change. You can use this in the catalyst for transformation. You need to be celebrating that you're in pain." That is still a very touchy subject in grief because people are so enmeshed in grief. It got to the stage where I was like, "I'm so unhappy with what I'm doing. I'm not making the connections. I'm not getting my message out."

Then I had the realization: I'm not even talking about my message. My authentic message is something so different and I'm not sharing it because I'm too busy being afraid of being judged and being criticized and of alienating people. I know how harsh it is. If you're in grief, and somebody says something that you don't like, you will turn, and you will rip them to pieces because I've watched it with other people who have said controversial things.

I'm like, "Wow, this actually isn't even my audience because the majority of people in grief don't want what I've got." People who want what I've got are not going to be looking for grief support. They're going to be looking for something different. I had this realization. Actually, truthfully, I ended up going away, and I did a twelve-hour, solo, overnight vigil in the woods, just me.

It's even in the title of my book, staring me in my face, because it's *Thriving Loss: Move Beyond Grief to a Place of Peace, Passion, and Purpose.* But what I had been doing was spending so much time talking about the grief, because this is what all the experts told me to do, to focus, to explore, to do this, to do that. I realized, "Wow, I'm not just about that. I'm about the peace, the passion, and the purpose. That's what I need to be about to attract people who want to work with my energy."

What was a really powerful moment for me was I was actually speaking to a client about this because she was at that stage that she was just setting up her own business. We'd worked through her grief, and this is where she was at in her own growth. I said to her, "Well, can I share this insight that I've had with you because it's so powerful. It's made me realize how not listening to this Inner Voice, in effect I've been lying to myself and I've been lying to other people. I've been inauthentic in what I'm doing, considering that I'm all about being open and honest."

I'd been having a huge lie, which I couldn't believe. I said to her, I said, "Well, if you think about it, if you think about my website," because she's always commented to me on my previous website. She said, "Oh, it's great, the layout, the design." I said to her, "Yes, but does my website accurately reflect the energy that's present in this call, when you and I are working together?"

She thought for a minute, and she went, "No." I was like, "There you go. My website is nothing about me. I have created this wonderful, attractive, appealing website to grief, that resonates with the natural images. Then my words are getting lost because the energy of my whole site is actually low. I can't get it out. From hearing her say that to me, it was like confirmation.

I basically said, "You know something, I'm actually sick of not trusting my intuition." I've reached a point where, okay, it's not huge, severe pain, but I have so much to give to the world. I really am able to make a huge contribution that can help swing humanity into evolution rather than the destruction that is so present. I know that with every fiber of my being. I've even got tears as I'm talking about it.

Kris: Me, too. I do, too. I have goose bumps. I am so enrolled in that. You are powerful. Absolutely. Oh, my gosh.

Tabitha: I've not been showing this. It's like, my goodness, I've been not only letting myself down, but other people as well. The realization of that was just like, whoa, this has been there all along. This is what I've been trying to get out over the last couple of years. I'm not going to regret anything that's taken me to where I am at this point, because everything unfolds perfectly.

But I know how much to actually say, "Okay, let's go with my intuition." It has been incredibly scary because my whole way of working, my whole way of approaching with clients—I've said, "All right, I can't take any more clients on until I've rebirthed who I am authentically." In effect, I've had to let go of the potential of income coming in at the same time.

But it has been absolutely fantastic. Even sometimes I can hear myself, and I'm like, "Tabitha, you're doubting yourself." It's like, you know something? Just trust. If there's one thing you need to do, just trust your intuition and go for it. The more I've practiced it, the more that it happens, the easier it is to maintain now.

It has been so funny because when I have actually listened to my intuition and taken action, the universe has actually given me confirming signs, confirming signals, that are saying, "This is right. This is a reflection to your intuition. This is right. Keep on going." So despite the fact that it's so scary, I am trusting myself and the world in a way I have never trusted myself or the world before because there's actually no other option.

All I can do is trust because I've been spending so much time not trusting and seeing the results that it's like the expression, "Let go and let God."

Kris: Yes. Yes.

Tabitha: I'm there, and I get it. Even if what my intuition tells me is completely random at times, I'm just like, "You know something? I'm just going to go with that. I'm going to go with it. It fits. It works." I'm like, "Wow, this actually is cool."

Kris: It is pretty cool. It's so interesting because I'm having a very similar experience where my Inner Voice is telling me, my intuition is saying, "Yes, keep going." I check my energy, and I'm like, "Are you sure?" I'm always kind of asking. It's like, "Yes, yes, yes." It's so interesting to me how all the little voices will come in and try to dissuade me, over and over and over again, from listening to my intuition.

But I say, "No. Thank you very much for sharing. I am moving forward." You're right. It gets easier and easier, and things open up. The validation comes very quickly.

Tabitha: What I'm finding is this is just like such a fantastic place to be in. Now that I've actually moved into it, I'm like, "Do you know

something? I'm going to do whatever it takes to maintain this, because it's so awesome." I never knew that it could possibly be like
this. If the Law of Attraction is true—and I've used the word "if"
because I do believe in the Law of Attraction—well, if it's true,
then I need to be and the great things are going to come naturally
because of the way that I am vibrating.

I didn't know I had this frequency of energy, or I've had insight
from glimmers into it before, but I've never known how to maintain it. It's like this whole taking in of, "Wait a minute, what do I
need to do? Oh, I need to go [outside]." I'm at the stage where I
spend about two hours outside in nature every day because that's
the source of my power, whether I'm sitting, whether I'm walking, climbing trees, or whatever.

I'm like, you know something, this is non-negotiable because I
need that moment to maintain my level of vibration.

This whole energetic shift—I mean, I look at my website, and I'm
just like, "Wow. That's me." I'm so excited, like, "Oh, my goodness, that is me." It truly reflects me. I'm bringing in these things
like talking to trees. Well, that's part of what I do, and my whole
program is a tree of transformation. That's one of my unique sell-
ing points, actually, to tell people that.

Kris: I think so, too. Your vision of grief is so powerful, too; it could
          also be something that I could see where people would really be
          jarred by it, and yet it is such a powerful message, and that is
          when you said, "I'm so grateful that my brother died." I don't
          know anybody, except for you who has said that—and I think
          that I could definitely get to that place, too, and I've had those
          moments where I've felt that gratitude about [something that
          seems so foreign to most people].

When someone is like, "Well, I really miss this person," and everything, and you say, "No, you miss the idea of the person." When you're really connected to the person and you know that you are, that you're a spiritual being, and you're still always connected to them, there is nothing to miss.

Tabitha: Exactly. Exactly.

Tabitha learned to trust herself and let go of her "expertise" around grief as she had been practicing it because she came to another level of clarity around it. Because she couldn't find anyone who saw things the way she now does, she held herself back, until she couldn't any longer. With courage, she began sharing her new, more conscious and enlightened view of the grief process, and because of that, her people are showing up. Owning her intuitive perceptions, her perspective, and her experience, then sharing it is what built up her conviction. She is living a life well spoken because she is enrolling people in a new way of seeing the world, and it's expanding her world as well.

THE WELL SPOKEN WORD

"In the beginning was the Word, and the Word was with God, and the Word was God."

—John 1:1

In the Christian tradition, Christ has been described as being the Word, the living Logos, of God. The Greek word logos is translated as "word." Logos also means "divine animating principle pervading the Universe," or (the divine) "through which all things are made."[20] Some say that the Gospel of John is describing Jesus as the living Logos, or living Word. Because the Word, or Logos, and the energy of it, is living, we have access to it, anytime

---

20 From http://en.wikipedia.org/wiki/Logos

anywhere and everyone must discover how to communicate with, and as, God in her own unique way.

God is consciousness, all pervasive, in and of everything. Jesus and Buddha, among other enlightened humans turned Avatars, were the ultimate thought leaders. In human form, they conquered the little voices, moved up the scale of consciousness, and shared their message from that place.

Am I saying you need to be enlightened to be happy, whole, and successful? No way! What I'm saying is that the way has been shown to us, through different forms, to step out of ignorance, to stop living in the past, in fear, in emotional turmoil, and if we choose to, we can be free.

A thought leader is someone who is embodying the Christ or Buddha Consciousness. Jesus taught, along with Buddha and other Ascended Masters who have walked the planet, that we can be as great and do "even greater things" as any enlightened being, even though (and because!) we are human. While they addressed the suffering of humanity, and even over-came it themselves, they also showed us a way to do it for ourselves, and it is right under our noses.

That level of awareness of our Divinity, of who we Truly are, and how abso-lutely inherently worthy we are, while still humble, while still recognizing that it is not from ego, but from a Source greater than us, is the mark of a thought-leader and someone who is here to transform the world. This is a level of awareness, consciousness, and belief that most people, myself included, do not yet fully embody. Why? Because we are human, we forget. And because most folks do not consistently take care of themselves or value themselves enough to foster that level of awareness.

In our subservience and approaching God from a place of unworthiness, from a place of less-than and needing to be saved, or pleading for help in-stead of looking for what's right and going well in the moment, we disown our Divinity. Most of us approach God from the perspective of our little voices. We are taught to do so from an early age. Each of us is created perfectly to listen to and express God in our own unique way. None is better than, or less than, any other. No one is left out. No one.

Honestly, sometimes I have this vision of God (when I'm feeling particularly irreverent) thinking out loud, "Lordy, would you people stop groveling already? I created you to be so much more than you think of yourselves. My love for you is never-ending and all-encompassing, but I'm getting a little annoyed by your resisting this! Just get over it, okay?" And the devil, if there is such a character, is on the sidelines wringing his hands in a mwah-hah-hah sort of way and whispering to the little voices, "Our plan is working! Keep tearing them down and I promise you'll be safe from my wrath."

But you and I know he's lying.

We human beings suffer because we are ignorant of the Truth. We pass on a little voice "truth" and perpetuate it through disowning the responsibility inherent in a Divine existence. The responsibility for oneself, others, and the planet. This lack of awareness and responsibility shows up in our health, relationships, work, bank accounts, and in the level of joy we feel in our lives. It shows up in the way we care for ourselves, for others, and the value we put on the packaging of ourselves, versus *knowing* ourselves.

I believe the best way to counter the little voices of fear, doubt, shame, guilt, etc. is to stop living in fear. Turn and face your bogeyman. Increase your awareness through shining your light. Stop speaking and writing from that place of fear; stop making decisions while in a fear state. Stop marketing and doing business from that place. Stop having conversations in the external boardroom that reflect the fears of the middle managers (aka little voices) in your internal boardroom. It is a choice—simple, but not necessarily easy. It is choosing, even when the whole world is in the throes of little voice hostile takeovers (politics, religious wars, bullying, defensive communication, etc.) to stand in Love, to stand in Truth. It takes an amazing amount of clarity, courage, conviction, and self-knowledge to do this.

If you have read this far, you are up to the task.

Aside from the clarity, courage, conviction, and prosperity that comes when we listen to and speak from our Inner Voice, there is an even more compelling, simple, and—dare I say *fun*—reason to listen to it: So that God can experience the ever-evolving expansion and unfolding of the Universe through us, as us, unencumbered *because it feels so darn good*.

Remember: There is nothing you need to fix. There is nothing "wrong" with you.

YOU ARE ENOUGH.

You always have been.

From My Heart to Yours,

P.S. Dear reader, thank you for your practice. Thank you for choosing consciously. Thank you for listening to, speaking from, and creating from your Inner Voice over and over and over again, especially when (and because!) it scares the devil out of you. May you be blessed beyond measure as a result.

APPENDIX

Tools and Techniques

Demonstrations and recordings of the following techniques can be found at: http://www.krisprochaska.com/life-well-spoken/ and www. LifeWellSpoken.com

QUICK ENERGY REBOOT
FROM DONNA EDEN

Reset Buttons: Helps reset polarity, primes system for other energy work. Tap K-27 points **just under the collarbone**, below the inner end points of the collarbones where a man knots his tie. These points are about ½ inch below the collarbone and one inch out toward the shoulder. It is a small indentation and may be tender to the touch. If you tap with 3-4 fingers of each hand on each of the points (at the same time), you'll likely hit the right spot.

Hook up: To get back "online," it's like plugging in your main circuits and affects all the chakras and meridians. Place the middle finger of one hand in your navel (belly button) and the middle finger of your other hand on the third eye spot on the forehead just above and between the eyebrows. If you can't stand having your finger in your navel, then place your palm over your navel and your other palm over your third eye. Do what works for you.Hold these two spots and gently pull upwards with both fingers so your skin moves slightly up toward the top of your head. Relax your shoulders, breathe, and hold for about thirty seconds to one minute. You may yawn, sigh, or notice a deep relaxation and sense of calm throughout your body. You may notice clearer thinking and ability to be present here and now. You may not notice a darn thing—all are okay. Just know it's working.

Zip-up: For protection, and to avoid taking on other people's emotions, thoughts, energies, etc. Take fingers or the open palm of one hand and hold about 2-3 inches off the body, starting at the pubic bone area. Slowly draw your hand up to your chin as if you were zipping up a coat with a tall collar. Stop at the cleft of the chin just underneath the lips. Repeat three times. After last time, make a figure eight with your fingers over your chin to lock it in place.

VOW BREAKING SCRIPT

By Divine Decree, in the name of my God Presence, my Inner Voice, and under the law of Grace, Karma, Forgiveness, Love and Divinity, I now break all vows I have made in relationship to_____. I break this vow to/of _____ in all directions, all dimensions, all life-times, all space, and all time. I break it on behalf of my ancestors and on behalf of my descendants and future descendants. I break it on all levels of my awareness and consciousness and on the behalf of all parts of myself. I break it in service to the highest and best good of all, including God, and all those involved or impacted by this vow, including myself. All consequences of this vow both potentially and possibly are now fading and a new pos-sibility is opening up to me. It is now being written in my Master Records. It is done—so it is!

CORD CUTTING SEQUENCE

Imagine in your mind's eye the person, place, or experience (in this case a person) you wish to cut cords with. Take either your right or left arm, whichever you prefer, and make a large sweeping or chopping motion, as if you were clearing a cobweb or chopping a tree branch, in front of your body, starting just above your head and ending mid-thigh. Make several of these sweeping, cutting motions in front of your face, torso, arms, legs, and even your back (as best you can). Just set the intention for the cords to be cut, even in the places where you can't reach. As you "cut" the cords, actually say something to that effect like "I now cut all cords that are not of 100 percent pure Love and Light, and I ask Archangel Michael to assist me with his sword of Truth." You can even ask him to cut all the cords for you on your behalf!

Next, ask Archangel Michael to gather up all your own energy and bring it back into your body. Imagine all the energy that you either sent to others or that they tried to get from you, gathering together and funneling back into your body and going wherever it needs to go. Send the other person or persons' energy back to them, with blessings attached. Then ask Archangel Raphael to seal up your aura and all the places where the cords were attached to you and to fill up your body and your aura with Love and Light.

THOUGHT-LEADER CREATION TURNAROUND

- **Stop what you're doing:** *Feel your body.*

- **Ground:** Sitting, or standing, feet flat on the floor, palms over your navel. Imagine you have cords (or roots) of energy coming out of the soles of your feet and going down into the center of the earth. Inhale through your nose, exhale through your mouth gently, and send those cords deep into the earth. *Feel that connection.*

- **Surround:** Picture a *large bubble around you* that surrounds you about three feet from your body in all directions. It is composed of beautiful golden white (or any color you choose) light. Now you may not feel or sense a thing, and that's okay—not to worry; it still works, and over time as you awaken more and more to the energy *around you and in you,* you will begin to *perceive the vibrations* of things and people in a powerful way that is uniquely yours. Notice how soothing it is to be surrounded by this light, how safe it feels. *Feel held.*

- **Intend:** How do you want everything to turn out? Set an intention for how you want to feel moving forward. Listen for the inspired action to take. *Feel creative.*

- **Act:** Move back into your day, into your activity with intention and awareness. *Feel on purpose and aligned.* Go ahead. Try it right now....

EFT or Tapping: There is plenty of information on the Internet about this, so I am not going to include it here. You can find out more at http://www.eftuniverse.com or find an energy therapy practitioner at http://www.energypsych.com.

Resources/Bibliography /Suggested Reading

BOOKS

ACEP Training Manual. ACEP Energy Psychology Certification Program, 2007. http://www.energypsych.org (includes information on Chinese Five Element Theory)

Adams, Marilee. *Change Your Questions Change Your Life.* San Francisco: Berrett-Koehler, 2009.

Ash, Mary Kay. *The Success Story of America's Most Dynamic Businesswoman.* New York: Harper & Row, 1981.

Beckwith, Michael Bernard. *Spiritual Liberation: Fulfilling Your Soul's Potential.* New York: Atria, 2008. Audio Book.

Bolte-Taylor, Jill. *My Stroke of Insight.* New York: Penguin, 2006.

Braden, Gregg. *The Spontaneous Healing of Belief: Shattering The Paradigm of False Limits.* New York: Hay House, 2008.

Cameron, Julia. *The Artist's Way.* New York: Jeremy Tarcher/Putnam, 1992.

Dale, Cyndi. *The Subtle Body: An Encyclopedia of Your Energetic Anatomy.* Boulder, CO: Sounds True, 2009.

Eden, Donna. *Energy Medicine: Balancing Your Body's Energies for Optimal Health, Joy, and Vitality*. New York: Penguin, 2008.

Fritz, Robert. *The Path of Least Resistance: Learning to Become the Creative Force in Your Own Life*. New York: Fawcett, 1984.

Goldberg, Philip. *The Intuitive Edge: Understanding Intuition and Applying It in Everyday Life*. Los Angeles: Tarcher, 1983.

Hale, Gill. *The Practical Encyclopedia of Feng Shui: Understanding the Ancient Arts of Placement*. London: Hermes House, 1999.

Hawkins, David R. *Power vs. Force: The Hidden Determinants of Human Behavior*. Carlsbad, CA: Hay House, 2012.

Heer, Dain. *Being You, Changing the World*. Santa Barbara, CA: Access Consciousness, 2013.

Hendricks, Gay. *The Big Leap: Conquer Your Hidden Fear and Take Your Life to the Next Level*. New York: Harper Collins, 2013.

Hill, Napoleon. *Outwitting the Devil: The Secret to Freedom and Success*. ed. Sharon L. Lechter. New York: Sterling, 2012.

Hill, Napoleon. *Think And Grow Rich*. Meriden, CT: The Ralston Society, 1937.

Holliwell, Raymond. *Working With the Law*. BN Publishing, 2008

Jobs, Steve. "Stanford Commencement Address: June 12, 2005." *People Magazine*, October 24, 2011.

Lipton, Bruce. *The Biology of Belief: Unleashing the Power of Consciousness, Matter, and Miracles*. New York: Hay House, 2007.

Neagle, David. *The Millions Within: How to Manifest Exactly What You Want...and Have an Epic Life!* New York: Morgan James, 2013.

Owen, Amanda. *The Power of Receiving: A Revolutionary Approach to Giving Yourself the Life You Want and Deserve*. New York: Penguin, 2010.

Parkyn, Chetan. *Human Design: Discover The Person You Were Born To Be*. Novato, CA: New World Library, 2009.

Pert, Candace. *Molecules of Emotion: The Science Behind Mind-Body Medicine.* New York: Touchstone, 1997.

Schneider, Bruce. *Energy Leadership: Transforming Your Workplace and Your Life from the Core.* Hoboken, NJ: John Wiley & Sons, 2010.

Snyder, C. R. and Lopez, S. J. "The Value of Wisdom and Courage." *Positive Psychology: The Scientific and Practical Explorations of Human Strengths.* Thousand Oaks, Calif.: SAGE Publications, 2007. p. 241.

Tolle, Eckhart. *A New Earth: Awakening to Your Life's Purpose.* New York: Penguin, 2005.

Williamson, Marianne. *A Return To Love: Reflections on the Principles of A Course in Miracles.* New York: Harper Perennial, 1993.

Wright, Kurt. *Breaking the Rules: Removing the Obstacles to Effortless High Performance.* Boise, ID: CPM Publishing, 1988.

WEBSITES

Association of Comprehensive Energy Psychology (ACEP): http://www.energypsych.org

Emotional Freedom Technique (EFT):
http://www.eftuniverse.com

Resonance: Gaiam Life website:
http://blog.gaiam.com/quotes/authors/daniel-goleman/57842

Myers-Briggs Type Indicator: http://www.myersbriggs.org

Human Design: http://www.humandesignforusall.com
(get a free Human Design report here)

Heartmath Institute: http://www.heartmath.com

EFT (Emotional Freedom Technique):
http://www.eftuniverse.com

INNER VOICE STORY CONTRIBUTORS

Roma Anjoy, Ph.D. http://www.romaanjoy.com/

Lynn Baldwin-Rhoades
http://www.powerchicksinternational.com/

Beth Buelow http://www.theintrovertentrepreneur.com/

Jessica Butts, M.A. http://www.jessicabuttscounseling.com/

Elizabeth Case http://www.yellowdogconsulting.com/

Dr. Perry Chinn, DC http://www.perrychinn.com/

Maria Dykstra http://www.tredigital.com/

Jacqueline Fairbrass http://www.jacquelinefairbrass.com/

Megan J. Huber http://www.meganjhuber.com/

Tabitha Jayne http://www.tabithajayne.com/

Dianne Juhl http://www.femininefaceofmoney.com/

Karen-Lynn Maher http://www.legacyoneauthors.com

Jennifer Pearson http://www.healingpathvet.com/

Julie Ramage http://www.rewiredforyoursuccess.com

Nadhira Razack http://www.birthyourownbusiness.com/

Megha Rodriguez http://www.meghasuccess.com/

Kristin Thompson http://www.speakservegrow.com

Marty Ward http://www.successcoachinfo.com/

Rachel Whalley, MA http://www.healingforgoodgirls.com/

Debbie Whitlock http://www.debbiewhitlock.com/

About the Author

Kris is familiar with the little voices of fear and doubt that can derail the best laid plans and cause miscommunication. After eighteen years in the world of psychotherapy, she is adept at seeing the root cause of an issue or challenge. As a leadership coach and intuitive consultant, she offers tools and solutions for entrepreneurs and leaders to help them be more effective, powerful, and emotionally balanced and perform to their highest potential. Her motto: *Everyone can be a thought leader.* It all starts with **leading and speaking from your Inner Voice.**

With her mixture of compassion, irreverence, and ability to put people at ease (even while she's calling them out with her laser insight), **Kris has helped hundreds of women own how truly valuable they are and create powerful conversations so they can have more joy, ease, and prosperity, while making a bigger impact in the world.**

Following her Inner Voice led her to relocate and recreate her business in a way that allows her to spend more quality time with her husband, Mike, and their two kids, Eli Orion and Anja Soleil, in Bend, Oregon. Hiking, biking, skiing, trail running, and yoga all provide lots of opportunities for her to listen to her Inner Voice; now if she could just do all those things in her cowboy boots, life would be perfect.

Visit Kris at: **www.KrisProchaska.com**

Inner Voice
Coaching Programs

Kris offers individual and group retreats, coaching, and consulting for entrepreneurs, corporate teams, and other professionals, all focused on performance, leadership, and living true to one's inner authority. An avid hiker and lover of both the outdoors and spa treatments, Kris incorporates adventure and luxury spa experiences in her work with her clients because that's what helps her connect with her Inner Voice and it's way more fun than sitting on a couch! For more information on Kris' Inner Voice Coaching along with inspiration, motivation and support for you and your Inner Voice visit: **www.KrisProchaska.com** and **www. LifeWellSpoken.com**